TOOLS FOR PEACE

TOOLS FOR PEACE

The Spiritual Craft of St. Benedict and René Girard

ANDREW MARR, OSB

iUniverse, Inc.

New York Lincoln Shanghai

Tools for Peace

The Spiritual Craft of St. Benedict and René Girard

Copyright © 2007 by Andrew Marr

iUniverse books may be ordered through booksellers or by contacting:

iUniverse
2021 Pine Lake Road, Suite 100
Lincoln, NE 68512
www.iuniverse.com
1-800-Authors (1-800-288-4677)

The views expressed herein are the sole responsibility of the author and do not necessarily reflect the views of iUniverse or its affiliates.

ISBN-13: 978-0-595-41245-7 (pbk)
ISBN-13: 978-0-595-85598-8 (ebk)
ISBN-10: 0-595-41245-9 (pbk)
ISBN-10: 0-595-85598-9 (ebk)

Printed in the United States of America

C O N T E N T S

▼

ABBREVIATIONS

RB. Rule of St. Benedict.

RM. *The Rule of the Master* (*Regula Magistri*), trans. Luke Eberle. Kalamazoo: Cistercian Publications, 1977.

TH. Girard, René. *Things Hidden since the Foundation of the World: Research Undertaken in Collaboration with Jean-Michel Oughourlian and Guy Lefort*. Stanford: Stanford University Press, 1987.

GR. Girard, René. *The Girard Reader*. New York: Crossroad, 1996.

NOTES ON TRANSLATIONS

1. All quotations from the Bible are from the New Revised Standard Version.

2. All quotations from the Rule of Benedict are from Terence Kardong, *Benedict's Rule: A Translation and Commentary*. Collegeville, MN: Liturgical Press, 1996.

INTRODUCTION:
A PAIR OF TOOLSHEDS

Pax, the Latin word for peace, is one of the catchwords for Benedict's vision of right living, but this word is rarely used in his Rule. This reticence does not mean that peace is not important to Benedict. There are some values that Benedict presupposes so deeply that he rarely mentions them except in an offhand way. Peace is one of them. Benedict makes the fundamental value of peace clear when he says that the goods of the monastery should be distributed in such a way that "all the members will be at peace" (RB 34:5). Typically, Benedict does not write about peace as a vague, cosmic ideal. For Benedict, peace is actualized in the practicalities of everyday life with other people.

Benedict's fundamental question to an aspirant is not whether that person seeks peace, but whether the aspirant "really seeks God" (RB 58:7). However, Benedict's vision of community life makes it clear that anyone who "really seeks God" seeks peace just as truly. Surely no applicant who did not appear to be seeking peace would be thought to be truly seeking God. Benedict's fundamental question shows that seeking God is the gateway to every other good. For all of his responsibility to provide for the monastery, the abbot is admonished, in the words of the Gospel, to "seek first the kingdom of God" (RB 2:25, Mt. 6:33). Surely this admonition applies to the discernment of vocations as much as it does to the material goods of the monastery. In any case, monasteries have almost always offered an alternative way of life to the violence that often afflicts society.

Benedictine peace is not achieved by renouncing machine guns. Such tactics create no bonding between people; they create no peace. The peace that Benedict would have us strive for is much more positive. Real peace involves actively making connections between people and learning the art of giving priority to the needs of other people. The more we care about other people, the more we care for peace. For Benedict, peace is established in a community whose members truly √ seek God to the extent that their mutual service is grounded in God.

My own quest for God as a Benedictine monk has caused me to be troubled by violence, and most particularly by violence inspired by religious convictions. To try and understand how this comes about and what might be done about it, I have consulted many thinkers who have examined this phenomenon. Of these thinkers, I have found René Girard and others who make use of his thought to be the most helpful and stimulating. Over many years, Girard has developed his perception that the human quality of imitation is not limited to copying the actions of others, but it extends to the desires of other people. Girard prefers to use the word "mimesis" rather than imitation, and he refers to his basic insight and its ramifications as mimetic theory. Girard demonstrates how mimetic desire, where two people desire what the other wants, can evolve into mimetic rivalry where two or more people imitate each other in a tit-for-tat fashion. When more people in society imitate this rivalrous behavior, the whole society can reach a crisis that threatens to destroy it. According to Girard, the only way a society in ancient times was able to avoid this catastrophe was to redirect its mimetic behavior toward collective violence against one of its members. Girard goes on to argue that this resolution of social crises is the origin of primitive religions and human culture. In short, a society gathers together around its victim. Such a theory is disturbing, but we should expect that *any* helpful theory about the causes of violence will be disturbing. Girard does not argue that humanity is condemned to endless cycles of collective violence. He believes that a way out has been offered by the revelations in the Hebrew Bible and the New Testament. These writings reveal the truth of sacralized violence and witness to God's initiative to gather humanity in such a way that a victim is no longer required for human bonding. I hasten to add that Girard has noted many instances where Christians have fallen back into the same scapegoating violence of the primitive sacred. We are still very much in need of the Gospel to pull us back out of it. Girard has forcefully denied that he is a theologian, but other thinkers inspired by his thought have done vital work to develop his thought theologically and work out a Girardian hermeneutic of the Bible. Gil Bailie, James Williams, James Alison, and Raymund Schwager are the writers who have made the most important theological contributions to Girard's thought to date. Perhaps the reader can sense already that Girard's fundamental insights have the potential to prompt a reevaluation of just about everything, Christianity included. That is true. As he does with everything else, Girard tilts the entire Christian tradition at a forty-five-degree angle, but the result is a fresh take on Christianity that looks suspiciously like the heart of the Gospel.

As a Benedictine, it was only natural for me to look for ways mimetic theory might deepen my understanding of the Rule once I became seriously interested in it. Not surprisingly, I have found that Girard's thought tilts the Rule of Benedict in much the same way that it tilts the Gospel. Like the Bible, the Rule has its uncomfortable moments with human passions. The chapter on the Prior of the Monastery and the chapters dealing with punishment are particularly problematic. As it happened, it was with these chapters that I found Girard particularly helpful, but I have found in Girard a most interesting companion throughout my study of the Rule and a source of many new insights into Benedict's wisdom.

Since Girard's thought is concerned not only with understanding violence but with overcoming it, his ideas present us with a strong challenge to apply them in daily life. Major strides have been made to spell out the implication of Girard's thought for Christian spirituality, most notably in the works of Alison, but much more needs to be done. The Rule of Benedict is a practical document rather than a doctrinal one, a rule to be *lived* rather than just thought about. It focuses on the practices that build community and notes those practices that threaten or destroy community. In short, Benedict guides us in the ways we can gather God's people in a new way that frees us from the old way of gathering society around a victim. With such a quarry of practical applications for living the Gospel, it behooves us to dig down into it and see what aids we can find there for living out the insights of René Girard. With his practical mind-set, Benedict includes a list of "tools of the spiritual craft" (RB 4:75). His whole Rule can be seen as a shed filled with the tools we need for living a Christian life of peace. René Girard also has a toolshed filled with many treasures that serve the same purpose. In this book, I will rummage around in both toolsheds to see what we can find to forge a spirituality of peace rooted in the Gospel.

In many ways, a sixth-century monastic figure and a twentieth-century thinker are worlds apart from each other. Even so, what Benedict and Girard have in common is an anthropological approach to life. Both focus their attention on concrete human behavior in its social dimensions. For Benedict, simple acts such as tending a garden or serving a meal are elements of the Kingdom of God. For Girard, a simple scenario of two people reaching for the same book on the sale table offers a clue to the beginnings of human conflict that undermines the Kingdom of God. It is important to stress that the anthropological approaches of neither Benedict nor Girard diminish the importance of God. Benedict presupposes the grounding of the human self in God before all else. René Girard's analysis of human behavior brings us face to face with the claims of the Gospel.

Since this book brings together two people who have not been brought together in this way, it is likely that few readers will be knowledgeable about both Benedict and René Girard. I begin, therefore, with an introductory chapter on the fundamental vision of the Rule of Benedict and an introductory chapter on the thought of René Girard and others who have developed mimetic theory. The rest of the chapters in this book examine a chapter or a group of chapters in the Rule of Benedict in dialogue with mimetic theory. In discussing the prologue and first seven chapters of the Rule, which deal primarily with issues in spirituality and the virtues that one should cultivate, I examine ways that Girard's thought enhances our understanding of these virtues and how these virtues, in turn, can strengthen our application of Girard's thought. With this grounding, I will go on to examine the nuts and bolts in Benedict's toolshed to show how they help us cultivate the virtues that are so important for meeting the challenges that mimetic theory poses for us. It is my hope that all of us will emerge from this dialogue armed with many news tools for crafting peace in the world.

PART I

▼

INTRODUCTIONS TO THE RULE OF BENEDICT AND RENÉ GIRARD'S MIMETIC THEORY

CHAPTER 1

▼

GATHERING A COMMUNITY IN THE SPIRIT: INTRODUCING ST. BENEDICT AND HIS RULE

Benedict and His Time

Benedict wrote his Rule in the first half of the sixth century. He did not compose it placidly in a serene environment. By Benedict's time, the Roman Empire had collapsed in Europe, and Gothic rulers held sway over the Italian peninsula. In 525, the Byzantine Emperor Justinian I made the situation worse by launching an invasion on the peninsula to win it back for the empire. The result was a civil war that lasted over twenty years. For Benedict and his monks, it must have been a bit like living in Vietnam during the conflict there. Moreover, the many times Benedict had to suggest ways of coping with serious difficulties in community make it clear that not even the monastery was entirely peaceful. These consider-ations suggest that Benedict's Rule may well be relevant to us in our conflicted time.

Considering the impact that Benedict has had on Western civilization, it is both astounding and strangely disconcerting that we know almost nothing about him. The only document that has ever claimed to offer biographical information about Benedict is Book Two of the *Dialogues* attributed to Pope St. Gregory the Great. Unfortunately, there are many reasons for doubting that this document gives us any reliable information about Benedict. The miracle stories recorded in the *Dialogues* are so fanciful and archetypal that even a person with a firm belief that miracles do happen can be forgiven for not believing in the miracles attributed to Benedict in this document.

More important is the radical difference between the personality we glean from the Rule and the charismatic wonder worker portrayed in the *Dialogues*. In the *Dialogues*, Gregory tells his deacon, Peter, that the man who performed these miracles "was also very well-known for his words of doctrine" and that Benedict's Rule is "remarkable for its discretion and elegant in its language." This Rule reveals the "life and habits" of Benedict, because "the holy man could not possibly teach other than as he lived."[1] The Rule is indeed remarkable for its discretion. The author is accurate to that extent. Unfortunately, there is nothing else in the *Dialogues* that betrays any knowledge of the Rule of Benedict whatsoever. Moreover, it is hard to credit that the practical, sober-minded author of the Rule would spend most of his waking hours wreaking havoc on the laws of nature for the convenience of his monks and the astonishment of his neighbors. A comparison between two corresponding chapters in The Rule of Benedict and The Rule of the Master strengthens this dichotomy. In chapters 4 ("On the Tools of Good Works") and 7 ("On Humility"), Benedict copied most of his material from The Rule of the Master. Where the two differ significantly is that the Master capped both of his corresponding chapters with long-winded descriptions of heaven, but Benedict pointedly omitted both of these passages. Much as Benedict believed that eternal life in heaven with God was the ultimate goal of the monastic life, he clearly had no room for fanciful speculations about it. The Benedict of the *Dialogues,* on the other hand, is constantly meddling with the hereafter when he isn't redefining the natural laws of this world.

In spite of these problems, long recognized by Benedictine scholars, there has been an understandable tendency to hope that the second book of *Dialogues* does give us a bare outline of Benedict's life: that he was a sixth-century dropout, that he lived in a cave as a hermit, that he accepted the invitation of the monks at Vicovaro to be their abbot only to have them attempt to poison him, and that he founded a monastery on the ruins of a pagan temple on Monte Cassino. Unfortunately for this biographical sketch, the research of Francis Clark has discredited the *Dialogues* as a legitimate historical source even to this minimal extent. Clark makes a very strong case for attributing (or blaming) the authorship of the *Dialogues* to an anonymous cleric working in the Vatican archives during roughly the mid-seventh century.[2] Among many strong arguments in favor of this conclusion, one of the strongest is the total lack of a cult of St. Benedict until the middle of the seventh century.[3] Clark's reasoning is that if Pope Gregory had written the *Dialogues* in 593, as has been claimed, then it would have had a high circulation from the start as did the works known to be composed by this Pope, and Benedict would have been highly acclaimed as a saint starting from that time. Moreover, there are *no* references to this work that can be safely dated to the late sixth century to indicate that it was known by anybody at the time.[4] Clark also undermines the claim in the *Dialogues* that Benedict founded a monastery on Monte Cassino by demonstrating that there is no other historical evidence that anyone built a monastery there during the sixth century, nor is there any archaeological evidence for such a thing.[5] I cannot go further into the highly detailed arguments that Clark puts forth in this book, but I am sufficiently convinced of his conclusions to feel that prudence and intellectual honesty require that we not rely on the *Dialogues* of "St. Gregory" as a likely source of information about Benedict.

What we are left with is a monastic rule attributed to Benedict that was most likely written, almost certainly in stages, sometime during the first half of the sixth century. The many references to known Roman liturgical practices in Benedict's outline of the Divine Office suggest that Benedict and his community were probably located in or near Rome. The references to farming in the Rule suggest that they were far enough from the urban center to have farmland around them. Beyond that, we have only the Rule itself to shed any light on the kind of person Benedict was. For that reason, I will use only the Rule of Benedict for the purposes of comparing Benedict with René Girard. There are some narrations in Book Two of the *Dialogues* that are ripe for a Girardian analysis, but that will have to be a separate project for another day.

Benedict had inherited two centuries of monastic tradition by the time he wrote his Rule. He respected the radical asceticism of the eastern Desert Fathers who ate very little, slept very little, maintained strict silence, usually lived alone, and prayed nonstop in their cells. However, Benedict felt that the communal life with its more moderate asceticism, which other monastic figures developed, was more realistic for those who aspired to the monastic life in his time and place. With this focus, Benedict says specifically that he wrote his Rule for followers of the cenobitic life. What Benedict means by that term is a community whose members "serve under a rule and an abbot" (RB 1:2). It is not enough, then, to define the monastic life as a vocation to prayer. Rather, the monastic life is a vocation to a *community* of prayer. Central to the community's structure is the abbot. The abbot is elected by the community, but, once elected, he holds much authority in the exercise of that office. In representing Christ to the community, the abbot has a strong claim of obedience upon the monastics under him. Representing Christ, however, also means *acting like Christ*. That is, the abbot should live a sacrificial life devoted to nurturing others.

Benedict is quite clear that community life is best fostered by a moderate middle way between radical asceticism and a life of indulgence: Monks should eat adequate amounts of food, but not too much; they should have adequate amounts of sleep, but not too much. Another example of Benedict's sense of balance is his stress both on quality relationships in community and solitude. Most important, Benedict demonstrates an uncanny balance between a realistic appraisal of human behavior and an idealistic hope for what people can become by the grace of God. He knew that even those who choose to devote themselves to a life of worship will have their foibles, and any change for the better will take many years of struggle. Benedict did not urge his monks to storm heaven and win salvation in a day. Rather, he enjoined an asceticism more relaxed than that of the early monks, an asceticism that prompted one to take a gradual but inexorable journey to God in which one never loses sight of the goal. The practice may be moderate, but its direction is inexorable.

The three vows that a Benedictine makes at profession are stability, obedience, and fidelity to the monastic life (conversion). These vows give us a strong indication of how communally oriented Benedict's monastic vision is. (The famous triad of vows—poverty, chastity, and obedience—are a twelfth-century innovation by other religious orders.) The vow of stability is a promise to stay in the monastery of one's profession, the vow of obedience promises just that to both abbot and community, and the vow of conversion is a promise to persevere in faithfully living the monastic life. One can see that these three vows are nearly synonymous. All three are also oriented to life in community rather than to individual virtues such as fasting or personal prayer. Each of these Benedictine vows will be discussed more fully in the pertinent chapters below. It will also be seen that the explicit vows of poverty and chastity that came later in the tradition of religious orders are implicit in the Benedictine vows.

Overview of the Rule of Benedict

Benedict absorbed so much of the monastic tradition he inherited that his Rule is a less original document than it was once thought to be. Of particular importance is an anonymous monastic rule known as The Rule of the Master. Many long passages in the Rule of Benedict are identical with portions of The Rule of the Master. Many of these passages, in turn, were borrowed heavily from the writings of the monastic writer John Cassian (360–435). It was assumed for some time that the Master cribbed from Benedict and did a bad job of it. Since then, research has demonstrated that Benedict cribbed from the Master and did a great job of it. Although we have had to renounce any romantic notions that Benedict was an original genius, a renunciation after Benedict's heart, comparison of the two documents has proven to be a vital exegetical tool for understanding Benedict's monastic vision. Observing what Benedict copied from the Master and what he did not copy and noting where the two works differ gives us many valuable clues as to Benedict's personality and outlook.

The Rule of Benedict is, for the most part, a practical document that gives directives and recommendations on what the members of the community should *do* to live a communal life grounded in Christ. The prologue and the first seven chapters deal with fundamental virtues of monastic spirituality such as obedience and humility, but even here Benedict refers to concrete practices that cultivate these virtues. There is some emphasis on the inner work required of the individual to become humble and obedient, but this inner work is clearly placed in a communal context. The two peaks in this section, the chapter on the abbot and the chapter on humility, put personal cultivation in relationship with the structure of communal obedience. The rest of the Rule is devoted to specific directions in areas such as the structure of the Divine Office, disciplinary procedures, food and clothing allowance, and hospitality to guests. Many of these chapters are sprinkled with brief, didactic comments in which Benedict packs a powerful punch in just a few words. There is no more powerful way to demonstrate the importance of trivial everyday activity for achieving the deepest and most advanced level of spirituality than to embed deep spiritual teaching in discussions of mundane affairs as Benedict does.

Worship provides the structure of the day in Benedict's timetable. A night office before sunrise is followed by seven offices spaced throughout the day, ending with compline at the day's end. This sacred time is woven into everything else a monastic does throughout the day with the result that each day becomes a tightly woven garment held together by prayer. Here we have a reversal of the way time is usually structured—in fact, has to be structured—in non-monastic settings. Most of the time, no matter how much we may prefer prayer to everything else, work controls the day, and prayer is worked around these commitments. The monastic schedule reminds all Christians of the true priorities, even when their daily timetables simply cannot (and ought not) embody them.

A life of worship of itself is not Benedict's ideal, however. His ideal is that worship and work together form a unified life devoted to God and neighbor. Work is not a distraction from prayer. On the contrary, prayer must be grounded in concrete acts of work that keep us in touch with the reality of the material world. Keeping in touch with the material world, in turn, keeps us in touch with the Creator. Moreover, putting work in the context of a life of worship changes our perspective on work. In this perspective, we work for the sake of doing the job itself rather than primarily from ulterior motives such as making money or making a name for ourselves. Taking care in our work and in the way we handle tools has a salutary effect on our interiority, which opens the way to deeper prayer.

Study is a fundamental practice that adds further balance to worship and work. In the Benedictine tradition, however, the perspective on study is quite different from what we normally experience in academic institutions. Benedict envisions study as a means of growing close to God rather than as something we do just to get a diploma. Reading and meditating on scripture and the classic texts on Christian spirituality are fundamental to monastic study. Such reading feeds the mind, but more importantly, it feeds the heart so that we get a *feel* for the love of God revealed in scripture and in the writings of God's most faithful servants. The deeper our feeling for this love, the better we can judge how deeply God's love has been captured by other writers. Given this foundation, there is a wide variety of reading that can also draw us closer to God, ranging from insightful novels to historical studies to books on nuclear physics.

Work, study, and prayer may seem to be disparate activities that tend to pull away from each other. There is, however, a fundamental ascetical practice that unites these three activities and many others besides: attention. Work, study, and prayer all require attention if they are to be done well. What a person must pay attention *to* differs with each activity, but the need for attention is the same. What is demanded of us is that we become attentive people. The best way to deepen our prayer life while working is to concentrate on the *work*. The more we pay attention to the work we do, the more attentive we become. The more attentive we become in our work, the more attentive we will be at study and prayer as well.

Simone Weil articulated the importance of attention in a valuable essay with the cumbersome title "Reflection on the Right Use of School Studies with a View to the Love of God." As the title implies, Weil wrote this essay to help students understand how their studies cultivate attention, but the opening sentences point to much broader applications:

> The key to a Christian conception of studies is the realization that prayer consists of attention. It is the orientation of all the attention of which the soul is capable toward God. The quality of the attention counts for much in the quality of the prayer. Warmth of heart cannot make up for it.[6]

Weil goes on to insist that even an academic subject that has no practical use for a pupil is still valuable for what it teaches in the discipline of attention. This is true of many other undertakings that seem dull and of little value to us.

One might think that practicing attention is easy. The reality is that it is a stiff challenge, a challenge in which we fight evil. Weil warns us of the challenges:

> Something in our soul has a far more violent repugnance for true attention than the flesh has for bodily fatigue. This something is much more closely connected with evil than is the flesh. That is why every time we really concentrate our attention, we destroy the evil in ourselves.[7]

In fighting evil with attention, we must also seek truth with equal passion: "Above all our thought should be empty, waiting, not seeking anything, but ready to receive in its naked truth the object that is to penetrate it."[8] When it comes to directing attention to human beings, it becomes an instrument of charity. "Not only does the love of God have attention for its substance; the love of our neighbor, which we know to be the same love, is made of this same substance."[9] Weil goes on to say that what the most unhappy people in the world need most is for someone to give them the gift of attention:

> The capacity to give one's attention to a sufferer is a very rare and difficult thing; it is almost a miracle; it *is* a miracle. Nearly all those who think they have this capacity do not possess it. Warmth of heart, impulsiveness, pity are not enough.[10]

Attention is not important only for living out the Rule of Benedict. When we look at René Girard's mimetic theory, we shall see that the discipline of attention is of great importance for living out the implications of his principles. Giving attention to the things of the world, to other people, and to God fosters a deep respect to all, which blossoms into love.

Benedict's Realism

One of the constant dangers in monasticism is the trap of overachieving. Benedict was sufficiently aware of this problem to temper his idealism with a realistic view of human nature. In a time when so much idealism has broken down under the weight of harsh realities, we can take heart from Benedict's sober realism that never loses sight of high ideals. Benedict knew that neither personal nor communal problems can be solved with the wave of a magic wand. There is no substitute for grinding away at our foibles day in and day out. When we become frustrated from trying "instant solutions" that don't work, Benedict's conviction that we can become better people in the long run if we are patient with ourselves and with others will strengthen us for the long haul.

There are many statements in his Rule where Benedict makes it clear that he does not expect his monks to become automatically perfect the moment they are clothed in the monastic habit. On the contrary, he often gives the impression that he *expects* things to go wrong. When the signal is given to rise for morning prayers, the monastics need to encourage one another "on account of the excuses of the sleepy." Benedict goes on to say that a monastic is late for the morning office only by coming in *after* the *Gloria* of Psalm 95, for which reason "we want it said very slowly and with pauses" (RB 43:4). Here we see Benedict giving his monastics some slack while also making it clear that tardiness is not acceptable. This is one of many examples of Benedict's acceptance of human limitations even as he goads his monastics on to do better.

Just as monastic history has its ups and downs, the most conscientious monastics experience the same rhythm of fervor and lassitude in their observance. A monastic vocation is not a fantasy life of serene prayer that overlooks our common humanity. That would hardly be a strong witness to the Faith. Rather, it is a monastic's struggle to live rightly and to become ever more open to God's grace, which gives the monastic something to share with others in the Church and the world.

Ministry

It is impossible to truly seek God without affecting other people as well. Service to God is invariably redirected by God to the rest of God's people. The act of prayer itself is a ministry to the Church and the world as much as it is to God. I once had the opportunity to reflect on the significance of our prayer as ministry when a guest asked me why there was so little overt intercessory prayer during the Office. Part of my answer was that we solicit requests for intercessory prayers in our newsletter, and these prayer intentions are distributed among the community so that we can pray the Office for those intentions. Moreover, the comprehensiveness of the Psalter in its various moods ranging from despair to joy suggests that in the Divine Office we are praying the Psalms for the whole people of God. A deeper point is the mystery that we do not, and ought not, know what God does with our acts of prayer. We pray with the conviction that prayer is, in itself, a good thing to do and that it pleases God. The value of prayer cannot be measured by practical considerations any more than the value of a deep friendship can be measured by what we hope to "get out of it." We pray with the trust that God will use our prayers for the benefit of others in whatever ways God sees fit.

The one apostolate to people outside the community that is mentioned in the Rule, but one given a strong emphasis, is ministry to guests. Except for a detailed description of how to greet a guest, Benedict says little of how his monastics should minister to guests during their stay, except to say that they should be treated "as Christ" and "proper respect should be shown to all" (RB 53:1–2). Benedict probably did not give them retreat addresses. Perhaps he offered counsel to some. Such pastoral work is quite common in monastic guesthouses these days. No matter what a community does for its guests, the most important feature of its guest ministry is offering them the opportunity to share in the worship of the community. Worship is in itself a teacher that offers a new perspective on the burdens one carries in life. So it is that any words of counsel from a monastic will be deepened greatly by prayer with the community. Guests also have the opportunity to have quiet time for study, prayer, and reflection that they often do not get in their usual environments. With the help of their personal reflections, many guests discover that workaholism is a problem that has been cutting them off from the depths within themselves where God would speak with them.

The Benedictine life is not utopian in the sense that it posits an ideal social structure that will automatically solve human problems once people adopt that structure. I pointed out above that St. Benedict starts with monastics where they are, and then encourages them to change for the better in the Lord. The same principle applies to society. Many people, even people deeply committed to the economic structure of this country, may yet feel the need for an improved society. A different lifestyle, such as one lived in a monastery, will not give the rest of the world all the answers, but the attempt to live the monastic life does offer society alternate cultural values, some of which may suggest possible changes in the way we live. As monastics, we may not necessarily set a good example for others to follow, but our own struggles to live with ourselves and with each other may foster the hope that, with the grace of God, change for the better is possible for individuals and for society. Perhaps the greatest use for a monastery is that, because it does not make sense in worldly terms, it points to the reality of eternity that governs all our lives whether we acknowledge it or not.

Benedict for Today's Laity

When Benedict wrote his monastic rule, it could not have occurred to him that fifteen centuries later numerous non-monastics would study his Rule and ponder its applications for their lives. There was some precedent for some non-monastics applying the Rule to their lives in medieval times when monastic leaders encouraged their noble patrons to devote as much time to praying the Divine Office and attending Mass as they possibly could. The modern development is different. When Esther De Waal was living in the cathedral close of Canterbury Cathedral, a place redolent with Benedictine history, she began to study the Rule of Benedict and reflect on it. At the time, she was serving her family as wife and mother. Many teachings in the Rule resonated with her experience of communal dynamics in her family, and she began to study the Rule systematically for the insights it might give her in her state of life. As a result of her study, she organized a program called "The Benedictine Experience," where non-monastics could experience a Benedictine rhythm of worship, work, and study, the latter fueled by her own meditations and lectures by a Benedictine monk or nun. De Waal's writings on Benedict's Rule have received much acclaim from laypersons, parish clergy, and Benedictines. The modest movement she started remains a significant presence in many churches today. Many other able writers have added to the literature on Benedictine spirituality for laity. One of them is Joan Chittester, who, although herself a Benedictine sister, shows a knack of discussing the Rule for non-monastics. More recently, Kathleen Norris has written about Benedictine life and spirituality with much insight and sensitivity. It is in the spirit of De Waal, Chittester, and Norris that I have approached the Rule of Benedict, hoping that the dialogue with Girard's mimetic theory will strengthen the vision and practice of Benedict's lay disciples today. It is also my hope that the sons and daughters of Benedict who live in monasteries will also gain new insights into the Rule through this dialogue.

CHAPTER 2

▼

VIOLENCE AND THE KINGDOM OF GOD: INTRODUCING THE ANTHROPOLOGY OF RENÉ GIRARD[1]

Biographical Sketch of René Girard

René Girard was born in Avignon in 1923. In 1947, he graduated from the École des Chartres in Paris with a degree in medieval studies. The next year, he moved to the United States, where he has lived out the rest of his academic life. He received his PhD from Indiana University and then was asked to teach some courses there in French literature. It was at this time that Girard wrote his first works of literary criticism. His next major appointment was in 1957 at Johns Hopkins University, where he served in the Department of Romance Languages. It was during the winter of 1959 that Girard experienced a conversion to the Christian faith and became a Roman Catholic. Between 1971 and 1976, Girard taught at the State University of New York at Buffalo. At this time, in 1971, he wrote his seminal book *Violence and the Sacred*, which was translated into English in 1977. When this book appeared in English, it gained much interest in the academic community. While the book was still hot off the presses in its French version, Raymund Schwager, a theology professor at the University of Innsbruck, read it and immediately traveled to Avignon, where Girard was spending the summer, to discuss it. From this time up to Schwager's untimely death in 2004, the two collaborated closely in the development of mimetic theory. In 1978, two years after joining the faculty of Johns Hopkins University, Girard wrote his most important book *Things Hidden Since the Foundation of the World.* It was in this book that Girard came out of the closet as a Christian, to the consternation of many academic colleagues, especially after its English translation was published in 1987. By this time, Girard had been the Andrew Hammond Professor of French Language, Literature, and Civilization since 1981. Girard retired from this post in 1995 but continues to serve Stanford University as a professor emeritus.

Discovering Mimetic Desire in Literature

For René Girard, mimesis is the fundamental anthropological characteristic of human behavior. Human beings are creatures who imitate. Without mimesis, there would be no human culture. We learn to talk and act in society by mimicking the behavior modeled for us by others. It is not this external imitative behavior that most catches Girard's interest, however. What Girard focuses on most is our tendency to imitate the *desires* of other people. Although we tend to think our desires are autonomous, that they originate from ourselves alone toward certain objects, Girard suggests that our desires are primarily stirred by the desires of others. As a result, our desires, far from being autonomous, are intertwined with the desires of other people. This focus on the mimetic quality of human desire does not deny human beings' basic biological drives. These drives are very real. But the mimetic quality of desire is so strong that the natural biological drives are caught up in it.

The mimetic quality of desire is often observed in the nursery. When one child reaches for a toy, another child suddenly wants that same toy rather than any of the other toys in the room—at which point the first child wants the toy even more than before. Before long, several children are fighting over one toy, while other toys lie around, neglected. Girard calls this imitation of desire "mimetic rivalry." Although we adults might shake our heads over this childish behavior, we often end up acting like the children in the nursery.[2] When one man shows an interest in a woman, chances are a friend of his will suddenly become interested in her as well, even if he hadn't given her a thought before.

It was the insights of the greatest novelists of the past five centuries that first called Girard's attention to the mimetic quality of human desire. He noticed that when Don Quixote chooses to imitate Amadis of Gaul in all things, it is Amadis of Gaul who chooses Don Quixote's objects of desire for him.[3] Since Amadis of Gaul is a fictional character and a far greater knight than Don Quixote could ever be, Don Quixote's mimetic relationship to Amadis of Gaul is not harmful, except for the bruises he suffers when he attacks some windmills. A problem in our cultural reception of this book, however, a problem with serious consequences, is that both Don Quixote and many of his readers fail to realize that "chivalric passion defines a desire *according to Another*, opposed to this desire *according to One-Self* that most of us pride ourselves on enjoying." So deeply do Don Quixote and Sancho Panza borrow their desires "that they completely confuse it with the will to be Oneself."[4]

The situation is quite different when the desires of one person are aroused by another living person who has roughly equal power and ability. Girard finds this sort of mimetic rivalry throughout the novels of Stendhal. At the beginning of *The Red and the Black*, M. Rênal, mayor of his village, assumes that M. Valenod covets the tutor, Julien, whom he has hired for his own children. M. Rênal follows up his fantasy by resolving to offer his tutor more money. Suddenly, Julien has become more valuable simply because he *seems* to be desired by a second person.[5] Advertising appeals primarily to this same mimetic drive with its basic message: Everybody wants this product; not everybody can have it, but *you* can—if you buy it *now*.

A short story by Shirley Jackson illustrates mimetic desire so clearly that one who believes in time travel might be inclined to think that Jackson moved forward in time to read Girard's books and then wrote the story to illustrate his theory. The title of the story is "Seven Types of Ambiguity."[6] A college student haunts a bookstore that has a rare copy of William Empson's book *Seven Types of Ambiguity*, a somewhat rarified study in aesthetics. A hefty man comes into the store with his wife. Having recently come into a lot of money, this man wants to buy a large number of books to make up for many lost years when he did not have the opportunity to read. The student guides the customer through several books in the store, advising him as to which books seem best suited to his needs. At this stage, the customer is desiring these books through the desires of the student in a constructive way. By reading the recommended books, that desire can deepen within himself even as the two share it. But the student also lets on that he desires the rare copy of the Empson book. It is obvious to the reader that while the Thackeray novels are a suitable recommendation, the customer is clearly not at all equipped to get much out of William Empson's book. And yet, when the customer comes to the cash register, he casually adds Empson's book to the rest of the books that he is buying. Clearly, he desires the book *only* because the student desires it, and not for any intrinsic value it can have for him.

Girard calls the scenario where the desires of two people converge on the same object a mimetic triangle. In *The Red and the Black*, M. Rênal and M. Valenod formed a mimetic triangle with the tutor, Julian. Much more commonly in literature, mimetic triangles are formed by two men desiring the same woman or two women desiring the same man. Given the fantasy that accompanies the formation of these triangles, as Stendahl's example amply proves, one would expect that mimetic triangles would be inherently unstable. Shakespeare's *A Midsummer Night's Dream* shows us how unstable such mimetic triangles can be. At the beginning of the play, Lysander and Demetrius both pursue Hermia, Helena having been forsaken by Demetrius. But halfway through the play, due to Puck's mix-up of enchantments ordered by the Fairy King Oberon, Lysander and Demetrius both forsake Hermia and chase after Helena. The fanciful setting of a forest where fairies play their pranks on the humans while simultaneously acting out their own mimetic triangles highlights the power of mimetic desire to enchant those who fall sway to it. Hermia herself pinpoints the dynamics of mimetic desire when she cries out, "Oh hell! To choose love by another's eyes!"[7]

If desire is as mimetic as Girard suggests, then it follows that one person's love for another will sometimes need to be validated by somebody else. This validation occurs if the second party's desire is inflamed in the same way as the first's. Fyodor Dostoevsky illustrates this dynamic of mimetic desire quite clearly in his novella *The Eternal Husband*. After the death of his wife, Pavel Pavlovitch Trusotsky searches out the men who were rivals to his wife's affections. He finds Velchaninov and becomes his companion. Later, when Trusotsky decides to remarry, "he cannot hold to his own choice inasmuch as the appointed seducer has not confirmed it."[8] That is, his rival must desire the same woman he desires. Velchaninov does just that, and Trusotsky loses the woman to his rival. Understanding this dynamic of mimetic desire makes the otherwise puzzling opening scene of Shakespeare's *A Winter's Tale* intelligible. Leontes urges his best friend, Polixenes, to admire his wife, Hermione, but as soon as he does, Leontes becomes insanely jealous and sets off a wave of violent reaction that is only partially resolved at the end of the play.

Dostoevsky builds much of the plot of *The Brothers Karamazov* around the mimetic triangle created by Fyodor Karamazov and his son, Dimitri with Grushenka. For her part, Grushenka not only actively fuels this rivalry, but she tries to stoke the fires further by drawing yet another Karamazov, Alyosha, into the fray. Alyosha, however, being a devout follower of the holy man Zossima, declines to play the game. Alyosha's charitable behavior leads Grushenka to repent of her actions, and she no longer tries to fuel the rivalry between Dmitri and his father. Unfortunately, Fyodor and Dmitri Karamazov prove that the presence of Grushenka is no longer necessary for them to pursue their mimetic rivalry with each other, with tragic results. In contrast, Alyosha weans a gang of boys away from their scapegoating behavior toward another boy, Ilyusha, and brings that boy back into fellowship with his mates by inspiring the boys to imitate his desire for Ilyusha's well-being. It is important to note here that Dostoevsky is showing how mimetic desire can be a good thing when the shared desire is for a good that can be shared. All of the boys can share in the love for Ilyusha, and they do.

Since so much of Girard's literary analysis and study of anthropology stresses the negative consequences of human mimesis, it is important to elaborate further on the potential for good in mimesis as it is illustrated in *The Brothers Karamazov*. In an interview with James Williams, Girard points to the constructive mimesis on the part of Jesus:

> As to whether I am advocating "renunciation" of mimetic desire, yes and no. Not the renunciation of mimetic desire itself, because what Jesus advocates *is* mimetic desire. Imitate me, and imitate the father through me, he says, so it's twice mimetic. Jesus seems to say that the only way to avoid violence is to imitate me, and imitate the Father. So the idea that mimetic desire itself is bad makes no sense.[9]

We shall see further on that, in Girard's eyes, it is Jesus who gives us the clearest model of mimetic desire as a fully constructive force. It is no accident that the one member of the Karamazov family who manages to break free of the mimetic violence in his family is influenced by a holy man who has given himself over to the imitation of Christ.

The object of a peacefully shared mimetic desire becomes more substantial in the eyes of the beholders. In Shirley Jackson's story "Seven Types of Ambiguity," the novels of Thackeray grow in importance when the student stirs the customer's desire to read them. But when mimetic rivalry sets in, we get the opposite effect: a shrinking object. Girard explains: "As rivalry becomes acute, the rivals are more apt to forget about whatever objects are, in principle, the cause of the rivalry and instead to become more fascinated with one another. In effect the rivalry is purged of any external stake and becomes a matter of pure rivalry and prestige."[10] When the heat of mimetic rivalry dissolves the original object of the rivalry, the rivalry degenerates into conflict for the sake of conflict. So it is that the reality of William Empson's book becomes invisible to the customer, as he has no idea what he is adding to his collection of books. The identities of Hermia and Helena are blurred when they are triangled by Lysander and Demetrius in *A Midsummer Night's Dream*. The rivalry between Dmitri Karamazov and his father becomes all the more intense when Grushenka drops out of the triangle. The rivals become mirror images of each other, returning tit-for-tat endlessly. They become what Girard calls "mimetic doubles."[11] The more intensely two people engage in mimetic rivalry, the more likely it is that more people will join in. It is possible for such a conflict to reach epidemic proportions to the extent that the existence of a society is threatened. When Girard followed up his literary studies with anthropological research into early human cultures and their sacred institutions, he came to the conclusion that almost always, and probably always, humanity went the way of Fyodor and Dimitri rather than the way of Alyosha and Zossima.

Sacred Violence

The study of conflict resulting from mimetic desire in the confined social network of the novel led Girard to examine the impact of this behavior on larger social groups. In noting that mimetic rivalry is contagious, Girard argues that "if the number of individuals polarized around a single object increases, other members of the community, as yet not implicated, will tend to follow the example of those who are." The resulting escalation can easily reach a boiling point where "the mimetic frenzy has reached a high degree of intensity," where we can "expect conflictual mimesis to take over and snowball in its effects."[12] This snowballing of mimetic conflict threatens to destroy the whole society. And yet, Girard noted that in archaic societies, peace suddenly and mysteriously emerged out of the mimetic conflict of all against all. How did this happen? Girard speculates that right at the crucial point, when a society teetered on the brink of destroying itself, the mimetic contagion suddenly focused on one person. This one person, and this person only, was deemed responsible for the social chaos. First, everybody had imitated everybody else in reciprocal violence. Then, suddenly, everybody imitated everybody else in blaming one person for the social chaos. The responsible person was then killed or possibly expelled through spontaneous mob violence. The immediate relief of peace and order was dramatic. So great was the sense of awe in the face of what happened that the person killed was then worshiped as a deity. The person who earlier was deemed totally responsible for the social violence suddenly was deemed totally responsible for the peace. Girard refers to this process as the scapegoating mechanism. This "solution" was not the result of human ingenuity. Rather, the social escalation of mimetic contagion

itself triggered the mechanism of collective violence. In order for collective vio- ↲
lence to stabilize a society, it is essential that *nobody* suffer a moral hangover as a
result of the event. One dissenting voice would be enough to spoil everything.
Moreover, the lynching of the victim *must not* be seen for what it is. There must
be a total forgetting of what actually happened.

Although it was necessary that the truth of collective violence be forgotten, it
was also necessary that society both sustain the camaraderie generated by that violence and find ways to prevent these crises from happening again as much as possible. The camaraderie was sustained by ritual and myth, and the repetition of
mimetic conflagration was controlled by prohibitions designed to prevent scenar-
ios of mimetic rivalry. After using mimetic theory to reconstruct societal meltdown and its "solution," Girard examines these three effects of this "solution"
that became the three pillars of human culture: myth, ritual, and prohibition.

In many cases, animal sacrifice became a substitute for human sacrifice. But if
the catharsis of animal sacrifice was not enough to sustain a society, then human
sacrifice was reinstituted. The Aztecs are only a particularly notorious example of
this practice. Far from being an isolated phenomenon, the practice of human sacrifice constantly turns up in ancient cultures throughout the world, thus lending
support to the importance Girard gives it as a fundamental practice of the primitive sacred.[13]

It is, however, in his analysis of mythology that Girard's insights are particularly interesting. In myths scattered throughout the world, Girard finds both
hints of their violent origins and attempts to cover up that violence. Many deities
created the world through a process of their own dismemberment. Purusha, for
example, created the cosmos and then the castes out of various parts of his body.
Other myths, such as Marduk's defeat of the sea-monster Tiamat, tell of strife at
the dawn of creation. Sometimes the mimetic doubling in a community is portrayed in a myth of two brothers who fight to the death, such as the slaying of
Remus by Romulus. In a myth of the Yahuna Indians, Milomaki, a singer who
enchants the populace with his music, is deemed responsible for numerous deaths
through fish poisoning. He is cremated on a funeral pyre and from his body
grows the first paxiuba palm tree in the world.[14] Oedipus, deemed responsible for
the plague that has stricken Thebes because he killed his father, King Laius and
then married his mother, is duly expelled from the city. The myths of Milomaki
and Oedipus are good examples of the mimetic crowd activity of adulation and
persecution. Even today, we can see that celebrities and heads of state are common targets for social opprobrium. There is no question of giving a fair trial to
the likes of Tiamat, Milomaki, or Oedipus. To question the guilt of any of these

victims would spoil the mechanism of collective violence. It is essential that the victim have no voice. Gil Bailie points out that the root of the Greek word *mythos* is *mu*, which means to close or keep secret.[15] Aeschylus understood the importance of silencing. When Agamemnon was about to sacrifice his daughter, Iphigenia, he ordered that his daughter's mouth be gagged.[16] In this understanding of religion, there seems to be no place for God. That is precisely Girard's understanding of the case. God has nothing to do with a religion that operates on the basis of sacred violence.

Girard also finds traces of mimetic crises in common prohibitions that are also found worldwide. The fear of mimetic doubles makes intelligible some taboos that otherwise make no rational sense, such as the dread of twin births that often led to the infanticide of at least one of the children. Girard also suggests that ancient prohibitions such as the one against incest are best understood in this way:

> The most available and accessible objects are prohibited because they are most likely to provoke mimetic rivalries among members of the group. Sacred objects, totemic foods, female deities—these have certainly been the cause of real mimetic rivalries in the past, before they were made sacred. That is the reason they were. Therefore they become the objects of strict prohibitions.[17]

The structuring of society along hierarchical lines also creates safeguards against societal breakdown through a mimetic crisis. When an object of desire is not attainable because the desired person is of a much higher social class, or economic factors make the material objects unattainable, then mimetic rivalry is significantly reduced. Unfortunately, this "solution" requires victims just as much as sacrificial rituals do as such societal arrangements inevitably institute violence perpetrated on those placed in lower ranks. That the four castes of India's social system are carved out of the pieces of the dismembered Purusha is a particularly vivid illustration of the connection between sacred violence and social structures.

Those who believe that religion is primarily or solely derived from humanity's sense of mystery before the forces of nature might be startled by Girard's theory, which goes counter to this notion. I have heard Girard scoff at the idea that early humans had the time to speculate about nature and nature's mysteries. I don't think it is necessary to underrate this human tendency to prefer Girard's speculations of sacred violence as the more fundamental explanation. I think that humanity's awe of creation is natural and very real (Rom. 1:19–21), but the overwhelming power of mimetic crises and their "solution" hijacked this natural awe. That is, awe before creation was overtaken by awe over the relief from a mimetic crisis through the collective violence against a victim. Girard's theory also makes human culture a more dubious phenomenon than is often thought to be the case. Normally, one thinks that it is a good thing to be "cultured." Girard does not deny that many good things have developed in human culture, but he does insist that, as long as a culture is founded on sacrifice, a culture's foundation is inherently unstable. We shall soon see how Girard thinks that human culture can be put on a much firmer and humane foundation.

The Hebrew Bible

There seems to be no way out of the human dilemma of the primitive sacred as René Girard sees it. If the solution to societal crises requires a social act whose truth must be concealed, how can humanity possibly come to see the problem? Even if a few people *could* see this reality clearly, they would almost certainly become mute victims themselves before they had a chance to spread the word. Girard does not, in fact, see how it is possible for humanity, on its own, to see the truth of sacred violence *and* act effectively to abolish it. In the Hebrew Bible and the New Testament, Girard sees a record of God's revelation of this fundamental truth at the root of human culture and the opening of a way out of the mechanism of sacrificial violence. Not surprisingly, there is much tension in the Bible between God's revelation and the old projections of human violence on God. It takes time for God to wean humanity from the old means of keeping society from falling apart.

Girard points out many instances in the Hebrew Bible that provide a radical contrast with the mythology of the primitive sacred, even when, superficially, they seem to be very similar. Like Romulus, Cain kills his brother and becomes the first founder of a city (Gen. 4:17). It is significant that no clear reason is given why Abel's offering should have been more acceptable to God than Cain's. In a crisis generated by mimetic rivalry, nothing matters except the rivalry itself. The crucial difference between this story and that of Romulus and Remus is that the blood of Remus is mute, but the blood of Abel cries from the ground. The victim has been given a voice.[18] Although Joseph's brothers blame Joseph for their violence against him, the narration makes it clear that Joseph is a victim of his brothers' jealousy. More importantly, Joseph becomes an agent of reconciliation as a live human being rather than a dead one. Saul was driven to a murderous rage when David was credited with slaying tens of thousands and Saul only thousands (1 Sam. 18:7). Not only that, but when his son, Jonathan befriended David, Saul tried in vain to draw his son into his mimetic rivalry with David. Through his renunciation of that rivalry, Jonathan witnessed to a new way for humans to relate to one another in the fear of God.

Although the Jewish religion is founded on violence, there is a radical differ- ence in its story from the founding mythology of other religions. This time, the story is told from the viewpoint of the victims rather than the victimizers. The Jews are the collective victims of the Egyptians who had enslaved them. God's deliverance of the Jews from slavery did not, however, heal them of their own problems with mimetic rivalry and collective violence. Violent tensions erupted periodically during the journey through the desert. In some instances, the people ganged up on Moses and Aaron. In other instances, the people ganged up on somebody else. After scoring a major victory at Jericho, Joshua suddenly suffered a defeat at Ai that seemed inexplicable until the casting of lots revealed Achan as the one responsible for stirring God's anger by taking some of the booty for him- self, as if it is likely he was the only one who committed this crime (Joshua 7). The divinely sanctioned stoning of Achan and his family rightly horrifies sensitive readers. It is important to note, however, that far from constructing a myth to cover the collective violence, stories such as this show the collective violence for what it really is.[19] That such violence was projected onto God in the Hebrew Bible shows that the association of God with violence was still alive even among the chosen people.

The sacrificial violence practiced by the other nations proved to be a constant temptation to Israel. The prophets constantly denounced the people for "offering up their sons and daughters to Molech, though I did not command them, nor did it enter my mind that they should do this abomination, causing Judah to sin" (Jer. 32:35). Josiah tried to abolish this human sacrifice, but, unfortunately, he did it by having all the prophets of Baal slain on their altars (2 Kings 23:20). Even in the act of fighting the victimization of the innocent, Josiah created more sacrificial victims than there already were. This problem of defending victims by creating victims remains a pitfall for many advocacy groups today.

Although Israel's sacrificial cult did not involve human sacrifice, it still received denunciations from prophets in oracles such as

I hate, I despise your festivals,
and I take no delight in your solemn assemblies. (Amos 5:21)

Or,

I have had enough of burnt offerings of rams

and the fat of fed beasts;
I do not delight in the blood of bulls,
or of lambs, or of goats. (Is. 1:11)

Isaiah draws a close correlation between sacrificial rites and social violence where widows and orphans are sacrificed to the interests of those making the sacrifices.

When you stretch out your hands,
I will hide my eyes from you;
even though you make many prayers,
I will not listen;
your hands are full of blood.
Wash yourselves; make yourselves clean;
remove the evil of your doings
from before my eyes;
cease to do evil,
learn to do good;
seek justice, rescue the oppressed,
defend the orphan, plead for the widow (Is. 1:15–17)

Raymund Schwager says, "If, according to its basic structure, the sacrificial cult is a ritual repetition of the scapegoat mechanism, then it cannot by itself pave the way to the true God."[20] Bible scholars and theologians debate whether the prophets intended to abolish the sacrificial cult or maintain the cult and add social justice to it. Ezekiel, a member of the priestly caste, did prophesy the institution of a reformed sacrificial rite rather than its abolition, but most other prophets seem to have demanded its abolition. In any case, the oracles of Isaiah and Amos challenge the practitioners of the sacrificial cult to prove that one can both make sacrifices *and* act justly in society. The implication is that if justice does not happen, it may be a sign that the cult should be abolished. These oracles also provided an ethical alternative to sacrificial rites that the rabbinic tradition could build upon after the Temple in Jerusalem was destroyed in 70 AD. Schwager observes, "How little belief in Yahweh depended on sacrifices is shown by the fact that it could survive undamaged the cultless periods after the first and second destructions of Jerusalem."[21]

The Psalms, too, question the sacrificial cult by linking it to social injustice, but much more often, they deal directly with collective violence as experienced by the victim. The psalmist is often surrounded by enemies who combine violence with lying: "More in number than the hairs of my head are those who hate me without cause; many are those who would destroy me, my enemies who accuse me falsely. What I did not steal must I now restore?" (Ps. 69:4). Schwager says that this psalm "says of its deadly enemies that they are very numerous, are deceitful, and hate without cause. These three elements can be found again and again in the description of the enemies."[22] These are, of course, fundamental elements in Girard's theory where the collective has lost touch with the cause of its violence and it depends on lies to cover up what it is really doing. Schwager goes on to point out that when the Psalms give us the voice of the "single individual suffering collective violence, it is clear that that person does not face many individual enemies separately, but they unite against him or her."[23] The opening lines of Psalm 2 where "the rulers take counsel together, against the Lord and his anointed" is a particularly clear example of this conspiratorial thinking. But even while complaining of acute suffering at the hands of others, the psalmist does not claim to be innocent of all wrong doing. The psalmist claims to be innocent only of the specific accusations of the enemies. This lack of innocence is particularly noticeable in the psalmist's cries for vengeance on the persecutors with such choice imprecations as, "Let their eyes be darkened so that they cannot see, and make their loins tremble continually" (Ps. 69:23). These sentiments are understandable, but they also demonstrate that the psalmist is still caught in the encompassing violence that requires victims.

The scenario of all against one reaches its most powerful disclosure in the Hebrew Bible in the Songs of the Suffering Servant in Isaiah. As in the complaints in the Psalms, it is stated clearly that the Servant of Yahweh was persecuted without cause. "By a perversion of justice he was taken away. Who could have imagined his future? For he was cut off from the land of the living, stricken for the transgression of my people ... although he had done no violence, and there was no deceit in his mouth" (Is. 53:8–9). These Songs of the Suffering Servant, along with many of the "Passion" psalms, Psalm 22 in particular, have often been understood as prophecies of the Passion of Christ. Mimetic theory suggests, however, that these prophets were not predicting the future by gazing into a crystal ball. The prophets were disclosing the very same story that was being repeated time and time again, and would be repeated yet again when the Logos came into the world and became flesh (Jn. 1:14).

Sandor Goodhart, a Jewish thinker involved with mimetic theory, tells us that Isaiah's disclosure of collective violence entails a disclosure of *our* participation in that violence: "The pain he bears and the disease he carries are the product at least in part of our own behavior toward him—although we commonly deny responsibility for that behavior.... We blamed him for our transgressive behavior and that constituted his wound."[24] As a Jew committed to mimetic theory, Goodhart wrestles with how to articulate the relationship between the Jewish tradition and Christianity. Understandably uncomfortable with any supersessive outlook, Goodhart insists that the theory of the innocent victim is "an old Jewish theme."[25] He goes on to suggest that Christianity makes central "the persecutory structure" that "comes to dominate Jesus' life ... a structure which in the Jewish context is subsumed with the more general formulation of the anti-idolatrous."[26]

The Lamb of God

The New Testament bears witness to the life and judicial murder of an innocent man, Jesus of Nazareth. This occurred at a time of social turmoil when groups of people, who normally were at loggerheads with each other, united against Jesus and him put him to death. That this scenario should be at the heart of Christianity suggests that Girard's mimetic theory and his understanding of sacred violence are far from peripheral observations about human nature.

As an inheritor of the Jewish tradition, Jesus needed to exercise careful discernment as to which of many messianic models in that tradition his heavenly Father was calling him to follow. One model put forth in much apocalyptic literature was that of a powerful warrior appearing from heaven to avenge all of the enemies of God with violent wrath. But, as Schwager says,

> From that overflowing world of images [Jesus] took hold only of the one idea of judgment at hand, and at the same time he understood this judgment in a quite different way. Whereas the judgment according to the visions of the apocalypticists takes place in the struggle against the enemies of God, Jesus proclaimed his Father as a God of love for one's enemies and interpreted the judgment as a self-condemnation of those who shut themselves away from this love.[27]

What Jesus did was proclaim the fatherly love he experienced from God when he called God *Abba* and preach that it is this love that defines God. Grounded in this love, Jesus not only rejected "the victorious and violent Messiah," but he embraced "the completely different tradition, according to which those sent by God must before the final event suffer violence from their enemies."[28] This is the tradition that we find in the Psalms of persecution, the Book of Wisdom, and, most powerfully, in Deutero-Isaiah. The Gospels are quite frank about how difficult it was for Jesus' disciples to accept this model, and Jesus himself had to struggle to hold this course. Every time Jesus tried to warn his disciples that he expected to follow the way of suffering and persecution, he met serious resistance. Ironically, it was precisely at the times when Jesus told his disciples that he would be handed over to the authorities to be crucified that they squabbled over who was the greatest among them or who would get the places of honor in the coming kingdom. It is, of course, this same behavioral pattern in humanity that made it necessary for Jesus to take the route that he did. In response to his disciples' rivalry, Jesus held before them a helpless child, such as the disciples tried to keep away from him, and held the child up as a model of the Kingdom of God (Lk. 9:46–47). When Peter rebuked Jesus for predicting an ignominious death, Jesus called Peter "Satan," because he was tempting Jesus to follow the wrong model. The frantic tone of this rebuke suggests that Jesus was seriously tempted to follow Peter's catastrophic advice. It is no wonder that, during the Last Supper, Peter had trouble allowing Jesus to wash his feet![29]

Girard attaches much importance to the biblical meaning of the word *skandalon* with its graphic meaning of "stumbling block." In calling Peter "Satan," Jesus is accusing him of being a *skandalon*, a stumbling block. That is, Peter is, inadvertently perhaps, trying to trip Jesus up so that he fails to fulfill his mission. Girard laments the disappearance of this word from modern Bibles in English and French. "The new translations do not convey the idea of something that simultaneously attracts and repels."[30] That is, a "*skandalon* designates a very common inability to walk away from mimetic rivalry which turns it into an addiction. The *skandalon* is anything that attracts us in proportion to the suffering or irritation that it causes us."[31] It is in precisely this way that the disciples make themselves *skandala* to each other when they argue over who is the greatest among them.

It should come as no surprise that Jesus, like the prophets, was deeply aware of the connection between mimetic rivalry and violence, and that he warned his listeners against it. "Beware of the scribes who like to walk around in long robes, and love to be greeted with respect in the marketplaces, and to have the best seats in the synagogues and places of honor at banquets. They devour widows' houses and for the sake of appearance say long prayers. They will receive the greater condemnation" (Lk. 20:46–47). The suggestion here is that the competitive jockeying for position results in the oppression of the most helpless members of society, the widows and orphans. The danger of these denunciations was that Jesus and his listeners might become self-righteous over their condemnation of the bad guys, a self-righteousness all the more satisfying for being directed against their social and religious superiors. This attitude would leave them in the grip of mimetic rivalry. For that reason, Jesus also admonished his followers to follow precisely the opposite behavior than that modeled by the practice of reciprocal violence. "You have heard that it was said, 'An eye for an eye and a tooth for a tooth.' But I say to you, Do not resist an evildoer. But if anyone strikes you on the right cheek, turn the other also" (Mt. 5:38–39). Schwager points out that the right inner attitude is enough. The New Testament texts "never separate inner disposition from outward action."[32] Likewise, Girard says,

> Violence is the enslavement of a pervasive lie; it imposes upon men a falsi-fied vision not only of God but also of everything else. And that is indeed why it is a closed kingdom. Escaping from violence is escaping from this kingdom into another kingdom, whose existence the majority of people do not even suspect. This is the Kingdom of love, which is also the domain of the true God.[33]

The preaching of Jesus goes hand in hand with his ministry of healing. Prominent among the acts of healing are exorcisms. Schwager reminds us that in the Bible, "illness is a disorder in the totality of human behavior, in one's relationships to self, neighbor, and God."[34] That is why Jesus confronted the demons who had taken over human personalities through violence. The story of the Gerasene demoniac in Mark 5:1–17 illustrates the social dimensions of healing. Girard argues that "Mark's text suggests that the Gerasenes and their demoniac have been settled for some time in a sort of cyclical pathology."[35] In short, the possessed man had become a perpetual scapegoat for the community. It is curious that the swineherds asked Jesus to leave in response to a healing that one might think was to their economic advantage. Girard argues that the swineherds actually were angry over being deprived of their scapegoat.[36]

As the Kingdom encountered more and more resistance, Jesus emphasized the reality of collective violence in his teaching. When the Jewish leaders declared Abraham to be their father, Jesus retorted that *their* father "was a murderer from the beginning and does not stand in the truth, because there is no truth in him. When he lies, he speaks according to his own nature, for he is a liar and the father of lies. But because I tell the truth, you do not believe me" (Jn. 8:44–45). The phrase "from the beginning" makes it clear that Jesus is accusing all of humanity and not just one ethnic group. The twin allies of violence and untruth are unmasked with one stroke. Not surprisingly, the listeners proved Jesus' point by picking up stones to throw at him. The famous parable of the wicked tenants who kill the servants and then the heir of the vineyard also zeroes in on the theme of collective violence (Mt. 21:33–46). This parable is one occasion among many

in the New Testament when Psalm 117:22 is quoted: "The stone that the build-
ers rejected has become the chief cornerstone." The one who is expelled will be
the source of the true human order of goodness grounded in God.[37]

Although Jesus provoked the Jewish leaders many times, his cleansing of the
temple was the last straw. This action put Jesus firmly in the footsteps of prophets
such as Isaiah and Amos. At the very least, overturning the tables of the money
changers flung a stiff ethical challenge to the sacrificial cult and the economy
built around it. Since Jesus' disruptive actions must have closed down the system
for at least a day, right at Passover time, it is quite possible that Jesus' intention
was to close down the system for all time. In any case, when Jesus served bread
and wine at his last meal, he started a ritual that did not depend on the sacrifice of
victims of any kind but would be firmly grounded in the memory of Jesus' sacrifice on the cross. In Jesus' critique of temple worship, Goodhart sees "an internal
Jewish affair."[38] In fact, in order to be Christian, we must recognize that we have
been Jewish first and "to own the specifically Jewish Toradic critique of sacrificial
violence as [our] own in order that violence be rejected and peace established."[39]

The Passion narratives reveal the truth of sacred violence by disclosing, in
detail, the combination of mob action and judicial murder for what it is with no
punches pulled. The Gospel writers show with unrelenting clarity how mimetic
contagion takes over the crowd in Jerusalem until all awareness of the truth is
lost. It was the same crowd that threw palm branches on the road in Jesus' honor
that cried out for Jesus' crucifixion. So great was the contagion that Jesus' closest
disciples fled when their leader was arrested, and Peter denied that he knew Jesus
rather than separate himself from the crowd in the courtyard of the high priest. In
the end, Jesus was executed on a cross, the most dishonorable death possible at
the time.

Contrary to much popular teaching, the Gospels do not present Jesus' death as
in any way a sacrifice offered to an angry god to appease that god's wrath over
human sin by punishment that fits the crime. This "logic" assumes that
punishment is the *only* action that can ever right a wrong, a "logic" that fuels
never-ending cycles of vengeance. The Gospels say nothing about *God's* wrath at
the time of Jesus' arrest, trial, and crucifixion, but they say much about the wrath
of humans. What the Gospel texts show clearly is that the death of Jesus was
committed entirely by a collective effort of human beings who blamed Jesus for
all the social tension in Jerusalem. When Jesus said that it was "necessary" that he
undergo suffering and death (Mark 8:31), the necessity that he was referring to
was *human* necessity, not God's.[40] Caiaphas stated the logic of sacred violence

straight out: "You do not understand that it is better for you to have one man die for the people than to have the whole nation destroyed" (Jn. 11:50).

If Jesus had stayed dead, the Gospels as we know them would never have been written. But Peter recovered from his mimetic contagion enough to hear the cock crow. Then, he and the other disciples recovered from scattering in their blind fear and regathered in a locked room. But how could such a small group that was running scared end up proclaiming the truth of Jesus' death with such boldness? It was humanly impossible for the disciples to overcome the mimetic contagion to that degree. But God did what humans could not do. God had not sacrificed Jesus in any way. What God did was raise the crucified Jesus to life. More importantly, the risen Christ did not come in anger to exact revenge on those who betrayed him or those who killed him. Schwager tells us that in Jesus' parable of the evil workers in the vineyard, the owner's "goodness finds a limit and makes way for retributional punishment," so that this parable remains "within the limits of human thought." Schwager goes on to say that

> The action of God in Jesus' fate goes a fundamental step beyond the behavior of the owner of the vineyard. If the latter reacted to the killing of his son with the killing of the wine-growers (Mark 12:9), the heavenly Father sent his risen Son back to murdering humanity and to the disciples in their failure with the words: "Peace be with you" (John 20:19). If even the greatest misdeed against his own Son provoked no reaction of revenge, then there is no other thinkable deed which God would not willingly forgive.[41]

Indeed, far from seeking revenge against the disciples, the risen Jesus came to them through locked doors and breathed the Holy Spirit on them to give them the gift of God's life. Girard says,

> It is, of course, the Risen Jesus who re-gathered the disciples and gave them this power. The Resurrection is responsible for this change, of course, but even this most amazing miracle would not have sufficed to transform these men so completely if it had been an isolated wonder rather than the first manifestation of the redemptive power of the Cross.[42]

In his anthropological approach, Girard does not try to tackle ontological questions. However, he insists "the Son alone is united with the Father in the fullness of humanity and divinity." Jesus is the "only mediator, the one bridge between the kingdom of violence and the Kingdom of God."[43] In short, the acts of Jesus *are* the acts of God. Another way to express this conviction is to note that

Jesus himself modeled for us the right way to embody the human quality of mimesis, a way that acts out the model Jesus learned from his heavenly Father. What Jesus did was carry out the works his father gave him to carry out (Jn. 5:36). He did not speak and act for himself. It was the Father, living in him who was doing the work (Jn. 14:11).

In the famous hymn in Philippians, St. Paul urges all Christians to follow the model of Christ "who, though he was in the form of God, did not regard equality with God as something to be exploited, but emptied himself, taking the form of a slave" (Phil. 2:6–7). Many times St. Paul stresses the importance of being an example for others (Phil. 3:17, 1 Th. 1:7). All of us are called to model Christ to each other. Alison suggests that the more an infant receives a sense of life as a gift from its parents, the less need the infant has to grasp at life in a competitive way.[44] Hence the importance of our not being a *skandalon* to the "little ones" (Mt. 18:6). The persons of the Holy Trinity imitate one another in love with no competition between them. That is the model revealed by Jesus Christ.

The Intelligence of the Victim

The collective violence of all-against-one requires the avoidance of truth of what they are really doing. In order to avoid this truth, the society must project its violence against the victim onto God. It is no accident that the pacifistic verses in the Sermon on the Mount are accompanied by solemn warnings against the distortions of projection: "Why do you see the speck in your neighbor's eye, but do not notice the log in your own eye?" (Mt. 7:3). The tendency to project violence back onto God leads many readers of the New Testament to think that Jesus was throwing a tantrum at those who rejected his message when he uttered apocalyptic sayings of doom. Girard, however, stresses that the "wars and rumors of war" are simply the natural consequence of choosing mimetic violence rather than the kingdom of God.[45] That is, it is not God who inflicts violence on humanity as a punitive measure for being bad, it is humans who inflict violence on other humans as a sign of their collective rejection of God. When we insist on choosing to act in this way, God delivers us over to our own passions and allows us to live with the result (Rom. 1:18–25). Girard also brings up the theme of projection in his interpretation of the parables that come at the climax of Jesus' teaching ministry. In the parable of the talents, the master says, "I will judge you by your own words, you wicked slave! You knew, did you, that I was a harsh man, taking what I did not deposit and reaping what I did not sow?" (Lk. 19:22). It is the lazy servant who said that the master was hard, not the master.[46] Likewise, it was the listeners of the parable of the wicked servants in the vineyard who said that these servants would come to a bad end. As noted above, the risen Christ did not, in fact, come to destroy those who had crucified him; the risen Jesus restrained himself from any show of strength against those who killed him or forsook him. By offering forgiveness and the strength to imitate the Lamb of God in word and deed, the risen Christ definitively countered the worldly tendency to resolve human issues through the competitive use of power.[47] Instead, Jesus revealed himself as "the forgiving victim."[48]

From the truth of the risen and forgiving victim, it follows that any act, or even any thought, of making another person a victim casts a veil over the truth. It also follows that only the voice of the victim can reveal the truth. Alison calls this "the intelligence of the victim."[49] The writers of the Gospels do not tell the story of Jesus' judicial murder from their own point of view. "It is the victim's intelligence that is allowed to provide the lines which make the story what it is."[50] The victim's intelligence also reveals that God has nothing to do with death. "Jesus was working out of an imagination which was simply untinged by death, so that he could work beyond it."[51] Jesus demonstrated this imagination by commending his life to his heavenly Father so that he could receive life from the heavenly Father he had given himself over to. It is through the intelligence of the victim that St. Paul proclaims Jesus Christ as Lord. The God who said "Let light shine out of darkness" is the God "who has shone in our hearts to give the light of the knowledge of the glory of God in the face of Jesus Christ" (2 Cor. 4:5–6). True knowledge is not derived from our intellects; true knowledge is derived from the face of the victim.

Here is the crux of the matter: The reality of the victim is the bedrock for discerning truth. There is much in mimetic theory to fuel a hermeneutics of suspicion. Even some of the greatest saints in the Church have suffered the ill effects of mimetic contagion. However, unlike deconstructionism, mimetic theory does not deny that there is any truth or that a search for origins is illusory. On the contrary, mimetic theory asserts that there is truth and the truth *can* be known. Where? In the place of the victim. More than once, I have seen Girard challenged in a panel discussion to admit that we cannot discern truth beyond our subjectivity. Each time, Girard has replied with the truth of the victim. When we are presented with a victim, he says, we *must* ask the question, are the accusations *true*? Yes or No. Girard often brings up the infamous Dreyfus Case to prove his point. The imbroglio of that affair confronted the people of Girard's native France with the question of truth over the falsehood of mimetic contagion. Girard reminds us that if Dreyfus' supporters "had admitted, as have some in our day, that to believe there is such a thing as truth is the fundamental sin—then Dreyfus would never have been vindicated, and the lie would have won the victory."[52]

There is no question that the example of Jesus has triggered an enormous amount of sympathy for victims from the hospitals for lepers that sprouted in the early Christian centuries to the extensive ministry to those suffering from AIDS in our own time. Unfortunately, the notorious examples of sacred violence committed by Christians are too many and too well-known to need enumerating in this book. As an example, Girard begins his book *The Scapegoat* with an analysis of a document by the fourteenth-century poet Guillaume de Machaut. This writer explains why the Jews are entirely to blame for the Black Death plague and, on that account, deserve the collective violence that has been inflicted upon them.[53] Such examples should caution us against being too quick to assume that possession of the Gospel saves us from perpetrating sacred violence. Often, the disciples who fought over who was the greatest prove to be a more attractive model to Christians than Jesus, who "humbled himself and became obedient to the point of death" (Phil 2:8). Because we perpetuate the mimetic rivalry of the disciples, we perpetuate the scapegoating mechanisms to try and hold society together. It stands to reason, then, that the Christian tradition would develop over time. The process of absorbing the "intelligence of the victim" is a slow one. It isn't that God had a change of mind and heart somewhere along the line and became a more easy-going deity than before. What has been happening is that it takes God's people time to understand how wide the kingdom of God really is and then to adjust to that reality.

One of the interesting signs of our times is that it has become "politically correct" to show sympathy for victims, ranging from unpopular groups within society to animals and the environment. There is much in Girard's theory to gratify anybody who is serious about being "politically correct." There is also a serious caution. As the example of King Josiah reminds us, there is always a danger that we might defend victims at the cost of creating victims. S. Mark Heim suggests that this problem of creating victims in the name of sympathy for victims is a particularly Christian problem, a problem that first manifested itself as anti-Semitism. "The moment we point a finger at some 'they' as Jesus' killers, we have enacted the sin that the cross specifically revealed and meant to overcome. We cut the branch behind ourselves."[54] The example of King Josiah shows us that this problem was developing in Judaism as it revealed the truth of victims. Another danger is that we can focus so intently on certain victims that the impact of our actions on other victims is not noticed. Worse, a victim may claim entitlement to vindictive behavior that keeps the cycle of violence going. Alison warns us,

> If you know the crucified and risen victim, you know that you are not yourself the victim. The danger is much more that you are either actively, or by omission, or both, a victimizer.... The person who thinks of himself or herself as the victim is quick to divide the world into 'we' and 'they.' In the knowledge of the risen victim there is only a 'we,' because we no longer need to define ourselves over against anyone at all.[55]

We are living in a precarious time. Girard argues that the reason this is so is because Jesus has destroyed the mechanism of sacred violence once and for all. The old ways of stabilizing society can only fail now that Jesus has blown the cover on sacred violence. When we resort to sacred violence anyway, we splinter society into small groups, each united around one victim or group of victims. Instead of one victim providing the centerpiece of a society, we have several victims providing several centers. This leaves us no center at all. Since these acts of violence no longer "work," the violence escalates. Add the tendency of reform-minded people to defend victims in ways that create more victims, and we have the perfect recipe for social chaos. That's the bad news. The good news is that God continues to gather all of us into the Kingdom of God's peace through the Holy Spirit. The Holy Spirit, the Paraclete, is our advocate, our lawyer for the defense. We have to realize, of course, in the depths of our hearts, with God's grace, that the Holy Spirit is the advocate of *everybody*. Following Jesus means becoming an advocate of *all* God's people. God does not exclude anybody from the Kingdom. We can exclude ourselves, however, by excluding others.

A Girardian analysis of human behavior suggests that when the desires of two or more people become enmeshed in one another, conflict is the usual result. This conflict is not absolutely inevitable, however. It was possible for Jonathan to desire the kingship for David rather than for himself. The more our human desires are enmeshed in the desires of Christ, the more we desire that the life we receive from God be given to all other people. Then, and only then, do we have the courage to model ourselves on Jesus, who laid down his life in the faith that the heavenly Father desired, not death, but abundant life.

PART II

▼

THE RULE OF BENEDICT IN DIALOGUE WITH RENÉ GIRARD'S MIMETIC THEORY

CHAPTER 3

▼

A CALL TO CONVERSION: THE PROLOGUE TO THE RULE OF BENEDICT

"Listen!" This opening word of Benedict's Rule is a call to obedience. Benedict goes on to admonish us to listen to the master's teaching with the "ear of [our] hearts" so that we will turn away from the "inertia of disobedience" to "the labor of obedience" (Pr. 1). Listening with the ear of the heart is not a passive act. We have truly listened only if we *act* upon the words that we listen to. We must "renounce self-will and take up the powerful and shining weapons of obedience to fight for the Lord Christ, the true king" (Pr. 3). Benedict says that the "inertia of disobedience" is "self-will," but if we turn to the "shining weapons of obedience," we will fight for "the Lord Christ, the true king." Here, Benedict is as specific about what he would have us turn *to* as he is about what he would have us turn *from*.

Benedict's use of formal terms for Christ, such as "the true king," is typical of Benedict's reverential attitude. De Waal notes that Benedict does not even use the name "Jesus" in the Rule, but he always sticks to the title "Christ."[1] Concern with the Arian heresy that denied the full divinity of Christ may be one reason for this formality. The Gothic rulers of the Italian peninsula in Benedict's time were Arian, so concern about their theology would have been very much on his mind. It is very possible that Benedict wanted to be sure to safeguard Christ's divinity under these circumstances, but deference and respect for authority, both human and divine, are at the heart of his communal vision. De Waal admits that although Benedict's formal language may seem to create a gulf between Christ and humanity, it has the virtue of giving us "the sense of the power and the presence of the risen Christ" and it "makes the paschal mystery central and inescapable."[2] De Waal goes on to say that this formality is balanced by the parable of the prodigal son echoed in the opening words of the prologue, which "address each one of us as the prodigal and at once plunge each of us immediately into that story."[3] In light of Girard's mimetic theory, we might define conversion as turning away from mimetic rivalry and turning toward a generous willing of the good of the other person. Chittester, ever conscious of the social implications of Benedict's teachings, reminds us that "if we live in an environment of corporate greed or personal violence, we cannot grow from it spiritually until we allow ourselves to recognize it."[4] For Girard, recognizing the systemic presence of sacrificial violence in society is the first step toward overcoming it.

Benedict's contrast between "the labor of obedience" and "the inertia of disobedience" (Pr. 2) suggests that disobedience is the default mechanism if we do not exert the effort obedience requires. We have to make a conscious choice in favor of the communal good and then constantly renew that choice with an energetic effort. Benedict uses two recurring images in the prologue to prod us into making this choice and acting on it energetically. The first image is combat: "Therefore we must prepare our hearts and our bodies to wage the battle of holy obedience to [God's] precepts" (RB Pr. 40). Those of us who are horrified with the effects of war may wish to back away from Benedict's use of military imagery. Moreover, Girard's thought alerts us to how strongly mimetic rivalry drives war, even so-called "just wars." But even if we throw away all swords and guns, we must not forget that resisting the powerful currents of destructive mimesis requires a military-type discipline. Kardong points us in this direction by noting that "the early monks considered their battle against sin to be a continuation of the conflict of the martyrs against pagan persecution." In their struggles against sin, "they frequently expressed warm devotion to the person of Christ. The love of Christ kept the early Church from descending into a mere struggle of wills with the Roman state."[5] It is precisely military discipline that strengthens us to resist entering into violent relationships with others. Benedict's second recurring image is running. When referring to John 12:35, Benedict substitutes the verb "run" for John's use of "walk" in that verse when he urges us to "run while you have the light of life (RB Pr. 13). De Waal says that Benedict's change of a gospel word "tells us a lot about his sense of urgency."[6] Further, Benedict tells us that "if we wish to dwell in the tent of [God's] kingdom we shall not arrive unless we *run* there by good deeds" (RB Pr. 22, italics mine). Likewise, we must "race along the way of God's commandments" (RB Pr. 49). Clearly, the effort required by the "labor of obedience" will be as strenuous as a marathon.

Benedict trumpets reveille with this warning issued each morning at the beginning of Matins: "Today, if you hear [God's] voice, harden not your hearts" (RB Pr. 10, Ps. 95:8). This verse is an allusion to the murmuring of the Israelites in the desert. The spring from which Moses produced water by striking the rock was named Meribah, which means "Contention." In the midst of this contention, Moses was threatened with collective violence until he succeeded in making the water flow. Here, the "inertia of disobedience" is the tendency for discontented members of the community to imitate each other's discontent until it snowballs through the whole community, at which point everybody bands together against either the leader or some other member deemed responsible for the present crisis. In prescribing the use of this psalm at the start of each day, Benedict uses God's warning as a daily wake-up call against the contagious vice of murmuring and its destructive effect on a community.

Benedict then throws out this question from Psalm 34: "Which of you desires life and longs to see good days?" (Pr. 15, Ps. 34:13) and combines it with the parable of the workers in the vineyard where the Lord himself is "seeking a worker for himself in the crowds" (RB Pr. 14, Mt. 20:1–16). In the parable, the crowds consist of the idle laborers who have not yet been hired, those still sunk in "the sloth of disobedience." Since the master offers a job to everybody in the crowd by the end of the day, this call is not limited to a chosen few, but is addressed to all people. From a Girardian perspective, it is noteworthy that the workers have emerged *from* the mimetic crowd once they have heard God's voice. These workers are not romantic individualists; they have joined a different collective, but one governed by the desires of the divine master rather than that of the crowd. Our fundamental choice is either to imitate those who are idle and do not respond to God's call or to imitate those who are working in God's vineyard and do the work the other workers are doing.

Benedict then tells us that "if we wish to dwell in the tent of [God's] kingdom we shall not arrive unless we *run* there by good deeds" (RB Pr. 22, Ps. 15:1, italics mine). The one who "will dwell in [God's] tent or "will rest on [God's] holy mountain" will be the one who "speaks the truth candidly and has not committed fraud with his tongue, and has not listened to slander against his neighbors" (RB Pr. 27, Ps. 15:1–3). Slander, of course, is the spreading of lies about other people, an essential ingredient of scapegoating. This is one of many instances where the Psalms inundate us with exhortations to speak the truth and shun lies. Girard has shown us how collective violence requires lies to perpetuate itself. The psalmist shows us that renouncing collective violence leads to seeking the truth and speaking it. Seeking the truth and speaking it, in turn, builds up the good of the community. When the devil suggests telling lies, committing fraud, and listening to slander (Satan is an accuser and a liar from the beginning), these thoughts must be smashed against Christ (RB Pr. 28). Once again, Benedict uses an expression that stresses exertion. We easily fall into the trap of just pushing disobedient thoughts away, but if that is all we do, we are in danger of sweeping the house clean only to clear space for the exorcized demon to bring back seven companions worse than itself (Mt. 12:43–45). This is why it is important to turn our thoughts to Christ and follow Christ as our model. Otherwise, we remain preoccupied with the models offered by the devil. By smashing the devil's thoughts against Christ, we realize that we cannot take credit for the good that we do, because our good actions are dependent on the grace of Christ, the rock upon which we must build the house of the obedient life (Pr. 33–34, Mt. 7:24–25).

Strenuous as the exertion is that Benedict urges on us, we remain totally dependent on the grace of God. As we "fight for Christ our true king" with "the shining weapons of obedience," we must also "beg [God] with insistent prayer to bring [our good work] to completion" (RB Pr. 3–4). Even as we run to God's kingdom by good deeds, Benedict reminds us that "the fear of the Lord keeps these people from vaunting themselves for their good performance, for they know that what is good in themselves could not have come about except for the Lord" (RB Pr. 29). This sort of juxtaposition does not amount to a theological treatise on grace and works in Benedict's Rule. Rather, Benedict plunges us into God's energizing call, which *stirs* us into action. We cannot enter into the race unless we are energized by God's wake-up call. Once we are so energized, God *shows* us the way to the vineyard that he calls us to. As we expend our energy in *running* the race before us, the *energy* for running that race comes from God.

Mimetic theory also brings us to this same tension between God's initiative and human effort. Girard says that we should take Jesus at his word when he said on the cross, "Father, forgive them; for they do not know what they are doing" (Lk. 23:34). Girard goes on to say that here Jesus "expresses the powerlessness of those caught up in the mimetic snowballing process powerless to see what moves and compels them. Persecutors think they are doing the good, the right thing;

they believe they are working for justice and truth; they believe they are saving their community."[7] Girard goes on to say that "scandals are above all a kind of inability to see, an insurmountable blindness."[8] Unfortunately, Girard does not show us what we can do once the truth of sacred violence has been revealed to us by the Gospels. Schwager is much more helpful here with his teaching on the work of the Holy Spirit. After Easter, Jesus' disciples

> were inwardly so deeply pervaded by the Spirit that they began to speak and act in a new way, and yet they maintained in the experience of the Spirit a distinctness, so that they did not attribute the new power to themselves.[9]

What the Holy Spirit did for the disciples, the Holy Spirit does for each one of us. Benedict reminds us that it is through the Spirit that we "heap praise on the Lord working in [us], saying 'Not to us, Lord, not to us, but to your name be the glory'" (RB Pr. 30, Psalm 115:1).

The prologue fleshes out the Benedictine vow of *conversatio morum*. In the past, this problematic Latin phrase has been translated as "conversion of life." A more accurate translation is "fidelity to the monastic life" (RB 58:17). Kardong admits that "since the word contains the evocative root *converti*, such an interpretation seems pretty bland, but the ancients assumed that acceptance of the monastic lifestyle would imply a thorough change of the person on a deep level."[10] This thorough change on a deep level is dramatized by the voice of God calling out to us and rousing us to turn from "the sloth of disobedience" and "run in the way of God's commands." All Christians, of course, are called to conversion as an ongoing process, not just monastics. In the course of studying the Rule, we shall examine the tools Benedict gives us for living this life of conversion.

The prologue presents us with the traditional choice presented by Deuteronomy 30:15: the way of life or the way of death. When the fundamental human choice is presented in those terms, there is an element of severity. Dire threats to the disobedient are not far around the corner. Benedict warns us to obey God so that he will not disinherit us "like an angry father does with his sons, nor will he, like a fearsome lord enraged with our offenses, give us over to "perpetual punishment as wicked slaves who did not wish to follow him to glory" (RB Pr. 6–7). It is important to remember, however, that Benedict does not suggest that God in any way *wants* anybody to be disinherited or handed over to everlasting torment. The *only* thing God wants is that we should "follow him to glory." God does not offer life *and* death. God offers *life*. If one does not accept the offer of life, then one has forfeited life because there is no other source for it.

Benedict does not conceive of the way of life as a grim choice that we make while gritting our teeth and looking ahead to a life devoid of pleasure. That is more in keeping with the attitude of the Master who ends his prologue with the Lord's threat: "I will punish their sins with the rod."[11] It is precisely at this point where Benedict parts company with the Master and reverts to the much more positive vision of John Cassian. Like Cassian, Benedict believes that the inner presence of God's joy can be experienced in this life as a foretaste of heaven. Choosing to accept God's gift of life and start on the path of salvation "can only be narrow at the outset," but as we progress, "our hearts will swell with unspeakable sweetness of love, enabling us to race along the way of God's commandments" (RB Pr. 49). Here is the counterbalance to the formal language Benedict uses in relation to God. Christ may be the Risen Lord and King, but this same Christ fills our hearts with "unspeakable sweetness of love."

CHAPTER 4

▼

A CALL TO COMMITMENT: THE KINDS OF MONASTICS

Fundamentally, there are two kinds of monastics: those who live under a rule and an abbot and those who don't. Among those who don't are anchorites. These monastics once lived under a rule and an abbot, but after having lived through "long testing in a monastery, have become able to fight against the vices without the help of other people but solely with the help of God" (RB 1:4–6). The other kinds of monastics are sarabaites, who live in twos or threes, and gyrovagues, who are "ever on the move and never stable" (RB 1:11). Benedict then announces that the rest of his Rule applies to the cenobites, "the most vigorous" kind of monastics (RB 1:13).

Benedict's pairing of rule and abbot, in that order, is important. Although the charismatic style of leadership can be salutary on a short-term basis, it does not sustain the monastic life over the long haul. Even the holiest of abbots have their blind spots, and they can be caught in mimetic conflict just as much as any other monastic. For that reason, there is need for a monastic rule that applies to the whole community, including the abbot. A rule legislates a common life so that the members of the community will normally eat the same food and drink the same beverage and pray at the same times. But for all the possible faults an abbot might have, Benedict insists that there must be an abbot who has the prime responsibility for interpreting the rule for the community and enforcing it. A look at the other three kinds of monastics who are not cenobites helps to clarify Benedict's vision of the cenobitic life where monastics live in community under an abbot.

The anchorites, or hermits, are the monastic pioneers whose noble spirituality continues to inspire idealistic Christians today. Benedict shows respect for anchorites, but he shows considerable reserve as well. He is treading carefully here, because both Cassian and the Master are part of a large and loud chorus that has "a higher opinion of anchoritism than of cenobitism."[1] But Benedict's heart is elsewhere. Closer to his outlook are the reservations that Benedict's predecessor, Basil the Great (c. 330–379), expresses for the hermit life. Basil insists that community life is "more advantageous than the solitary life both for preserving the goods bestowed on us by God and for warding off the external attacks of the Enemy."[2] Basil also frets over the hermit's peril of self-satisfaction because "the solitary has no one to appraise him of his conduct."[3] Most serious is the hermit's lack of opportunity to practice charity for other people. After noting that Jesus washed the feet of his disciples, Basil asks, "Whom, therefore, will you wash? To whom will you minister? In comparison with whom will you be the lowest, if you live alone?"[4] It should be added that many stories of desert monastics point toward similar dangers for a hermit. In one story, a monk left his community because he was always losing his temper with the other monks. After setting up his hermitage, he took a pitcher to the nearest water source, some distance away. During his return, he spilled the water repeatedly, and finally he broke the pitcher in a fit of anger. At that point, he realized that moving away from everybody else hadn't sweetened his temper after all and he moved back to his community. Other stories demonstrate the importance attached to charitable works, especially the obligations of caring for the sick and offering hospitality to visitors. Although Benedict respected the vocation of anchorites who had been trained in community, he was unwilling to consider the eremitical calling a graduation from community life. Kardong, in the spirit of Benedict, cautions us that "to relegate common life to the ancillary task of forming anchorites cuts at the very heart of community," making the communal life merely an "instrumental means" for using "others for personal growth" and then leaving them "behind when convenient."[5] As far as Benedict is concerned, there is no higher calling than the cenobitic life to graduate to.

I think Girard would agree with Benedict that problems in human relationships are not solved by withdrawing from other people. If we try that, our mimetic entanglements are sure to follow us to the hermitage. Girard has gone so far as to say that "the mimetic is itself a desire and is therefore the real 'unconscious.'"[6] With that being the case, a fundamental human task is to become conscious of how the desires of other people infect our own desires while becoming conscious of how we infect others. When a group of people live together, whether in a family, a monastery, or some other community, they have the opportunity to learn how to be infected by the right spirit (i.e., the Holy Spirit) in others and to resist infection of a bad spirit of mimetic desire from these same people. Likewise, we can see our own spirit mirrored in other people as we become aware of how we influence them. Maybe we can even see (please God!) the influence of the Holy Spirit moving through us to them. But outside of community, all the mimetic entanglements remain inside, very much alive, to the extent that they may become overwhelming. Living alone heightens the danger that faces us all, that we will come to regard our inner life as our own possession. "These are *my* feelings, *my* thoughts, *my* hangups." At this point, we are filled with mimetic desire even as we become fully convinced that we are not affected by other people.

In spite of these concerns, hermits deserve a good word before we move on. At their best, hermits witness to the vital importance of each person's individual relationship with God. When this relationship is real, it is not *individualistic*; it is rooted in the divine persons. The horror of collective violence causes one to think that we must learn to stand up to the crowd to stop the atrocities it commits. Girard, however, offers no hope that individuals can do that by human strength alone, but with God, even this becomes possible. A powerful example of an individual's resistance to collective mimesis is the prophet Micaiah in 1 Kings 22. All of the other prophets were vigorously prophesying to King Jehoshaphat and the king of Israel that their proposed military venture will succeed. Only Micaiah dissented. He dissented because he had seen "the Lord sitting on his throne" and he heard one of the attending spirits tell the Lord that it would send a lying spirit to "all of the prophets." This narrative borders on blaming God for the subsequent misadventure, but one should bear in mind that it is the lying spirit who says what Jehoshaphat and the king of Israel have already decided they want the Lord to tell them. This degree of holding firm in God against "all of the prophets" is the strength of an eremitical vocation. The more deeply we are rooted in God, the more deeply we are immersed in the love that God has for *all* creation. It was in the solitude of her cell in Norwich that Lady Julian gained the courage politely but firmly to question the Church's article of faith that many people will be damned, as

> it seemed to me that it was impossible that every kind of thing should be well, as our Lord revealed at this time. And to this I had no other answer as a revelation from our Lord except this: What is impossible to you is not impossible to me. I shall preserve my word in everything, and I shall make everything well. And in this I was taught by the grace of God that I should stand firm and believe firmly that every kind of thing will be well, as our Lord revealed at that same time.[7]

Benedict has nothing but condemnation for the sarabaites and the gyrovagues. The "wretched" sarabaites "have been tested by no rule." Like gold that has not been tested in the furnace, "they are as soft as lead" (RB 1:6). These "monastics" live in small groups with no structure of authority and therefore no accountability. "Their own opinions and desires they call holy; what displeases them they say is not permissible" (RB 1:9). Mimetic theory rings several alarm bells here. If we live only by our own opinions and desires, then we are really at the mercy of the opinions and desires of others. De Waal notes how much our culture encourages us "to become more and more inward-looking; narcissism is rife and the tools for self-analysis and self-help are so readily available that I can easily enclose myself in a sheepfold of my own making."[8] Chittester notes that Sarabaites might live good and moral lives, but still only lives of "moderate contentment." We need to remember that "it's not all that uncommon for people of all eras to use religion to makes themselves comfortable."[9]

The gyrovagues are the worst of all "monastics." They are always on the move, never staying long in any one place, never staying with the same people. Gyrovagues might be congenial people, but they have no commitment whatsoever. Even more than the sarabaites, they are "slaves to their own wills and the delights of the palate" (RB 1:11). Benedict's feelings about this lifestyle are so strong that stability of place is the first vow he asks a monastic to take at profession. That is to say, more than a life of prayer in community, the Benedictine life is one of *commitment* to a life of prayer in a *particular* community. It is only those persons who have known us on a long-term basis who can most really challenge our foibles and encourage us to grow. A person who flits from one acquaintance to another without forming lasting relationships avoids these challenges at a great cost. Unfortunately, commitment is precisely a quality that is often lacking today. Not only does lack of commitment show up in divorce statistics, but it governs career choices as well. These days, many people spend much time and expense to be trained in a skill with the *intention* that they will practice it for only a time and then move on to something else. It won't do to take rigid positions that imprison people in horrific marriages, bad employment situations, or a broken down monastic vocation, but the chances of a marriage and a job holding up on a long-term basis are much better if they are entered into with *commitment*.

The current mimetic process in today's society makes commitment all the more challenging, as it is all the harder to be committed to people who are not willing to be committed in their turn. When faced with this dilemma, it is all the more important to make a decision as to whether our model will be the people around us who are uncommitted or Christ. Christ is committed to us, and he is just as committed to those who are not faithful. The Resurrected Christ gathered the community that his death had scattered, and the Holy Spirit continues this work of gathering. Can we do less?

The external stability of place that Benedict prescribes is intended to foster an inner stability in each person. Being rooted in community leads to being rooted in God. De Waal says that such roots "let something grow, reach maturity, produce fruits from deep inside myself."[10] De Waal goes on to contrast stability which is fruitful from "staticness" which is unproductive. True stability allows for flexibility, the flexibility that a tree needs to grow properly. If the roots hold firm, then the tree can bend freely to the wind of the Holy Spirit. A good example of this sort of stability was modeled to me by a theology professor I had in college. He believed that one should pick a good thinker, use that thinker's concepts as the basis for one's own thinking, and take those concepts as far as they can go. This sort of rootedness, he reasoned, could bear much fruit. My professor's choice was Alfred North Whitehead. A few years later, taking this basic advice to heart, I settled on Thomas Aquinas. On becoming a Benedictine, the anthropology of Benedict became the lens through which I examined Thomistic thought. In the past dozen years or so, Girard has taken over as my primary thinker, but I still believe that Thomas' thought offers the most satisfying philosophical and theological outlook. I have also found that listening deeply to other people and to the Gospel has caused me to change my mind and heart on some matters. These are ways in which my roots have allowed for a still-growing tree of bewildering richness.

It is well-known among Benedictines that joining a monastery and living under a rule and the guidance of an abbot does not guarantee that one will not become, in essence, a sarabaite or a gyrovague. Even within a community, one can fall into living with one or two other members or even alone over/against the superior and the customs and rules of the house. Or, one can become inwardly scattered, seeking distractions from the common life as much as possible so as never to settle down under the guidance of the superior and the other members of the community. To be a cenobite is to live *with* other people in sufficiently stable relationships so that one can be affected by others and learn how to affect others rightly.

CHAPTER 5

▼

THE AUTHORITY OF CHRIST: THE ABBOT

Benedict's teaching on the abbot is put in bold relief when we contrast that with Girard's insights into sacred kingship. Although many people equate kingship with strength, the king being the man who has grasped power by beating out his rivals, Girard sees "monarchy as at first nothing but the will to reproduce the reconciliatory mechanism."[1] That is to say, monarchy is created for the purposes of designating the sacrificial victims that are periodically required to maintain the unity that collective violence creates for society. Girard goes on to say that "the king is at first nothing more than a victim with a sort of suspended sentence."[2] Many puzzling details about kingship collected by anthropologists fall into place when we look at kingship from this perspective. Such details include ritual (but nonetheless real) abuse inflicted on the new king, and mock (but nonetheless real) battles as part of the coronation rite. Most striking is the requirement that the king break the most sacred taboos, even the prohibition against incest, after which he is executed for his "crimes." (Oedipus has no monopoly on this story!)[3]

It is possible, of course, that the royal victim might turn the tables on his persecutors if he can sufficiently lengthen the time before his sacrifice so that he can "consolidate progressively more power over the community."[4] In such a case, the king retains his power by being the one who creates sacrificial substitutes for himself. That is, the king avoids being the victim only if he creates victims. Indeed, the ancient monarchs who lived to have the tale of their reigns told boasted of their numerous conquests of other people. The many kings who were sacrificial victims we hear about mostly in their culture's mythology. So it is that the king's role in society is inextricably entwined with sacrifice; "he is the *sacrificer* but also the *sacrifice* in periods of crisis."[5] With this understanding of kingship, we can readily understand why Yahweh accused Israel of betraying him when they asked for a king like the other nations (1 Sam. 8:7). Indeed, the Hebrew Bible demythologizes sacred kingship by revealing its sacrificial elements and revealing the naked mimetic struggles in which the king and his rivals are involved. James Williams points out that 1 Samuel recounts more sacrifices than any other book in the Hebrew Bible and suggests that "this is so because the emergence of the monarchy is itself a sacrificial event."[6] The first king, Saul, proves to be a sacrificial victim. As he struggles against his mimetic doubles, Samuel and David, it seems that Saul does not have a chance in the world of doing anything right. He doesn't. He is killed in battle right after violating his own ban against wizards and mediums (1 Sam. 28). Williams says of Saul's demise, "The combination of the failure of the first king as sacrificer and the failure of sacrifice itself is generated from the heart of a religious vision that begins to replace kingship with the writing of history and sacrifice with law and Scripture."[7] Although the imaginations of many have hoisted much glamour upon King David, the Second Book of Samuel shows quite frankly the extent to which David himself was a great sacrificer of other people for the sake of attaining and maintaining his position. A particularly blood-curdling example is David's handing over seven descendants of Saul to appease the vengeful Gibeonites, who had been the victims of Saul's violence (2 Sam. 21:1–9). The author's placing this event at the end of the book, out of its chronological order, adds considerable emphasis to the story and makes it part of the concluding summary of David's reign.

When we consider the full biblical record of King David, not to speak of the kings who followed him, we realize that we must be very careful about what we mean when we say Christ is our king. To think of Christ as a king like David is to invite moral catastrophe. Jesus *redeemed* the Davidic kingship, not only by his death and Resurrection, but by the way he turned the institution of kingship and all other authority on its head in his life and teachings. Like ancient sacred kingship, the kingship of Christ is founded on a victim of collective violence, but with a radical difference. Jesus reigns *as* the victim, not a dead victim, but the *risen* victim. It is the slain Lamb of God who stands on the throne in Revelation. Jesus does not reign by diverting violence from himself to other people. Neither does Jesus reign by instituting a rigid society of inflexible authoritarian laws. Jesus reigns by orienting society toward sympathy for the victim as victim. Before his death at the hands of the authorities of his time, Jesus reminded his disciples of how "the rulers of the Gentiles lord it over them and their great ones are tyrants over them." But it is not to be so among Jesus' followers. "Whoever wants to be great among you must be your servant and whoever wishes to be first among you must be your slave; just as the Son of Man came not to be served but to serve, and to give his life a ransom for many" (Mt. 20:25–28). The word translated here as "ransom" is *lytron*, that is, the price of release. Williams points out that this is "an obviously sacrificial word" used to "break out of a sacrificial worldview."[8] Williams explains that this ransom is not sacrificial but is "God's free offering of release to human beings through Jesus as the divine son, … the king who rules through serving."[9] Yet another powerful example of Jesus redeeming the Davidic kingship is his healing the blind and the lame in the temple right after riding into Jerusalem on a colt and then cleansing the temple (Mt. 21:14). The blind and the lame are the very people David had insisted be driven away from the temple (1 Sam. 5:8).

When he writes about the abbot of the monastery, Benedict uses much of the patriarchal language that supported the Roman ideal of the *pater familias*. Chittester, however, insists that Benedict is envisioning "a different kind of life than the sixth-century Roman ever saw."[10] Kardong reminds us that "all of the images for the abbot used by Benedict and the ancient monks are drawn from the Bible and not from contemporary politics."[11] It is well-known that Roman law gave the father of a family unrestricted rights over all who were dependent on him, including the right to decide if a child should live or die. Benedict's concept of fatherhood is very different. The word "abbot" is derived from the Aramaic word *abba*, the word Jesus used of his heavenly Father. For Jesus, his heavenly Father was the one who overwhelmed him with the love of one who will, in the words of the Lord's Prayer, provide daily bread to all, forgive all, and save all from overwhelming trials. We have already noted that the Gospels radically subvert the old system of sacred kingship and offer a radically different alternative. It should not surprise us if Benedict proves to be as revolutionary as the Gospels.

Benedict reveals his subversive vision of authority right at the start when he says that the abbot "is believed to represent Christ in the monastery" (RB 2:2). This loaded phrase is the gunpowder that explodes the old system. Placing the abbot in the place of Christ puts the whole community, the abbot included, in a precarious position. Insofar as one views reality through the old system of sacred violence, this designation seems to have the effect of investing absolute authority in the abbot. If the Christian is expected to obey Christ in all things, then the Christian is expected to obey one's superior in the same way. There is the danger that a person in authority will identify with Christ as the Lord but not as the savior who gave his life to save all people. The next step is to blur the distinction between the leader and God. The result is precisely the same social configuration that produced and sustained the sacrificial kingship in ancient times.

It is essential, then, to hold fast to the truth that the abbot holds the place of a person *other* than the abbot himself, a place that no human may usurp. In this way, the authority of the abbot is relativized, even deconstructed, in significant ways. The sacred king did not represent God; he *was* God. The abbot *represents* or *holds the place* of another human being who is God. The abbot's authority, strong as it is, is a derived authority. The abbot himself is not the measure of right and wrong. The measure of right and wrong is the Gospel and the Rule. The abbot is not allowed to teach anything contrary to the Law of God. The abbot's authority is relativized in another significant way through the image of the shepherd. A shepherd takes care of a flock that belongs to somebody else. The monastics entrusted to the abbot's care do not belong to him; they belong to Christ.

Holding fast to the couplings of abbot and rule, and abbot and Gospel ensures that the abbot is a *member* of the community. In a sacrificial system as understood by Girard, the victim is both partly a member of the community and partly outside of the community. By forcing the king outside of the normal laws, such as those prohibiting incest, the king was, in effect, expelled from the community. In those cases where the king managed to consolidate power and sustain it by sacrificing others in his place, the sacrificial victims were first expelled from the community and so lost the protection of the law. We find to this day that those in positions of authority are tempted to think that their position puts them above the rules and laws that others are subject to, or even to go so far as to blur the distinction between law and self. Louis XIV's famous declaration—"*L'État c'est moi*"—is the end result of that path. In any community, then, the first step toward preventing a sacrificial order is for all to make sure that those in authority are *members* of the community and not in any way *above* the community.

Kardong says that "the abbot makes present Christ as the object of obedience, and not the 'obedient Christ.'"[12] This truth gains its fullest perspective when we note that the Rule identifies those who are sick and the guests, especially those who are poor, with Christ. This is a far cry from an image of Christ as an almighty monarch devoted to ordering people about. Instead, Christ issues authority from his own helplessness on the cross. Obedience to Christ is not, then, primarily obedience to the powerful; it is obedience to those who have no power. In their helplessness, the sick and the poor command the very obedience that the superior commands from the community. This line of thought further suggests that the abbot exerts authority through his own poverty and weakness more than with his own strength. More importantly, the abbot represents Christ by bearing the burdens of the other members of the community. Any sensitive person given a position of leadership knows that the weaknesses and pain of those under his authority weigh much heavier than they did before taking on that position. This bearing of burdens is all the more painful when there is nothing that can be done for another except to bear the pain he is bearing.

Benedict reinforces the importance of the abbot's being a member of the community rather than someone above it by insisting that the abbot "should demonstrate everything that is good and holy by his deeds more than by his words" (RB 2:12). Although "gifted disciples" might benefit from words, the more recalcitrant and naive do not. For these people, the abbot "must model the divine precepts" (RB 2:12). The abbot, of course, can only be a model that the others in the community can imitate if he does what everybody else should be doing. This teaching already had a long history in the monastic tradition by Benedict's time. Typically, a younger monastic would learn through living with a more experienced monastic and doing the same things that the elder did. These elders rarely had to explain anything in words because their actions did all the teaching. Benedict knows instinctively that an elder's modeling must not become a stumbling block (*skandalon*) for others. Saying one thing and doing another makes an elder such a stumbling block. That is why followers are rightly scandalized by this phenomenon. Or they should be! Benedict says that such an abbot will be reproached as a sinner: "'You noticed the speck in your brother's eye, but did not see the plank in your own'" (RB 2:15, Mt. 7:3). Surely, when an abbot has to discipline a monastic, he must examine himself to see if he is in any way guilty of the same offense. If he does this, then "the warnings he gives to others for improvement serve to effect the correction of his own vices" (RB 2:40).

A more insidious way that a superior might become a stumbling block to others is by holding authority in a rivalrous way. This imposes a classic mimetic double bind on everybody else. In this double bind, the model says, imitate me and don't imitate me. In examining this potential dynamic of the master-disciple relationship, Girard notes that the master wants others to take him as a model, *but*

> if the imitation is too perfect, and the imitator threatens to surpass the model, the master will completely change his attitude and begin to display

jealousy, mistrust and hostility. He will be tempted to do everything he can to discredit and discourage his disciples.[13]

This sort of impasse is avoided if the abbot imitates Christ, as Benedict says he should, and the other monastics imitate the abbot's imitation of Christ. Christ is enriched when his creatures share his being, so there is no competition there. The generous love that caused God to create the world in the first place continues to be poured out to all creatures. Benedict has also reminded us that God's love is poured out most especially to victims, such as the sick and the poor. When both master and disciple participate in the being of Christ that is constituted by self-giving, they receive more of Christ's being, which leads to further self-giving, quite the opposite of a rivalrous relationship.

Many times mimetic rivalry asserts itself not through assaults on the position of leadership itself, but through seeking power and influence on the one in authority. If a person cannot be a king, the next best role is to exert influence *through* the king. In fact, this can be the safer position since it is the king who is the sacrificial victim with a suspended sentence. Or is it? One handy way for a king to deflect mimetic rivalry away from himself is to manipulate the courtiers around the throne to fight over the spoils. A king's favorites then become pawns in a game of who can sacrifice whom. The danger of mimetic contagion in such a situation is great. When one or two people are seen to vie for subversive influence with the king, others are likely to join the fray for fear of being left behind and "losing out." In this way, power brokers working behind the throne have often been convenient scapegoats for the monarchs when such a service was required by circumstances.

It is surely this kind of danger that leads Benedict to insist that the abbot not play favorites in the monastery. "He should not love one more than another, unless he finds him more excellent in good deeds and obedience" (RB 2:17). The more susceptible a person in authority is to surface appearances, the greater the danger that he or she will be used to further the personal ambitions of those people. Insofar as an abbot or any other leader plays favorites, there are bound to be serious distortions of truth. People vying for favor and influence will represent both themselves and their competitors falsely. Like Samuel, such a leader is swayed by appearances, while it is God who sees the heart (1 Sam. 16:7). Here is the crux of the matter: If a person in authority falls into mimetic games of retaining power through manipulating other people, then it becomes impossible to see those people as God sees them. Benedict echoes St. Paul when he reminds us that God's view is that "we are all one in Christ, and under one Lord we bear the same yoke of service" (RB 2:20, Gal. 3:28). In holding the place of Christ, the abbot holds the place of the One who loves each person individually, equally, and unconditionally. There is no place in this all-embracing love for mimetic favoritism.

Only within the embrace of God's love for all is there a chance that an abbot can see others truly and make true distinctions among them. The only acceptable reason for advancing one monk over another is if that person be found "superior to others in good works and still humble." (RB 2:21) One can see that an abbot who is playing power games of any kind will fail to see true humility when it is present or will fail to value it. Moreover, the truly humble person will not strive for a higher place in the community for the sake of having a higher place. Such a person will also be more in tune with God's all-embracing love than with personal ambition. We shall see later, when examining the chapters dealing with rank in the community, that part of an abbot's job is to make sure that there are no favors available for the ambitious to strive for. The only "rewards" available should be opportunities to serve the community more diligently than ever.

The even-handed treatment of all monastics heightens the abbot's awareness of the reality of others. One of these realities is that people are different. Even while weighing in against favoritism, Benedict hinted that there are legitimate reasons for treating different people differently. The important thing is to avoid unjust treatment that is skewed by mimetic distortions. Fair and equal treatment means giving each person the treatment appropriate to his or her reality. A cookie cutter approach will not do. The abbot should "vary his approach according to the situation" (RB 2:24). At the level of material things, the abbot will likely discern that some monks need more things for their use than others. The abbot should "pay attention to the weaknesses of the needy and not the bad will of the envious" (RB 55:21). When it comes to correcting the members of the community, the abbot, again, should adjust his approach to each individual. He should "discipline the unruly and restless rather sharply, but entreat the obedient, mild and patient to make more progress" (RB 2:25). "Let him tailor his approach to meet each one's character and understanding" (RB 25:32).

A truly equal treatment is to give each person what that person truly needs. This is tricky, because what a person wants and what a person *needs* are not always the same thing. If a person's desires are driven by mimetic forces, then these desires are likely to be at variance from what God wants for that person. The self-giving quality of authority boils down to attentiveness to the true needs of the *other*. It is also important for the abbot not to be caught in the mimetic desires of others who might then be envious of what another monastic is given by the abbot. The very act of granting something extra to a weaker monastic may cause others to desire the same thing simply because the other has it. When faced with this level of mimetic desire, it is easier for the abbot either to give everybody the same, even though it is not appropriate for everybody, or deny the weak person what that person truly needs. However, only by staying the course of granting what is appropriate to each person can the abbot model a right way of navigating through the confusion of mimetic desires.

Benedict lays a heavy, even an oppressive, emphasis on the abbot's accountability before God. "Let the abbot know that the shepherd will bear the blame if the owner of the sheep finds them less than profitable" (RB 2:7). He must not forget the bad end of Eli, who failed to discipline his evil sons (RB 2:26, 1 Sam. 2–4). There is a fine line that an abbot and anyone else in authority must walk here. Intervening between two or more people at the first hint of trouble can do more harm than good. Leaders are responsible for their relationships with each person but not for these people's relationships with each other. If two people in a community have difficulty getting along, it is up to them to fix the relationship. Nobody else can do it for them. The danger that Benedict is warning against here is that some people, if given too much latitude, might snatch undue power over others and exercise tyranny over them. Benedict's concern for the "weaker" members of the community surely extends to protecting them from any who would browbeat them. An abbot's accountability for the behavior of those under him, however, is not absolute. If he has really tried to reform "a restless and disobedient flock" (RB 2:8), and they have not responded, he is no longer held responsible for them.

The deeper issue of the responsibility we all have for each other is that we all influence each other through our words, our deeds, and even our thoughts, and we need to be mindful of the effects we have on other people. We do not live just to save our own souls; we live to save the souls of everybody. In one of the most moving passages in Dostoevsky's novel *The Brothers Karamazov*, Father Zossima recounts the story of his brother's spiritual awakening, which led him to insist on the responsibility of every person for everybody else, to insist that "each of us is guilty of everything before everyone, and I most of all."[14] Far from being an expression of abject penitence, these words are part of a joyful vision of God's created world. The sense of being guilty before all made Zossima's brother wish to serve all, to hope that all people will give up quarreling, boasting, and remembering each other's offenses. Later on, Father Zossima shows the influence of his dead brother when he admonishes his listeners to

> Keep company with yourself and look to yourself every day and hour, every minute, that your image be ever gracious. See, here you have passed by a small child, passed by in anger, with a foul word, with a wrathful soul; you perhaps did not notice the child, but he saw you, and your unsightly and impious image has remained in his defenseless heart.[15]

Here, Dostoevsky is warning us against being a *skandalon* to others. The hypersensitivity of such reflections can easily become oppressive, however, and it is important to heed them against the backdrop of our oneness in Christ in whom each of us is loved.

The abbot is responsible for the material provisions of the community, and on that account, he has a duty to deal carefully and responsibly in mundane affairs. These days, the abbot must often do fundraising on behalf of the community, an activity that requires much attention to and respect for other people. More seriously, asking for funds puts one in a vulnerable position before others. Yet, in the midst of such activity, the abbot "above all" should "neither neglect nor undervalue the welfare of the souls committed to him by paying more attention to fleeting, earthly, perishable matters" (RB 2:33). There is more to this than giving the "spiritual" priority over the temporal. Dealing with business affairs almost inevitably has a competitive element that can consume anyone who is not securely centered on God. There are times when it is better to have less money and more integrity in one's spiritual life. An abbot can likewise be consumed by "fleeting" and "perishable" matters if he enters a competitive relationship with members of the community where "winning" by gaining their forced submission to his wishes becomes the most important goal.

Benedict's mature reflections on the qualities of the abbot in chapter 64 are among the most attractive statements in the Rule. In a list of maxims for the abbot, Benedict reiterates the servant style of leadership. The abbot should "realize he should profit others rather than precede them" (RB 64:8). That is, abbatial rank should not be the occasion for hauteur on the part of the one who holds it. Again, the abbot is instructed to discern the appropriate way of dealing with each person in each situation as it comes up. In this later chapter, however, this servant style of leadership takes the form of exercising mercy over judgment. The abbot should "hate vices but love the brothers" (RB 64:11). More importantly, "He should aim more at being loved than feared" (RB 64:15). He must be prudent in correcting others so as not to break the vessel while trying to remove the rust (RB 64:12). Especially touching is the counsel that the abbot, aware of his own weaknesses while correcting those of others, not "break the bent reed" (RB 64:13). Kardong tells us that this verse is rich in biblical overtones. In Isaiah 42:3, the Suffering Servant refrains from breaking the bent reed, meaning that he refuses to use power in his dealings, especially with those weaker than himself. Therefore, Benedict compares the abbot to the Servant, which also connects him to the nonviolent Jesus, who preferred to be crucified rather than return evil for evil (Mt. 12:48).[16]

There can be no clearer way of showing that an abbot's authority should not be coercive than this reference to "losers" such as the Suffering Servant and Jesus Himself. Correcting the behavior of another is no fun. In fact, it is one of the hardest actions a person may have to take. (Anyone who *likes* correcting others is in serious moral and spiritual peril!) The gentle approach enjoined by Benedict here entails suffering *with* the person who needs to be corrected. De Waal says, "In using that image of the person as a vessel, he is saying something incarnational. Is he not telling us that each person is a Eucharistic vessel?"[17] The answer is surely yes.

Correcting another is a way of entering the Paschal Mystery on a small scale where one suffers with the other. In taking this gentle approach, there is a very real possibility of "losing." It is important to realize that only so much can be done at any given time. Sometimes a person will not understand what has been said no matter how clearly and pointedly it is expressed. Sometimes a person will understand clearly and simply refuse to obey. In such a situation, the abbot has a choice of escalating a mimetic contest of wills or going away defeated. It is with impasses such as this that Benedict would have us take a long-term approach and "meditate on the prudence of holy Jacob, who said: *If I make my flock walk too far, they will all die in one day*" (RB 64:18, Gen. 33:13). As Chittester says, "Benedict wants a community that is lead, but not driven."[18] It is, of course, *driving* a community that makes its members sacrificial victims, much as the Israelites were victims at the hands of the Egyptians. This is what happens if an abbot becomes "restless and troubled, extreme and headstrong, jealous and oversuspicious," all of which, Benedict says, the abbot should not be (RB 64:16). The more the abbot is at peace, the more the abbot can "arrange everything so that the strong are challenged and the feeble are not overwhelmed" (RB 64:19). When one challenges others without trying to overwhelm them, one is fostering their growth in God and thereby is fostering one's own growth in God as well.

CHAPTER 6

▼

MIMETIC DECISION MAKING: ON CALLING THE COMMUNITY TO COUNSEL

Mimetic theory offers us many insights into the dynamics of communal decisions. It warns us that the entanglement of mimetic rivalry can lead to catastrophic decisions. On the other hand, if mimetic desire should work in a constructive direction where each desires the good of the community, then the mimetic dimensions increase the chances of making a good decision. Although it may be less messy in the short run for a superior to make decisions unilaterally, the superior, in doing so, moves to the margin of the community, precisely the place of the sacrificial victim. In such a case, any mimetic rivalry in the community will pull the superior in different directions, and yet nobody who pulls the superior to a certain decision will take responsibility for that decision if it goes badly.

Benedict's chapter on community consultation navigates both the hazards and the opportunities in decision making. This is one of the most attractive divergences on Benedict's part from The Rule of the Master. The Master has only a short section in his chapter on the abbot about consulting the community. Even there, Kardong notes that the Master is reluctant to consult anyone, "which is not surprising considering his very low estimate of the wisdom of the average cenobite."[1] Benedict shows a much greater spirit of collegiality and genuine respect for what his fellow monastics might have to say. The very act of gathering the community together suggests that making a major decision should be a cooperative endeavor rather than a competitive one. Moreover, Benedict strongly reinforces the importance of the abbot's being a *member* of the community rather than someone above it by following the chapter on the abbot with this chapter on communal decision making.

Mimetic theory calls our attention to the entanglements of desire that complicate the process of group decision making. We tend to assume that each person knows what he or she wants. If a tug-of-war takes place, it is because different people want different things. What is often overlooked is the problem of discerning what each of us *really* wants. Girard would not encourage us to expect to get to the bottom of our *personal* desires, desires that belong to us and nobody else. The entanglement of our desires with those of others is too deep. It may be that something becomes more desirable because somebody else wants it. If that is the case, then does each individual really want it? It is true that some basic desires are innate, or seem to be so. I don't like watermelon or cola drinks and no bandwagon, no matter how crowded, is going to change that. On the other hand, it is worth noticing if an entree on a restaurant's menu seems more attractive if somebody else at the table expresses an interest in it. Or, if I go to a concert and like the piece that was played but a respected friend expresses distaste for the same piece, my liking for that piece may very well drop, at least for a time. On the other hand, if most other people like the piece, it increases the likelihood that I, too, will decide I liked the piece even if I wasn't so sure at first. This problem leads to the joke of the concertgoer who has to read a review of the concert before deciding how good the concert was. Some people try to solve this dilemma by always taking a stance that is at odds with that of most other people, but if that isn't being governed by others' desires, I don't know what is. Of course, increased experience of listening to the *music* itself, and enriching my own listening experiences with the insights of others, can put me sufficiently in tune with what it is that *I* like in music so as not to be totally a slave of the reactions of others. Listening to the *content* of each position put forth in a meeting can also give us some freedom from being entangled with others' desires.

We need not despair over this entanglement of each other's desires. The whole purpose of coming together as a group to make a decision is to try and have *some* effect on others while letting others have some effect on ourselves. The individual responsibility of participating in a decision does not mean that we isolate ourselves from each other. On the contrary, a sound communal decision requires a strong connectedness between the members of the community. Although it is unavoidable that each person will be affected by the desires of others, it is possible to be aware of the effect of others' desire upon us and where those effects might lead us for good or ill. This awareness can help to anchor our thoughts in the actual matter that the decision is about.

One way that a mimetic process can skew a community's decision is by leading it to a premature consensus. We all know how one or two people can get a ball rolling so quickly that it gathers momentum until it is nearly unstoppable. Then the decision is made before anybody has even had a chance to think. Sometimes decisions are made this way because the question is a no-brainer, or the issue is so innocuous that it isn't worth a lot of time or effort. But for important decisions, it is important to be careful of this hazard. We all know that as soon as a bandwagon rolls in, it is easy just to follow the bandwagon's banner and not give the matter further thought. When the community is of "one mind," however, Girard would have us pause to make sure that this unanimity is not at the expense of somebody. After all, decisions to lynch somebody are made in precisely this way. The fundamental danger, of course, is that the bandwagon might roll over the issues so that nobody sees them any more. I am sure every community has made *some* bad decisions in this way. The example Benedict himself gives for such a disaster is the possibility "that a whole community may conspire to choose a person [as abbot] who will go along with their vices" (RB 64:3).

A true consensus occurs when everybody looks carefully at a particular issue and sees it roughly the same way or is genuinely persuaded to do so. Reaching a decision by such a consensus does much to build up peace within a community. The mimetic tendency within humans increases the likelihood that such a consensus can happen at appropriate times. However, it is important to make sure that the *right* consensus has been reached. When the chain reaction of mimesis leads to a consensus, that consensus still needs to be measured by the rule and the Gospel and plain old, ordinary common sense.

It is important to be mindful of how mimetic rivalry can cloud decision making. A person at odds with another may not want to be on the same side as that person on any issue, and so will be sure to want the opposite of what the other wants. As I noted above, in such a case, the desire of one person has fully captured the desire of the other. The actual issue at hand becomes irrelevant in this scenario and even disappears as does the ostensible bone of contention of two people obsessed with each other in naked mimetic rivalry. This danger is all the greater if the two are locked in any sort of power struggle for control of the community. If mimetic rivalry has the potential of leading to a meltdown that is resolved by collective violence whose reality must be denied, then truth is sure to be a casualty of the mimetic rivalry that clouds the attempt to reach a decision. There is no chance of gaining a correct discernment of a matter if some people are more interested in "winning" than in coming to the right decision. It is well-known that arguing through smooth talk, dynamic delivery, or sheer temper-tantrum tactics can lead to a "victory," but all of these tactics cloud the issues and almost always lead to bad decisions. Worse, such tactics cause bad feeling to simmer in a community until this resentment flares up the next time the community gathers to make a decision.

Given the danger that mimetic rivalry can pose for truth, focusing on the concrete issues presented to the community goes a long way toward avoiding the ill effects of mimesis while retaining its beneficial elements. When a community is faced with a practical matter that requires a decision, some aspects of the material reality at hand are true while others are not. There may be room for disagreement as to how much peeling of old paint is tolerable before repainting a monastery building becomes mandatory, but the peeling of paint itself is either real or it isn't. Likewise, the amount of money the job will cost and how much money the monastery has in its bank account are also real. All this is to say that there are intrinsic merits to each case presented to a community for a decision. Although one cannot be totally free of the mimetic process swirling around the deliberations, it is possible to direct one's attention to the intrinsic merits of the case, or lack thereof. What is needed here, then, is the skill of focusing primarily on the *issue* and not one's relationships with the other people. The more each member of the community can focus on what there is to see and the possible consequences of the alternatives, the more likely it is that a group decision will be well-informed and not overly skewed by the mimetic dynamics in the community. This is an example where the discipline of attention enjoined by Weil becomes very important in communal relationships.

For Benedict, the truth about an issue is grounded not in human perception alone, but in God's view of the issue. The best way for a community to reign in mimetic rivalry as it makes a decision is for all to "follow the Rule as their mistress" and not to "be so rash as to deviate from it in the slightest" (RB 3:7). The admonition to the abbot to "do all things according to the fear of God" as well as according to the Rule surely applies to the whole community. These parameters are still fairly wide, and human ingenuity can always make them wider still, but they give some basis for judging the worth of a proposal and its appropriateness for the community. Most important, this principle reminds us that it is not enough to disengage our own desires from mimetic processes. We must seek the desires of God and align our desires accordingly. Knowing when we are willing what God wills and not confusing our own will with God's is tricky enough. It is common for monastics to say that something is "not monastic" just because they don't like it. This judgment can be leveled at some awfully petty matters. This is why monastics need to "follow the Rule as their mistress." The experience of living the monastic life for many years helps one develop a kind of sixth sense as to what is "monastic" and what isn't. One of the most important things for a novice to learn is to discriminate between what requests are appropriate and which are not. A monastic who constantly has to be denied permission has not grasped the ethos of the life.

In discerning the truth of an issue and how God sees it, the *way* each person expresses an opinion is as important as its content. Benedicts asks that each member of the community offer "advice with all deference and humility, and not presume to assert their views in a bold manner" (RB 3:4). By presenting our opinions with "deference and humility," we allow the merits of the argument to speak for themselves. Such an approach shows respect both for the matters being discussed and for the others sharing in the decision. More importantly, it is easier to *listen* to a person who leaves space for us to consider what is being said. That, in turn, makes it easier to listen to God as well. On the contrary, pushing a point of view obstinately makes it harder for others to listen, just as it makes it harder to listen to God. Getting carried away with an argument quickly makes one lose sight of how sound or unsound the argument really is. When the volume keeps going up, one can no longer hear oneself think. The entanglements of mimetic rivalry hinder the art of listening and eventually obliterate it altogether. On the contrary, a humble presentation of one's views fosters the art of listening and offers us a way out of these entanglements.

Benedict says that the reason the *whole* community should be gathered to decide an important matter is "because the Lord often reveals what is best to the younger" (RB 3:3). Since we easily think the youngest people are the *least* likely to have a sound opinion, Benedict reminds us that God's will *could* be spoken by *anyone* in the community. We need to listen to *everybody* because *anybody* could have the best suggestion. What better way could there be of bringing home the necessity of carrying on a discussion with respect for *everybody* than to single out the advantages of listening to the one who usually has the *least* respect? Again, we are alerted to the need to transcend our habitual mimetic entanglements that predispose us to assume that some people are right while we automatically discount others.

Benedict's suggestion that God's will is often revealed to the youngest is not arbitrary. The youngest member of the community is the one who has had the least time to form mimetic relationships. That means that the youngest person may well have a fresh look that the rest of the community lacks. ("We've always done it this way" is a constant refrain in monastic houses.) On that account, the youngest member has a greater freedom to look at the intrinsic merits of a proposal without being confused by mimetic contagion than do older members. Benedict sees the same advantage with a visiting monastic. The visitor might point "out a shortcoming calmly and with loving humility," showing that such a one may have been "sent by the Lord for that very purpose" (RB 61:4). It often happens that a community becomes deadlocked over some matter so that it cannot move forward to a decision. Serious mimetic static is often the cause of this sort of logjam. When this happens, it is often an opinion offered by an outsider that gently breaks the logs apart. This person might not even have said anything very different from what was already said in the community, but hearing it said by somebody who is not part of the community's mimetic dynamics makes it easier for everybody to *hear* it.

It is significant that Benedict does not envision these decisions as being governed by majority vote. Voting, of course, can easily degenerate into a competitive match. In spite of that hazard, centuries of experience have shown that mandating a binding vote for some important decisions is the lesser of evils so as to avoid abuses of abbatial authority. Monastic constitutions consistently reflect this necessity. Even so, there are times when the buck stops at the abbot's desk and he has to make the decision. When there is a true consensus, there is no problem. When, after discussion, there is still division, the abbot faces a bit of a challenge. Even though the other members of the community are expected to obey the decision, it is the abbot's job "to arrange things with foresight and justice" (RB 3:6). First the abbot must *listen* and *ponder* the matter before making a decision. This decision should be as congruent to the current reality of the community as possible. That is to say, the abbot's decision need not be, and sometimes *should* not be, a decision that would have been feasible in an ideal world. Both the strengths and the weaknesses of the members of the community need to be taken into account. The result is usually a compromise of some sort that pleases few at the most but is one that avoids making "winners" and "losers" of anybody.

The most important result of all, whether the abbot makes a unilateral ruling after listening to everybody or there is a communal vote, is that everybody be listened to before the decision is made. It makes a huge difference in communal dynamics if the people who did not "get their way" at a meeting can still go away feeling that they were listened to rather than feeling they were simply ignored. We have to be careful here. Some people fall into the trap of assuming they are ignored and not listened to every time they do not get there own way! More important, the decision should be one "beneficial for salvation" (RB 3:5). It is easy to confuse mimetic contagion with the will of God. If a community is going to avoid this pitfall, it is imperative that all turn to God as the reference point against which the merits of the case are weighed. As Benedict pointed out, God just might use the youngest person or a visitor to offer a point of view from outside the daily mimetic process of a community to help the decision along, but ultimately it is God who is the outside source who can best raise us above our mimetic tangles and give us a clearer vision of what should be done in a particular instance.

CHAPTER 7

▼

THE TOOLS OF GOOD WORKS: THE CRAFT OF CHRISTIAN LIVING

At first glance, chapter 4 of the Rule of Benedict looks like a hodgepodge of maxims, seventy-four of them in all. With a closer look, we can see some verses grouped by theme, but, as Kardong says, "if this list has a structure or a logic, it does not easily reveal itself."[1] On a more positive note, this chapter offers us a comprehensive, if bewildering, catalog of the tools of the trade that belong in a monastic's workshop. Many of the maxims touch on topics that Benedict deals with at greater length elsewhere in the Rule. These are most usefully examined in the chapters focused on those themes. Other maxims, or clusters of maxims, get little, or no, attention elsewhere, so I will linger on them here. I will also try to give some sense of the panoramic view the details of this chapter gives of the spiritual journey.

In some ways, this chapter does not sit particularly well in its present context in Benedict's Rule. The same can be said for the corresponding chapters in The Rule of the Master. This awkwardness has given rise to the theory that this chapter is a treatise on basic Christian virtues that the Master either drew on or imported wholesale. This theory need not be correct in order for us to appreciate the fact that the exhortations here are generally applicable to all Christians and, for the most part, are not specifically monastic. Kardong says, "this should remind us that in its beginnings, the monastic movement was not all that distinct from Christianity itself." [2] That is, fundamentally, monastics are Christians who happen to follow the monastic life. Kardong goes on to point out that many people in Benedict's time entered the monastic life soon after converting to Christianity and that these people would need some basic catechism in Christian teachings and morality.[3]

Benedict's use of the word *instrumenta*, translated as "tools," is significant. The Master used the term *ars* (arts) in his title. Benedict's image suggests a more down-to-earth and practical attitude to these maxims. Kardong says that for Benedict, *instrumenta* does not mean "merely 'instrumental,'" suggesting that an instrument is merely a means to an end.[4] Here, Benedict differs from his mentor, John Cassian, who believed that "monastic practices are strictly instrumental" for the purpose of "producing a spiritual result, namely 'purity of heart' or the transformation of the human person."[5] Kardong goes on to say that Benedict's use of the term "instruments" "has the value of showing that monastic life is not merely a matter of ideas. What is at stake is not just conceptual clarity, but the salvation of the whole person."[6] This holistic view requires being down-to-earth enough to use the means to the end, which is God, but not being so earthly as to mistake the means for the end.

De Waal points out that "Benedict's concern is with the inner disposition and attitude, with the disposition of the heart, and in this chapter we are being given a practical yardstick that we can apply in our daily lives."[7] In short, this list of tools provides a dialectic between inward disposition and external action. Here is a holistic view from a different angle. A list of these traditional works of mercy— "Assist the poor, clothe the naked" and "visit the sick" (RB 4:14–16)—are blanketed by the attitudinal maxims "Deny yourself in order to follow Christ" (RB 4:10) and "Prefer nothing to the love of Christ" (RB 4:22). The maxim "love fasting" conflates the two as it commands both the outward action and the attitude behind it. These considerations should make it clear that for Benedict, there is a big difference between a collection of tools and a legal code.

The two great commandments of Jesus head the list of tools: "First, to love the Lord God with all your heart, all your soul and all your strength, then your neighbor as yourself" (RB 4:1–2). By placing these commandments at the top, Benedict makes it clear that he bases his anthropology firmly on our grounding in God, a grounding that leads directly to relationships with other people. These commandments usher in a whole different world from the one driven by mimetic rivalry. There is no conflictual mimesis in desiring what God desires, because God never desires anything at the expense of somebody else. Furthermore, since God desires the good for *everyone*, loving other people through loving God entails desiring *their* good. If we seek to love other people directly, even with good intentions, the danger of rivalry is great, because we have the tendency to enter into a struggle with them to see who can influence the other the most.

That the second commandment tells us to love our neighbors *as ourselves* is also of great importance, because it snuffs out any competition between oneself and others in one magical stroke. Søren Kierkegaard says,

> To love oneself in the right way and to love one's neighbor correspond perfectly to one another; fundamentally they are one and the same thing. When the law's *as yourself* has wrested from you the self-love which Christianity sadly enough must presuppose to be in every man, then and then only have you learned to love yourself. The law is, therefore: you shall love yourself in the same way as you love your neighbor when you love him as yourself.[8]

It is startling, but also enlightening, that Kierkegaard accepts the reality of self-love and uses that as the basis for loving others. That is to say, note how much you love yourself and then love your neighbor as much as that. Here, self-love ceases to be the basis of competitive relationships with others, but becomes instead the basis of reaching out to others. Actually, though, Kierkegaard is slyly suggesting that the term "self-love" is a bit of a misnomer. If true love of self occurs only when there is the same true love of others, then one's own self ceases to be an isolated object of love.

From a Girardian perspective, it is impressive that two clusters of maxims add up to a strong emphasis on renouncing mimetic rivalry and the cycle of vengeance that this rivalry leads to. The first cluster is "You should become a stranger to the world's way. Prefer nothing to the love of Christ. Do not act under the impulse of anger. Do not wait for vengeance" (RB 4:20–23). The second cluster is "Do not return evil for evil. Do not wrong others, but suffer patiently the wrongs done to you. Love your enemies. Do not curse those who curse you, but bless them instead. Bear persecution on behalf of justice" (RB 4:29–33). Kardong comments that to judge from the frequent references to Jesus' Sermon on the Mount in patristic literature, "this very demanding ethic was not discarded as impractical by the early church."[9] Benedict's placing of these maxims against vengeance right after the exhortations to "become a stranger to the world's way" and to "prefer nothing to the love of Christ" (RB 20–21) suggests that vengeance is the world's way and preferring nothing to Christ is tantamount to refusing to return evil for evil. Chittester calls this "a peacemaker's paragraph," one that confronts us with the Gospel stripped and unadorned." She goes on to say that non-violence "is the center of the monastic life. It doesn't talk about conflict resolution; it says don't begin the conflict. It doesn't talk about communication barriers; it says, stay gentle even with those who are not gentle with you. It doesn't talk about winning; it talks about loving."[10] Given that consideration, it is probably no accident that the next verse is "Do not be proud" (RB 4:34). Benedict's chapter on humility will develop this line of thought further.

In the next cluster of maxims, Benedict impresses upon us the need for deep honesty that goes well beyond renouncing the telling of lies: "Do not plot deceit. Do not give a false peace. Speak the truth both in your heart and with our mouth. [Do not be] a grumbler, nor one who runs down the reputation of others" (RB 4:24–25, 28, 39–40). Although politeness and charity may require showing more cordiality than one feels, it is important not to kindle a hidden anger or hatred of the other while presenting a pleasant face to that person. Neither is it helpful to pretend one is not angry with another when truly one is angry with that person. Benedict's interweaving of these maxims on inner honesty with those on non-retaliation suggests that these two qualities go hand in hand. The connection of inner honesty with non-retaliation alerts us to the need to change our inner disposition in some cases. Often, we are considered "honest" when we blow up at somebody just because that is how we actually feel at the time. The problem is, there is a very good chance that this "honest" anger is not congruent to the situation. If we feel anger at somebody else, we should raise the question as to how fair that anger really is to the other. Even if the anger does seem fair and congruent, there is still the question as to whether a nonviolent approach is preferable, in which case we should actively try to make peace with the other. If that is not possible or practicable, we can still decide not to act on that anger. If we take that route, then we simply have to let go of the anger, or at least admit to ourselves that we *choose* to carry the anger and take responsibility for it. Failure to be honest with our feelings toward others and to take responsibility for them makes us grumblers. A grumbler will seek vengeance under the pretext of a "false peace." Sooner or later, the grumbler will attempt to undermine the reputation of that person.

There is a great danger, a danger all the greater for clergy and monastics, of succumbing to the notion that the vocation we follow has *already* made us holy when common sense suggests that this is not the case. That is why Benedict warns his monastics: "Do not wish to be called holy before you really are; first be holy and then the term will be truer in your case" (RB 4:62). The more we *try* to be holy, the less likely we will become so. *Thinking* we are holy is inevitably fatal to the soul. This maxim also points to the danger of preferring a good reputation to the truth about ourselves. Wanting to be *called* holy makes us subservient to the desires of other people, which, in turn, alienates us from the desires of God. Worse, this attention to reputation easily leads to mimetic conflict where it becomes important to be *considered* holier than other people. Father Ferapont's jealousy of the starets Father Zossima in *The Brothers Karamazov* is a powerful illustration of what this mimetic thirst for holiness can do to a person. In short, efforts to be *considered* holy make us opaque so that others cannot see God through us. Renouncing this quest to be *considered* holy opens up the possibility of fulfilling what Chittester considers "the end of Benedictine spirituality [which] is to develop a transparent personality"[11] transparent to God.

Benedict's admonitions that show a firm belief in the possibility of hell may unnerve many people today: "Fear Judgment Day. Have a healthy fear of hell" (RB 4:44–45). Can the fear of hell be healthy? But if the fear of hell really *is* "healthy," then it is neither morbid nor vengeful. Schwager says, "it is necessary to see the doctrine of hell not only under the aspect of threat, but to consider it in relation to freedom."[12] So important is the reality of freedom for Schwager that he will go so far as to say that the heavenly Father will not "make his creatures happy even despite their wills."[13] Schwager does not see God acting in a punitive way; he sees God handing people over to their own choices. The maxim "Long for eternal life with the desire of the Spirit" (RB 4:46) turns the emphasis in a positive direction: We should long for eternal life. Benedict's reference to "the desire of the Spirit" is one of few times when the Holy Spirit is explicitly mentioned in the Rule, and it emphasizes the fact that what God desires for us is not hell but eternal life with God.

The injunction "Keep your eye on death every day" (RB 4:47) strikes many of us as morbid, but it isn't. Remembering the reality of death is beneficial in many ways. When we consider how the collective violence that leads to sacrificial rituals and mythology denies the reality of the death that was inflicted on a human being, it seems reasonable to suggest that facing the reality of death is a tool for turning away from violence and its lies. Moreover, there is impressive psychological research that suggests that repression of death's reality greatly increases our potential for directing violence toward others. In the book *In the Wake of 9/11: The Psychology of Terror,* Tom Pyszczynski recounts research that confirms Ernest Becker's thesis that the greater one's anxiety of death *and* the greater one's repression of this anxiety, the less one can cope with any challenge to one's world view, and the more likely such a one will react to any challenge with violence or will support the use of violence.[14]

When we consider the importance of chastity as a major monastic virtue, it is remarkable that Benedict mentions it explicitly only in this laconic maxim: "Love chastity" (RB 4:64). Chastity is touched on implicitly when Benedict says that monastics should "sleep in separate beds" and "receive bedding suitable to their monastic life" (RB 22:1–2). Given the kinds of things known to happen in bed when more than one person sleeps in it, especially if they are unclothed, as was often the case in medieval times, we know what Benedict is talking about here. The two words "Love chastity," however, speak volumes. Benedict is not asking us to grit our teeth and push away all sexual urges and then regret the imagined pleasures we are giving up. *Loving* chastity means renouncing our personal urges for the sake of *loving* other people and God. Anybody, whether married or not, can be attracted to another person sexually and have to hold back from acting on that attraction because of the harm it will do in some circumstances. Loving chastity means loving the person in a self-giving way that will not ask of another what that person does not want to give or *should* not give. Loving chastity means not subordinating the good of another person to our own stirring of sensuality out of love for that person. More than that, we should *love* other people so deeply that we feel this love and not the renunciation we have made. There is a tendency to confine chastity to preoccupation with our physiological urges and attempts to stifle them. Mimetic theory directly relates these urges to our relationships and the way these urges meld with the desires of others. When we participate in a mimetic triangle, we quickly lose sight of the reality of the other persons in it, and before long we lose sight of those persons altogether. The degree of love toward others that is required to overcome unchastity at any level is, as the first verse of this chapter reminds us, grounded in loving God.

Benedict's reticence on sexuality is itself an expression of chastity. Many times, long-winded condemnations of other people's sexual activity comes across as unchaste as the people being denounced. Talking about sex all the time, whether in praise or blame, indicates a serious preoccupation with it that makes mimetic doubles of both libertines and their puritanical critics. It is significant that Jesus was just as reticent on the subject of chastity as Benedict. Even when confronted with the woman in adultery, Jesus was much more concerned with the threat of collective violence than he was with any sexual acting out the woman may have done. This reticence about sex in both the Gospel and the Rule draws our attention to deeper currents of human mimesis and to the fundamental ways we relate to each other and to God. If we get the deeper level right, sexuality will likely fall into its rightful place.

Benedict concludes the list of "tools" with "And never despair of God's mercy" (RB 4:74). Mimetic theory draws our attention to our propensity to project our fear and violence onto God. When our attitudes toward others is vengeful, then we expect God to be vengeful to them and equally vengeful toward *us* if we mess up. The deepest truth about God, however, is that God is merciful. That means we are called to desire mercy for others and for ourselves as strongly as God desires mercy for us. The more we are immersed in mimetic conflict of any kind, the more tempted we are to despair of God's mercy. It is no accident that mimetic conflict seems inescapable when we are caught up in it. What Benedict would have us believe is that God's mercy is infinitely deeper than the merciless fury of mimetic rivalry. That means that God does not wait for us to renounce our vengeful way of living before offering us mercy; God offers us mercy so that we can renounce our vengeful way of living. A *healthy* fear of hell has no place for despair of God's mercy.

In his closing paragraph, Benedict brings us back down to earth by saying: "These, then are the tools of the spiritual craft" (RB 4:75). De Waal says that "these tools for my spiritual life are not so very different from the tools for my day-to-day life at work, in the garden or kitchen."[15] She goes on to point out that Benedict speaks of returning our tools on Judgment Day in precisely the same way that he speaks of returning the tools of the monastery after each use. Both should be "clean and intact" (RB 4:76, 35:11). Benedict then promises us that when we hand in our tools, we will be rewarded with "what eye has not seen nor ear heard, God has prepared for those who love him" (RB 4:77). As with the close of the prologue, Benedict ends with a promise of the joy God offers us both now and in the hereafter. Kardong says that this allusion to 1 Corinthians 2:9 "places the conclusion to the 'tools' precisely where it belongs, namely, union with God."[16]

CHAPTER 8

▼

OBEDIENCE:
THE ART OF PUTTING
ONESELF INTO THE
HANDS OF ANOTHER

The numerous abuses of authority that occur make obedience a problematic value, but abolishing authority does not abolish abuse. On the contrary, when there is a power vacuum, somebody will seize power and use that power to the detriment of others. Kardong points out that although we have much clarity on the abuses that arise from an authoritarian system, "many thoughtful people today are aware that self-will is still at the heart of many human problems. Unless we are freed from the insatiable demands of our ego, we cannot make spiritual progress."[1] In any case, questions about obedience and "self-will" are inescapable whenever one person shows up on our radar screen. We have to work out how we will negotiate our own desires in relationship with the other. Mimetic theory says that the desires of other people have a great effect on us and our desires likewise have a strong effect on them. Theoretically, this mutual effect can lead to a cooperative relationship, but in practice it is difficult to avoid having a contest of wills where each person tries to overcome the influence of another and dominate the other. We shall see that Benedict's concept of obedience is the opposite of a competitive relationship. For Benedict, obedience is a relationship of cooperation. The two chapters on the abbot already go a long way toward freeing us from a concept of obedience as subservience to tyranny by showing us that for Benedict, an abbot should be an authority who is *not* authoritarian.

Benedict opens this chapter by saying, "The basic road to progress for the humble person is through prompt obedience. This is characteristic of those who hold Christ more precious than all else" (RB 5:1–2). The virtue of humility is treated at great length in a chapter of its own. For now, it suffices to say that if humility is part and parcel of obedience, then obedience has to be a two-way street since humility is a virtue required of *everyone*, the abbot included. It follows that humility is not only required of the one following an order but is also required of the one who gives the order. Benedict points to the inner attitude that obedience requires when he says that the obedient person holds "Christ more precious than all else." We have already seen how Christ is the foundation of the abbot's authority. Now we shall see how Christ is the foundation of the disciple's obedience. That Christ is the foundation of both tells us, fundamentally, obedience has nothing to do with a contest of wills, but is an alignment of human wills with the will of Christ.

Benedict sets up a chain of command that begins with Christ, goes through the abbot, and ends with the disciple by quoting Jesus' words: "*Whoever listens to you listens to me*" (RB 5:6, Lk. 10:16). The context in Luke is Jesus sending out the seventy disciples to announce that the Kingdom of God has come near (Lk. 10:9). Earlier in the Gospel, Jesus defined the Kingdom as bringing good news to the poor, letting the oppressed go free, and proclaiming the year of the Lord's favor (Lk. 4:18). This proclamation of deep freedom is what the abbot is expected to teach his monastics. The "year of the Lord's favor" refers to the Jubilee, the time when all debts must be forgiven. A Christ-based obedience, then, is one where we give our wills over to the goal of creating a community of mutual forgiveness, one that constantly allows new beginnings for growing in God. This proclamation makes it clear that obedience has nothing to do with submission. Submission is the result of losing a power struggle. A Jubilee forgives all debts, which in turn abolishes power struggles. This verse from Luke, then, does not set up an authoritarian chain of command from Christ to abbot to servile monk. The obedience called for is the obedience to Christ who is present in the guest, especially in the poor and in the sick. That is, one is obedient to God when one is obedient to the true and legitimate needs of other people. For all the importance of the abbot, the whole community bears responsibility for listening to Christ by listening to others. Kardong reminds us that "the rather breathtaking equation in

Luke 10:16 of divine and human authority must not be used as an excuse to sweep aside the need for careful, even painstaking search for truth by all parties in cenobitic life."[2]

Benedict gives us an even deeper Christological model of obedience with these words of Jesus: "*I did not come to do my own will, but the will of the one who sent me*" (RB 5:13, Jn. 6:38). We call Jesus Lord, but far from being a drill sergeant barking out orders, Jesus is himself a model of obedience. It is important to stress the fact that Jesus' obedience to the One who sent him has no trace of competitive wrangling or browbeating. Rather, Jesus freely chooses what the Father also freely chooses. The obedience of Jesus took him to the Garden of Gethsemane and then to the cross. Schwager points out that Jesus' obedience is not obedience to a Father who *wanted* his son to be handed over and crucified. Jesus' prayer that he be freed from the cup of suffering "shows first of all that the creator does not will the suffering of his creatures in itself ... but the more comprehensive will to salvation reveals that God ... can 'use' even the failure of creatures in order to ... reveal something which goes beyond the possibilities of their natures."[3] This chapter of Benedict's Rule and Schwager's words show us that God does not intend suffering for us, but obedience to God could entail suffering from the sinfulness of others, just as the sinfulness of humans caused Jesus to suffer. Jesus, of course, in giving himself over to humans who mistreated him, also gave himself over to the Father, trusting that his Father was a God not of the dead, but of the living. Here, obedience is placed in a deeper supernatural context than the notion that obedience to a superior is equal to obedience to God. We follow Christ by giving up ourselves both to the needs of others and to God's care for us.

Benedict contrasts obedience with *voluntatem propriam,* a phrase usually translated as "self-will." These words are commonly used in monasticism to designate a personal preference for one's own will over that of the abbot and community. Kardong admits that this phrase "is an ambiguous concept, for it is not certain whether it means 'personal will' or 'self-will.'" We should not renounce a personal will because "it is a God-given gift and intrinsic to human maturity."[4] "Self-will," is the misuse of our personal will. We are not commanded to renounce having any will at all. We *are* commanded to renounce acting on our own will at the expense of others. We can hardly drop what we are doing to answer a call to obedience unless we have some cherished projects on our hands. If there is no personal will at all, then there is nothing to renounce. Clutching an individual project inappropriately could be an attempt to love Christ on our own terms instead of Christ's. If our hands become too full of our own projects, we do not want to empty them for the sake of Christ in another person. Kardong reflects that "to be focused on personal wants and projects means being correspondingly closed to the views of others and ultimately to the divine will."[5] The danger of the monastic concept of "self-will" is that it easily becomes a weapon to impose our own desires on others. Anyone who does not do what *I* want *must* be guilty of self-will, as if my own will cannot possibly be self-will.

The term "self-will" sounds a bit odd in a Girardian framework. If our desires our derived from the desires of others, then self-will, the sense that we have a will that is ours alone, is a delusion. But note how mimetic desire works: The more I want what somebody else wants, the more *I* think it is *I* who wants it. Advertising tries to convince each one of us that we personally desire what they are advertising precisely because everybody else wants it. Each person in a lynch mob is convinced that he or she personally wills that the lynching take place. In such cases, the good of other people is put on the back burner. In contrast, if we learn to desire what God desires for us and for other people, we gain freedom from the mimetic desires that we mistake for personal desires. We can see, then, that there is quite a lot of "self-will" in mimetic desire in that we try to appropriate the desires of others for ourselves. Mimetic theory also shows us further that "self-will" entangles our personal desires with those of others in a conflictual way. Even the desire to love Christ above all else can become warped into trying to love Christ better than anybody else.

We can hardly "hold Christ more precious than all else" unless we obey with a warm heart and good grace, and this is why Benedict emphasizes the disposition behind obedience as much as the act of obedience itself. "If a disciple obeys grudgingly and murmurs not only out loud but internally, even if he carries out the order, it will not be acceptable to God" (RB 5:17–18). Benedict says that the response to a command should be so quick as to make the two simultaneous and be done "with an alacrity caused by the fear of the Lord" (RB 5:9). Back in the prologue, Benedict had already commanded us to *run* in the way of obedience with this same alacrity. A favorite monastic story is that of the scribe who was in the middle of forming a letter when his abbot called him. With no hesitation whatever, he left the letter unfinished so as to answer the call. This sort of promptness reminds us that Benedict also urges us to *run* to fulfill God's commands. Benedict hastens to add here that "it is love that drives these people to progress toward eternal life" (RB 5:10). That is, it is the inner attitude of love that makes such prompt obedience pleasing to God and humanity.

The wrong attitude toward obedience is summed up in one word: murmuring. Murmuring is a problem that Benedict mentions often in the Rule. When acquisitive mimesis has been activated, murmuring rises up from the throat and up to the tongue. Benedict demonstrates how well he knows this problem when he tells his monastics that those who receive more should be humbled by their weakness. "Above all, the evil of murmuring must not appear for any cause by any word or gesture whatsoever" (RB 34:6). When we respond to an order with murmuring in our hearts, we are throwing ourselves into a conflicted relationship with the one who gave the order. If we follow the order only because we *have* to, we are acting in the spirit of a defeated warrior who is already plotting revenge for the "next time." On the contrary, obeying with alacrity, with love, is the attitude of one who does not act out of a sense of defeat, but out of a willingness to conform to the will of another. Many Christian writers wax eloquently on the beauty of obedience under heroic circumstances, especially the obedience unto death of the martyrs who shed their blood for Christ. But obedience is most challenging in the petty circumstances that we face day in and day out. Being asked to serve at table an extra time can easily set off a train of murmuring that undermines our act of service. After all, nobody gets put into the calendar of saints just for putting food on the table. In cases such as this, we must break out of ourselves and direct our attention to those who need to be served as well as to the needs of the person whose place we are taking. Murmuring is the vice that did much harm during the Israelites' journey through the desert. To murmur is to complain in such a way that no constructive action can be taken. This is why it is so secret, so much under the breath and so corrosive. The murmurer is not even trying to win by imposing his or her will on the community; the murmurer only seeks to ruin somebody else's "victory." Murmuring then, is a totally destructive vice that can have only a corrosive effect in a community by breaking the connections between people that obedience can forge. Schwager captures this deep level of obedience well when he tells us that saying "yes" to God "does not mean merely the following of individual commandments. It is essentially a matter of the standard by which individuals build up their world."[6]

Given the hard line that Benedict takes on obedience in this chapter, chapter 68 comes as a bit of a pleasant shock. As with chapter 64, where Benedict revisits the subject of the abbot, this chapter is surely the fruit of long experience and reflection that has deepened his understanding of the matter. Unlike the Master, who wouldn't even think of such a thing, Benedict provides room for negotiation between a monastic and the abbot. Benedict says that a monastic who feels that the imposed tasks are too heavy or even impossible should "accept the order of the superior with all gentleness and obedience" (RB 68:1). However, if the burden seems to be *too* hard, the monastic is invited to explain the problem to the abbot "patiently" and "without pride, obstinacy or refusal" (RB 68:2). Note that the inner attitude to obedience is as important as ever and that the *way* we express ourselves in such a case must reflect the right inward state. We should also remember that these are the same words Benedict uses for the way a personal point of view should be presented when the community is called to counsel.

Kardong points out that the word "impossible" indicates the point of view of the disciple and not that of the abbot. That is to say, Benedict does *not* support the old monastic trick of teaching obedience by giving impossible and absurd orders, such as planting a stick in the ground and watering it for thirty days.[7] The scenario here is one where a mutual obedience between abbot and fellow monastic comes into play. There is a real possibility that we will underestimate what we can accomplish and shrink from a request to do more than we think we can. In such a case, we may be greatly helped by being prodded by another to stretch ourselves until we find that we *can* do more than we thought we could. On the other hand, it is possible for someone to be asked to do something that one simply *cannot* do. An abbot needs to be obedient to the reality of the physical, mental, and psychological abilities of all in the community, and sometimes he has to be told when one really might be stretched *too* far. This attractive chapter, however, does not really change the basic teaching of obedience in chapter 5. Benedict makes it clear that if the abbot does not change his mind, the monastic must still obey lovingly, "confident in the help of God" (RB 68:5). Chittester quotes the modern saying, "There's no way out but through," and goes on to say that "the straight and simple truth is that there are some things in life that must be done, even when we don't want to do them, even when we believe we cannot do them…. The reality is that we are often incapable of assessing our own limits, our real talents, our true strength, our necessary ordeals."[8] Our inability to assess our own limits, talents, and strengths is the key here. Other people are just as fallible in judging what we can do as we are ourselves. That is why Benedict allows us to negotiate with "impossible" orders. By listening with the "ear of the heart," we will come as close as possible to our true limits, talents, and strengths.

Much of what has been said so far discusses obedience in a top-down fashion where a superior gives an order and the disciple obeys it, but fundamentally obedience is living in the context of other people. Benedict alerts us to this communal aspect of obedience when he says that "the blessing of obedience" should be shown not only to the abbot, "but the brothers should also obey one another" (RB 71:1). In short, each member of the community should be concerned for the well-being of all the other members. Obedience, then, is not so much a matter of following orders as it is being ever mindful of the welfare of the community. The abbot himself must be responsive to the needs and the abilities of the monks under his charge, as Benedict's admonition that the abbot remove causes for "justifiable murmuring" demonstrates (RB 41:4). Of course, the phrase "justifiable murmuring" is pretty much an oxymoron, but the point is that we all have some responsibility to avoid starting or fueling a mimetic chain reaction of murmuring.

When we put ourselves in the custody of another, we put ourselves in the *care* of another and accept the responsibility of caring for them in return. In chapter 72, Benedict takes this teaching yet one step further when he says that they all "must compete with one another in obedience" (RB 72:6). The obedience in which everybody should compete is defined as a situation where nobody pursues "what he judges advantageous for himself, but rather what benefits others" (RB 72:7). Benedict envisions a community where everybody tries to outdo everybody else in caring for everybody else. This is quite a contrast to the usual mode of human competition, where everybody tries to come out on top of the pack by making everybody else a loser. Benedict reminds us that God wants all of us to win our battles by making a winner out of everybody else.

CHAPTER 9

▼

SILENCE:
THE STILL SMALL VOICE
OF GOD

Both Kardong and De Waal express an initial disappointment in this brief chapter. Perhaps this disappointment stems from the rich experience each has had with silence that doesn't seem to be caught as effectively in Benedict's words as they are in writings by other spiritual masters. This is just one more instance, among many, of Benedict's diffidence about impressing us with eloquence. Time and time again, Benedict shows that he prefers to draw our attention to his teachings with the sparsest of words.

One of the paradoxes about speaking or writing about silence is that using words in any quantity is likely to undermine its subject. Indeed, the chapters on Silence in The Rule of the Master, from which Benedict took only a small portion, illustrate this pitfall. The Master is long and wearying. One can pick a few good points out of the morass, but they are engulfed in the overall garrulous style of the Master. This is an example of how a loquacious speaker causes us to tune out from what is said sooner rather than later. It is not just a matter of quantity of words; it is a matter of quality. We can listen to substantive speech for hours while five minutes of garrulous speech is too much. In contrast, we can see that Benedict embodies the practice of silence through the fewness of his words.

Silence is not a mere absence of words or thoughts; it is a positive and substantive reality. De Waal alerts us to the important distinction Benedict makes between *taciturnitas* and *silentium* (taciturnity and silence). *Taciturnitas* "simply means not speaking," while *silentium* has "the wider understanding of being still and silent."[1] Max Picard, a German philosopher, who has written on silence with greater elegance and depth than any other writer I know, confirms the importance of this distinction. He begins by telling us that "silence is nothing merely negative; it is not the mere absence of speech. It is a positive, a complete world in itself."[2] This positive aspect of silence is well expressed in the German title of Picard's book *Die Welt des Schweigens*. The verb *schweigen* is active rather than passive; it denotes silence as a purposeful act. Picard elaborates on the substantive quality of silence by claiming that "it is a primary, objective reality, which cannot be traced back to anything else.... There is nothing behind it to which it can be related except the Creator Himself."[3] Benedict shows his own awareness of this substantial reality of silence by saying that "we sometimes ought to refrain from speaking good words on account of the intrinsic value of silence" (RB 6:2).

We can further clarify the distinction between *taciturnitas* and *silentium* by taking note of how silence is compatible with words while taciturnity, of itself, has little or nothing to do with silence. In fact, silence requires a relationship with words in order to be itself. Picard says, "Speech came out of silence, out of the fullness of silence. The fullness of silence would have exploded if it had not been able to flow out into speech."[4] Picard deepens this dialectic by saying, "There is something silent in every word, as an abiding token of the origin of speech. And in every silence there is something of the spoken word, as an abiding token of silence to create speech."[5] Words, on the other hand, do not necessarily have any relationship with silence, and that is why mere taciturnity does not constitute silence. Words that merely create noise are chatter. We can hear words participating in the Word (the Logos) but chatter is totally disconnected from the Word. Music has the same dialectic with silence when it is *music* and not chatter. Many √ of the most powerful moments in music are the rests, those brief moments when no music sounds. The opening of Schubert's great Sonata in B-flat is a particularly dramatic example of the power of silence. Here, the grand pauses that punctuate the brief, tentative phrases and the off-key tremolos in the bass overwhelm the sounds emerging from the silence.

Curiously, Benedict does not begin his chapter with words floating serenely out of the primordial silence in the way Picard writes about it. Instead, he thrusts us into the struggle we experience to attain and maintain silence. Benedict extols the value of silence by quoting the opening words of Psalm 38 (39): "*I will guard*

*my ways so as not to sin with my tongue. I placed a guard at my mouth. I was speech-
less and humiliated, refraining even from good speech"* (RB 6:1). So far, so good.
But Benedict and his monastics would know from chanting the Psalter every
week the verse that follows: "I was silent and still; I held my peace to no avail; my
distress grew worse, my heart became hot within me. While I mused, the fire
burned; then I spoke with my tongue" (Psalm 39:3). This is nothing more than a
failed attempt at silence. With his heart becoming hot within him, the psalmist is
already experiencing a lot of interior noise, and it is no surprise that when this
noise bursts into speech, it is not speech with any connection with silence at all.
From this point on, the psalmist complains vociferously to God about everything
he doesn't like about the universe, noisier and noisier.

Benedict gives us an important key to the value of silence when he says that "it
is the master's role to speak and teach; the disciple is to keep silent and listen"
(RB 6:6). Kardong tells us that although this is the only time the word "listen"
occurs in this chapter, it "is not a throwaway word here, for listening is precisely
why the disciple is silent before the teacher.... It can be said to be the real node of
monastic silence."[6] Benedict is reminding us that in order for us to learn from
another, we must *listen* to that person. It is not possible to *listen* to another if we
are doing the talking or if our hearts are burning hot within us, ready to burst
into angry speech. We must stop talking before we can listen. In practice, the
hierarchy between master and disciple dissolves if real listening takes place,
because the master needs to *listen* to a disciple in order to discern what should be
taught. The point is, silence is not a virtue; in fact it is nothing at all, unless it fosters the art of listening. In contrast to the listening disciple, monasteries have
always been plagued by novices who know all about monasticism, and know even
more about the True Faith. On top of that, they know everything there is to
know about spirituality, and they will tell guests and their fellow monastics everything they "know." Novices such as these don't usually stay in the monastery very
long once they really find out what monasticism is all about. Mysteriously, the
longer one lives the monastic life, the less one knows about these things and the
less one has to say about them. Perhaps we should say that the more perfect the
disciple, the less that disciple will *want* to speak.

In discussing this magic word from the prologue that Benedict uses again here,
De Waal says that if she had to reduce the Rule of Benedict to one concept, it
would be "that of listening to the voice of God in my life." She goes on to say,

> When God's voice is drowned out by incessant clamor, whether inner or
> outer, in whatever shape or form, then continuous dialogue with God

becomes impossible. An inner monologue with myself, constant chatter with others, the invasion of the spoken word through the press and television are all the ever-present realities in my daily life over which I need to exercise some sort of discipline if I am to keep any quiet inner space in which to listen to the Word. This is the stillness of heart, the guarding of the heart, which touches the very deepest levels of my consciousness.[7]

In using the word "stillness," De Waal is giving it the meaning of the Greek monastic word *hesychia,* which means stillness and resting. Like the word silence in the sense of the German word *schweigen, hesychia* is an active word implying intentionality. That is, achieving stillness requires exertion, much exertion. The psalmist's difficulty with being still shows us that stillness can be a hard goal to reach. De Waal's reference to our inner monologues alerts us to where the problem is. Keeping our mouths shut will not create silence as long as we keep the fires burning within.

Although the quest for silence is in many ways an individual venture, most of Benedict's references to the practice of silence stress its importance in community life. Benedict's admonition to disciples to be silent in order to listen to teaching already points to a human relationship. Similarly, Benedict insists that at meals, where one of the monastics is reading to the community, "profound silence should reign" (RB 38:5). If anyone talks or even whispers during the reading, the reading cannot be heard. During study periods, older monastics need to patrol the monastery and "be on the lookout for the bored brother who gives himself over to frivolity or gossip and is not serious about *lectio.* Not only is he useless to himself, but he leads others astray as well" (RB 48:17–18). The word *lectio* is a monastic technical term for the prayerful and meditative study of scripture, the sort of study that can only blossom in an environment saturated with silence. Although Benedict is writing about individual study here, he is also making it clear that providing an environment for study so that it can lead to an encounter with God through God's Word is a *communal* effort. Even more important is the communal responsibility to protect the prayer of others with the gift of silence. When the Divine Office is finished, "we should all leave in deepest silence and show reverence for God" (RB 52:2). The phrase "deep silence" is another indication of the substantial weight silence has for Benedict. He goes on to say that the reason for leaving the church silently is so that anyone "who may wish to pray by himself not be hindered by the thoughtlessness of another" (RB 52:3). Silence, then, is not an individual matter at all. It is an integral part of *communal* life.

Although Benedict says little about the relationship between prayer and silence, his few words, such as those just quoted above, wrap prayer in silence.

Elsewhere, Benedict expresses his distrust of "much talking" at prayer, suggesting that such prayer will not be heard. Rather, "prayer should be short and pure unless perhaps it be prolonged under the inspiration of divine grace"(RB 20:3–4). John Cassian, one of Benedict's sources, says that a monastic's calling to seek "nothing other than the vision and contemplation of that divine purity ... can be acquired only by silence."[8] Kardong goes on to point out that Cassian's teaching demonstrates that prayer tends to evolve into wordlessness: "Since God is basically ineffable, true experience of God transcends words and even frustrates them."[9]

In laying out the times for silence and prayer, Benedict says that we should not "fraternize at improper times" (RB 48:21). The implication here is that there *are* times when fraternizing is proper. Monastic timetables normally provide for both conversation and silence by setting times for both. There are times for the community to gather at corporate recreation to socialize informally and there are times when all are to be silent. Of greatest importance is the Greater Silence that begins after Compline and extends through the early morning of the following day. Even here Benedict is flexible. As important as silence is during the night hours, he admits that charity to guests or some other command by the abbot might take precedence upon occasion.

Although words can be used constructively to build connections between people, words can just as easily be used to alienate people from one another. Refraining from speech that will hurt others is essential to creating and maintaining good relationships. This is why Benedict is so insistent that we refrain from "crude jokes and idle talk that arouses laughter" (RB 6:8). It is precisely this sort of chatter that slips into hurtful comments about other people. When we refrain from evil speech, we have a much better chance of becoming aware of what words will deepen our connection to another and which words might tear us apart. If the cellarer, the monk responsible for the goods of the monastery, is not able to furnish what is asked for at the time, he is admonished to "offer a kind word in reply" (RB 31:13). Likewise, the porter is expected to provide the weary traveler a prompt response "in the warmth of charity" (RB 66:4). Chittester shows us how words can build connections when she says that "the goal of monastic silence, and monastic speech, is respect for others.... The rule does not call for absolute silence; it calls for thoughtful talk."[10] When words are spoken between people in an environment of silence, these words are much more likely to be in tune with the Word. Words spoken outside of an environment of silence are more apt to be mere chatter.

Just as obedience must come from the heart, so silence must also come from the heart. It is very possible for there to be much noise and chattering beneath tightly closed lips. The "silent treatment" we give to people we have a grudge against is noisier than a tirade. Internal murmuring, of course, is an inner noise that destroys obedience as much as it destroys silence. In carrying out a command grudgingly, we cut ourselves off from each other with our interior noise. The more we are full of noise, the less aware we are of what is truly happening within us, to the point where we cannot "hear ourselves think." Such noise prevents us from listening to ourselves, to others, and to God.

When we consider mimetic theory in relation to silence and noise, we can see readily that acquisitive mimesis is a great noise maker. The mimetic rivalry that results from acquisitive mimesis wraps us so tightly with one another that it becomes impossible to *listen* to that person. At the same time, we think that the desires generated by the other are our own desires, because we are no longer capable of hearing the truth of what is in ourselves. It is worth our while to pause a moment and note what the chattering voices say inside us when they make so much noise. These voices are telling us how to trounce somebody in a debate or what to say in a long-winded lecture to make somebody *else* reform or how to make other people totally compliant to our desires to an extent that *never* happens in real life. In each of these examples, we can see our inner voices stirring up rivalry between ourselves and others. For some reason, in these fantasies we *always* win and everybody else always loses. When we direct our fantasies at people we hold a grudge against, whether for real injuries or imagined ones, our fantasies grind them deep into the dust. These interior voices can just as easily be filled with self-recriminations that echo the victimizing words drilled into us by others. As long as we allow the noise of these voices to overwhelm us, we are sacrificial victims who have acquiesced with our persecutors. In all of these cases, the noise of mimetic rivalry leaves us no room for God.

Alison offers us a dramatic presentation of how inner and outer noise prevented Elijah from hearing God until he was plunged "into the shamed silence of one who knows himself uncovered, and for that reason, deprived of legitimate speech" (1 Kings 18–19)[11]. Elijah could not hear God's voice in the wind, earthquake, or fire. And no wonder! Those phenomena echoed the inner noise that had filled Elijah with a sense of triumph when he defeated the prophets of Baal. Alison points out that what seemed to be a story of triumph turned out to be "the story of the un-deceiving of Elijah, ... the story of how Elijah learnt not to identify God with all those special effects which he had known how to manipulate to such violent effect."[12] What Elijah heard from the "still small voice" was what

Elijah could not hear when the crowd was cheering him on to his bloody victory over Baal's prophets. He had become a mimetic double of the prophets of Baal who had brought Yahweh down to Baal's level, a level of sacrificial violence. After hearing the still small voice, Elijah went away, his zeal all but extinguished. All he did afterward was choose Elisha to be his successor, a successor who pursued his ministry with a lot more healing and a lot less violence than did his master. Such was the result of the still small voice. This reflection on Elijah should caution us against glorying in noisy triumphs over other people, even (or especially!) in the name of God. The still small voice of God does not try to make a loser out of anyone.

Picard underscores the power of silence to heal human relationships when he says, "Within the realm of creative silence the individual does not notice any opposition between himself and the community, for the individual and the community do not stand against each other, but face the silence together. The difference between the individual and the community ceases to be important in face of the power of silence."[13] That is, silence dissolves the rivalrous impulses we are in danger of succumbing to. The practice of silence is a means of overcoming our own entanglements in mimetic rivalry as much as it is a means of grounding ourselves deeper in God. Benedict would be the first to insist that these two results of silence go together.

It is not possible to listen to God in silence without gaining a greater ability to listen to other people. Listening to others has the effect of quieting the noise of mimetic rivalry within ourselves. That is, it is not possible to *listen* to another and maintain the same noise level we had before. If we dedicate ourselves to maintaining a high inner noise level, we will not hear anybody else. Listening allows us to be nurtured by God in the silence of creation when the Logos first spoke. Insofar as we hear God in the nurturing silence, that nurturing silence will permeate the words we speak so that those words and their accompanying actions will nurture others.

CHAPTER 10

▼

HUMILITY:
RISING TO THE LOWEST PLACE

Benedict begins his chapter on humility with Wisdom's trumpet call: "Scripture *cries out* to us!" (RB 7:1). Like the school teacher raising her voice to call an unruly class to attention, Benedict shouts over our unruly affections to get our attention for an important matter. This alarm signal should be enough to alert us that humility is not a placid virtue but one that requires exertion and energy.

What scripture cries out is, *"Whoever is self-promoting will be humbled, and whoever is humble will be promoted"* (RB 7:1). These words of Jesus are recorded by Luke twice, first as a coda to the parable of the seats of honor (Lk. 14:11), and then as a coda to the parable of the Pharisee and the tax collector (Lk. 18:14). Both parables focus on mimetic rivalry so plainly that even (or maybe *especially!*) a small child can understand them. These parables are almost enough to make one think Girard himself invented them to illustrate mimetic theory.

The first of these parables makes light of our tendency to jockey for position at the expense of others. As each person rushes for the best places, they each have an eye only for the other people who are rushing for the same places. The host of the banquet is lost in the shuffle. In discussing this common human scenario, Alison tells us "that there are two possibilities: I can depend entirely on my peers, in which case … I'll have to do everything to keep myself well considered by them, receiving those whom they receive and excluding those whom they exclude." In this case, my "I" becomes "nothing other than a construction forged by the difficult game of keeping my reputation." The alternative is "that I receive my 'I' from God, and here's the rub; God has an awful reputation."[1] We could hardly find a clearer example of how mimetic rivalry and pride are intertwined. Jesus is not giving us a strategy for getting the best seats; Jesus is showing us that any notion that some seats are the best is a sorry illusion. If some seats are *thought* to be the best ones, it is only because everybody is going after them. Mimetic desire has made some seats more important than others. Jesus is telling us that we must renounce all mimetic rivalry for a "best" seat so that our Divine Host can place us in the seat that is best for each one of us.

In the second parable that uses this refrain, the Pharisee is supposedly focused on God. After all, he is praying! Or is he? The content of the prayer, however, makes it clear that the Pharisee is *not* thinking about God; he is thinking about how much better he is than this other person in the temple who happens to be a tax collector. Surely Benedict was well aware of how easily a follower of the monastic way could fall into the trap of "praying" in much the same way. The parable doesn't tell us if this tax collector, like Zacchaeus, changes his ways. All we have is Jesus' assurance that the tax collector's prayer for mercy has brought him up to a much higher place than the Pharisee, who thinks he is in an awfully high place. At the very least, there is hope that the tax collector will change for the better, but there is no such hope for the Pharisee as long as he "prays" with this attitude.

Alison uses examples from our everyday experience to illustrate the power of humility to diffuse mimetic rivalry along with the power of pride to spark and sustain it. Alison has us imagine two members of a teaching faculty who are competing with each other. If they become aware of what is happening, apologize, and back down, the problem dissolves. If these rivals lack the humility to take that step, and if they are sufficiently well-matched so that one is not likely to fully defeat the other, it becomes quite likely that these two professors will suddenly come to an agreement that the new teacher from Venezuela is the cause of the problem in their department. Accordingly, they will find a way to get the Venezuelan expelled, "and in their faculty peace reigns." That is, peace reigns until their rivalry breaks out again, "and they'll have to repeat the mechanism again, sacrificing, this time, Lord alone knows which expendable victim."[2]

Benedict follows his allusion to the two Lukan parables with a quote from Psalm 131 where a weaned child at its mother's breast provides an image of humility. There is some confusion in Benedict's quotation that Kardong suggests can be traced to a mistranslation in the Old Latin Bible that Benedict and the Master would have used. As quoted in the Rule, the Psalm verse suggests frustration, but the Psalm itself expresses the contentment of the child. Benedict's purposes seem to be served all the better by the truer text.[3] I don't think Benedict is romanticizing the innocence of infants here, especially when we consider the text he had to work with. Augustine of Hippo famously noted how an infant who has had its fill of milk will scowl at its foster sibling who sucks at the same breast that had just satisfied him.[4] (That's how quickly mimetic rivalry can set in!) What we need to focus on is not any intrinsic innocence of the small child, but the child's social position. A child on its mother's breast is not yet in a position to make a mad dash for the best seats at a banquet or to thank God for being better than other people. That will come soon enough, and that is the behavior that makes both children and adults childish rather than childlike. The person who has learned humility has put away such childish things and withdrawn from the rivalrous network of society. Such a one is as dependent and content as the weaned child on its mother's breast. De Waal says it this way: "When so often my own life seems to be dominated by struggle, expectation, external demands, I want now to stay with this image of the gentle, tender, and trusting relationship of mother and child, and to tell myself that this same absolute, unconditional trust in God is the prerequisite for embarking on Benedict's ladder."[5] Lest we think that perhaps we are being encouraged to remain immature by accepting our dependence on God, Chittester says that "no spiritual maturity can be achieved independent of a sense of God's role in our development."[6]

Like many other monastic writers of the early Christian centuries, Benedict uses the image of Jacob's ladder to map out the steps to spiritual growth. In Jacob's famous dream, the ladder connects heaven and earth. Likewise in Benedict's chapter on humility, his ladder connects our earthly lives with heaven. The ladder that we must climb refers to our own disciplined efforts to achieve the virtue of humility, but it is important to note that, as in Jacob's dream, the ladder itself is a gift from God. It is for us humans to *climb* the ladder, not to make it. "When the heart is humble, *God* raises it to heaven" (RB 7:8, italics mine). For Christians, the ladder between heaven and earth is Jesus Christ, who is both fully human and fully divine. Benedict quickly draws our attention to the *direction* we should climb on this ladder. We descend by pride and ascend by humility (RB 7:7). If we want to climb *up* to heaven, we must climb *down* the ladder of humility. That is to say, humility is the key to an Alice-Through-the-Looking-Glass world that turns upside down the world we have created for ourselves through mimetic rivalry. This same upside down movement is outlined in the famous hymn in Philippians 2:5–11: Jesus is exalted above every name *because* of his descent into human nature in the form of a slave who was put to death on the cross. As Alison says, a God who becomes a slave like that has a bad reputation.

With the first rung of the ladder, Benedict lays the foundation for humility: the constant remembrance of God. Kardong's literal translation, "To utterly flee forgetfulness by keeping the fear of God always before one's eyes" (RB 7:11), shows us that this step must be taken energetically. We must run up this ladder just as much as we must run the race before us. Keeping God in mind takes a lot of active attention. If we let up, we will fall into the default alternative of keeping other people constantly before our eyes instead of God. When we do that, we will most likely act like the people in the parable who elbow their way toward the best seats, desperate to stay ahead of everybody else and heedless of the host of the banquet. God, of course, is the host of the heavenly banquet. If we remain mindful of the Divine Host, we will cease to be so entangled with other people in a frantic rush to the best seats. Girard would have us understand that it is the lethal violence that results from this rush to the "best" seats that resolves itself through scapegoating violence. But when we are mindful of God, then God will show us our proper place where we are free from a mimetic desire for somebody else's place. Constant remembrance of God, then, is a major step in sparing ourselves and those around us from destructive mimesis.

While humans have to struggle to remember God constantly, God is always remembering *us*. The notion of an omniscient God who knows our every thought is oppressive if we project a Big Brother image onto God. Most of us think that anybody who knows *all* about us must despise us. Some of Benedict's comments on God's constant knowledge of us are intimidating. Not only that, but Benedict adds that the angels are constantly reporting our behavior to God as well (RB 7:13)! For that reason, "we must continually make sure … that God never sees us falling into evil and becoming useless people" (RB 7:29). But then Benedict quotes from Psalm 139 to suggest that God's constant knowledge of us isn't really so bad: "*You have known my thoughts from afar*" (RB 7:16, Ps. 139:3). Although God's searching and knowing us is an incentive to toe the line and behave well, there is more to it than that. God's eyes are fixed on us the way a mother's eyes are fixed on her child at her breast. When Jesus tells us that not a sparrow falls without the heavenly Father knowing it, and that every hair on our heads is counted, he is instilling in us his trust in the heavenly Father who watches over us, not out of a prurient interest in our faults, but out of a loving desire to take care of us. Psalm 139 celebrates God's intimate knowledge of our "inward parts," where we discover that we are "fearfully and wonderfully made" (Ps. 139:13–14). If we, like God, direct our attention to caring for every hair on each person's head, then we have lost track of where the "best" seats at the banquet are. As we move through the steps of humility, we will continue to find that the God who knows all about us responds to the truth about us with pure self-sacrificing love.

The constant remembrance of God heightens self-awareness. Since God knows all our thoughts, it behooves us to "guard ourselves at all times from sins and vice, that is, of thoughts, tongue, hands, feet or self-will, but also desires of the flesh" (RB 7:12). When we remember God, we remember ourselves. When we forget God, we forget ourselves and become lost in mimetic contagion. We cease to be conscious of our thoughts and so our thoughts rule us. However, when we remember God, who knows all our thoughts and desires, God will direct us back to our own thoughts so that we can monitor them and direct them in more wholesome directions. When we review our thoughts and desires in the memory of God, we can discern the ways in which we are affected by mimetic contagion before we lose ourselves in it. The opposite of a truthful review of self in the memory of God is the self-will that Benedict strictly forbids (RB 7:19). Kardong defines this vice as "the human drive for autonomy from every outside authority, including God."[7] As already noted, mimetic theory suggests that this autonomy is pure delusion. Self-will renders truth impossible. It is interesting to note that when we usually use the phrase "he was put in his place," we mean that the person was knocked down a peg or two. This is an example of how mimetic rivalry colors our thinking. In Jesus' parable, the host puts us in our places but *not* by knocking us down a few pegs but by putting us in the place *where we truthfully belong*.

In early monastic literature, the term *thoughts* means much more than the intellectual processes that run through a person's head. It is a translation of the Greek term *logismoi*, which refers to the whole bundle of emotions and desires inside a person. (Note the derivation of the word *logismoi* from *logos*.) The noisy, chattering thoughts that I enumerated as obstacles to silence are *logismoi*. The fantasies of rivalry against other people are *logismoi* as well. Given the struggles we have with *logismoi* such as these, there is a tendency to equate the word with bad thoughts or temptations. Benedict himself usually falls into this tendency, and no wonder, since John Cassian used this word for his list of capital sins with *logismoi* being equivalent to sins. Kardong says that *logismoi*, "like feelings and dreams, are the natural an inevitable content of the mind. They can tell us much about the state of our heart if analyzed with care."[8] Remembrance of God keeps us in touch with these *logismoi* that reveal the truth about ourselves. When we hold God in our memory, we can see the rivalrous fantasies for what they are and begin to see the contrast between our fantasies and God's regard of love for us.

As we ground humility in the remembrance of God, we come to see, in the second step of humility, how this virtue affects our relationships with other people. Just as Benedict earlier defined obedience as humility, he now defines humility as obedience. Where Benedict forbad the exercise of self-will in step one, he now ups the ante by commanding us to take the initiative and actively *renounce* self-will. Instead of taking "delight in satisfying our desires out of love for our own way," we should follow the example of Jesus, who said, *"I have not come to do my own will but the will of him who sent me"* (RB 7:31, Jn. 6:38). Remembering God entails remembering Christ, who is the model of humility.

In the third step of humility, Benedict tells us that we renounce self-will by submitting to the will of the superior. Benedict reiterates the Christological grounding of humility by quoting St. Paul's words: *"He became obedient to the point of death"* (RB 7:34, Phil. 2:8). If Christ does not insist on having his own way, why should we? The reference to the Paschal Mystery in Philippians shows us that Christ does not model obedience as cringing and slavish cowering before a despotic superior. The obedience of Christ is obedience to *our* needs to the extent that he is willing even to give up his life to meet those needs. This third step gives us fair warning as to where the fourth step will lead us.

The fourth step of humility plunges us into the Paschal Mystery of Christ, where we drink from the cup that Christ drank. We experience the obedience of Christ, not in external obedience, but from within where "obedience involves harsh, hostile things or even injustice of some sort," yet we "embrace them patiently with no outcry" (RB 7:35). Kardong tells us that the Latin syntax of this sentence is obscure and that a more literal translation might be, "One embraces patience quietly in the heart."[9] Once again, Benedict uses a strong active verb to impress upon us the active intentionality required in humility. We shouldn't just wait to receive the gift of patience; we should take the initiative and embrace the suffering that comes to us. In this way, we cultivate patience by entering into that which gives us much to be patient about. Benedict intensifies this painful embrace with this quote from the Psalms: *"All day long we are put to death on your account; we are considered as sheep for the slaughter"* (RB 7:38, Ps. 44:22). Worse, Benedict proves that we "ought to live under a superior" because Psalm 66 says, *"You have placed people over our heads"* (RB 7:41, 66:12). Kardong wryly comments that this reference to a conqueror's practice of placing his foot on the head of a defeated enemy "is a measure of the elasticity of patristic-monastic accommodation that this text could be used to bolster religious obedience, even of the most heroic kind."[10] Benedict then quotes Jesus' own teaching from the Sermon on the Mount, which embraces this same suffering: "When they are slapped on the cheek, they present the other one as well. When someone takes their shirt, they give up their coat as well. Pressed into service for one mile, they go two" (RB 7:42, Mt. 5:39–41). When we embrace the suffering, we embrace Christ who suffered before us.

The humble embrace of unjust suffering is counter to the temptation of retaliatory violence. Our instinctive reaction to an assault against ourselves is to strike back. After being attacked a few times, we even become likely to make preemptive strikes in self-defense. Striking back at one who committed an injury is not the reaction of a humble person, but the action of one who has been humiliated. When mimesis escalates into retaliatory violence, each side feels more and more humiliated by the other, and the need to inflict the humiliation they have suffered on the one who committed the injury becomes all the greater with each blow. It is not usual for physical violence to reach this level in a monastic community (but it has been known to happen!), but feuds that go on for years and decades are all too common. Usually, the parties to the feud reach a stalemate where the symmetrical acts of retaliation maintain a state of homeostasis that paralyzes the community. Such a retaliatory feud centers the community's life not on God, but on a tight knot of hatred.

The injuries we suffer from others show us how vulnerable we are. Since being on the receiving end of injuries is not most people's idea of fun, we defend ourselves by trying to arm ourselves *at least* as strongly as the other, if not more strongly. The trouble with this kind of arms race is that the protection we create to shield ourselves from other people also shields us from God. Our defenses and artillery are untruthful projections of ourselves that wipe out the memory of God. We may think that our lives depend on these fantastical protections, but it is these projections that prevents us from having a life. When we define our lives by our protective mechanisms, giving them up feels like death. A redefinition of our lives is the dissolution of everything that has held us together up to that time. If we do not clutch the ladder that extends from earth to heaven, which is Jesus Christ himself, how could we ever let go of our delusions?

Jesus was not nailed to the cross because he was too weak to fight back. He was nailed to the cross because he was strong enough to embrace the cross. Jesus said that we gain life by losing it, and then he died to prove it. The Resurrection is God's vindication of the Son who died for us. The Resurrection gives us hope that we receive life in the very giving of our lives, just as we receive only death when we deal out death to others. Benedict, however, does not defer the reward for giving up our lives to life in heaven. Rather, he stresses our participation in the heavenly life in the here and now. We receive life *now* so that we can take it with us when we die. Even in the midst of this painful chapter, Benedict includes words of encouragement that there is eternal light at the end of the tunnel. We should "bear such things without flagging or fleeing," because scripture says, "*Whoever perseveres to the end will be saved* (RB 7:37, Mt. 10:22). Better still, we can be "hopeful of divine vindication" and stay our course by saying, "*In all these things we triumph because of him who loved us*" (RB 7:39, Rom. 8:37). It is not the Passion of Christ by itself that anchors this fourth step of humility; it is the entire Paschal Mystery culminating in the Resurrection of Jesus that anchors us in the time of suffering envisioned here. When we embrace the suffering of injustice to the extent that we refrain from building protective and aggressive shells of fantasy, then the God-given life within us is free to grow. Where is the sting of death? The sting of death is the destruction of our resentments. Pulling out this stinger frees us to live our lives. When the risen Christ appeared to his disciples, he was full of life, not because he had been pulled out of the grave, but because he had not a trace of resentment toward those who had tortured and killed him.

Grounding the embrace of unjust suffering not on the crucifixion, but on the Resurrection of Christ protects us from equating the embrace of suffering with complacency. Contrary to some pious thought, this equation is not humility but pathology. Although the vulnerability that goes with humility means that we may suffer unjust injury, it does not mean that we should consider such injustice normal or acceptable. The last thing the fourth step is intended to be is a license for those in power to abuse their authority. We know by experience that these abuses come, but woe to the person through whom they come! A person who is unjustly treated has the opportunity to learn deep humility, but a person who intentionally oppresses another is obviously lacking that virtue! Masochism that revels in injuries received is retaliatory violence by another name. Such a one tries to use the suffering inflicted on him or her to get back at the oppressor. Far from being synonymous, humility and humiliation are really opposites. Humiliating another, besides being an act of severe pride on the part of a perpetrator, all too often causes pride in the injured one, who then makes extravagant claims of moral leverage in retaliation for that injury.

During the struggles with injustice that we experience in the fourth step of humility, the remembrance of God becomes more important than ever. When we are in such a position, we badly need God's help in revealing the truth of our own thoughts. Just because we *feel* injured, it does not necessarily mean that the injury was intentionally inflicted upon us. Circumstances themselves can be oppressive. More to the point, one does not always get one's own way in communal life. A necessary communal skill is the ability to swallow these disappointments when they come. We can easily come to the conclusion that we didn't get our way because others refused to listen to our suggestions. They did not listen to us because they wanted to suppress our brilliant ideas. Next thing we know, we are an object of oppression because other people envy our brilliance. In short, the perception of being a victim can quite possibly be a delusion. If we do not review our thoughts in God's presence, the likelihood of seeing such situations clearly becomes highly unlikely. However, if this review does seem to confirm the status of being a victim of injustice, the next step is to discern a *constructive* way to deal with it. As noted above, retaliatory violence leads to a stalemate from which no constructive solution can emerge. Destroying an opponent hardly qualifies as a constructive solution! It is not humility but the pride that tempts us to define our lives by our resentments. These resentments are the greatest stumbling blocks to finding remedies for unjust situations. So important can these resentments be to us that we prefer to retain an unjust situation and the resentment that goes with it rather than to let go of it. Such clinging to injustice and its hurt is what murmuring is all about. This is why Benedict denounces this vice at every opportunity.

The strong wording and Christological depth of this step of humility can easily mislead us into thinking that it refers to extraordinary circumstances. The opposite is often the case. Just as obedience can *seem* hardest in the most trivial cases, the patience that this step of humility requires can also be hardest at precisely those times when we might think it should be easiest. In his fine commentary on this chapter, Michael Casey reminds us that

> It is not so much the magnitude of events or the degree of pain which is the measure of patience. True patience is marked by tranquillity in all circumstances. Here we have to avoid quantitative judgments. We know from experience that it is sometimes harder to remain calm in small matters. Major disasters bring to the surface our best qualities. It is the itch of petty pricklings that particularly provokes our rage.[11]

If we remain mindful of our thoughts, we will notice how quickly we resort to murmuring as the solution to our daily problems and to the injustices we suffer, or think we suffer. If we take the fourth step of humility every day, every hour, we increase the chances of avoiding major crises in the community.

The fourth, sixth, and seventh steps of humility offer a neat if fearsome progression into the depths of the Paschal Mystery. But the fifth step seems to backtrack and take a break from this intense path. Benedict tells us to reveal humbly to a superior or some other wise listener "all evil thoughts that enter the heart, as well as the evils secretly committed" (RB 5:44). This step takes us back to square one: Be mindful of the truth of ourselves so as to preserve the constant remembrance of God. We have noted, however, that reviewing our *logismoi* is an essential element of the fourth step. In this respect, the fifth step is a natural progression from the fourth in its own way. Telling our *logismoi* to another takes humility, and the practice deepens our humility. Reviewing our *logismoi* will prove to be just as crucial with the sixth and seventh steps as it is to the fourth. By placing this fifth step where he does, Benedict roots our descent into the Paschal Mystery in the truth of ourselves and makes this self-knowledge the route into to the Paschal Mystery.

The sixth step takes us to a deep level of communal obedience where a monastic is expected to be "content with low and dishonorable treatment. And regarding all that is commanded him, he thinks of himself as a bad and worthless worker" (RB 7:49). Some translations of the Rule translate the opening sentence of this step so that it refers to material goods. Admonishing us to be content with inferior *items* is a worthwhile teaching, but it makes this paragraph incoherent. Interpreting the Latin so that it refers to the *treatment* we receive along with the lowly tasks assigned us makes for a smoother reading. However, if we zero in on Michael Casey's key word "contentment," then both meanings come together. "The most important element of the sixth step of humility is not the lowly status of the monk but his contentment." Attaining contentment entails denying "to external realities any automatic domination over our state of mind."[12] The "external realities" can just as easily be material goods granted or denied us as they can refer to the jobs we must do.

Both Chittester and De Waal emphasize the social ramifications of this sixth step of humility. Chittester notes how "status is snatched in normally harmless but corrosive little ways. We are a people who like embossed business cards and monogrammed leather briefcases and invitations to public events.... We measure our successes by the degree to which they outspan the successes of the neighbors. We have lost a sense of 'enoughness.'"[13] Again, we are reminded of how big the most trivial and petty competitive acts can be. De Waal says of this step, "I am gradually being stripped of all those pretensions and games that allow me to say that I am better, superior, more interesting and more worthwhile than other people. It is all part of the process of removing the mask. God does not want an ambitious and competitive person, but one who is content even in the lowliest of occupations." Then De Waal echoes Casey by saying that "contentment is the key word."[14] These comments make it clear that Benedict is probing deeply into the human heart to turn us away from the pull of mimetic desire that would have us outdo other people in collecting status symbols, be they material items or the positions we hold and the jobs we do.

While the fourth step focuses on injustice inflicted upon us by other people, this step deals more with the "injustice" that is built into life itself. That is to say, it isn't on account of human malice that floors need vacuuming and dishes need to be washed; it's just the way things are. The problem is that we tend to assign different levels of status to different tasks that need doing. "Women's work" is a term that relegates all the tasks assigned to women as inferior to the jobs that men do, an attitude that is justly labeled as "male chauvinist." Vacuuming a hallway is onerous in any case, but if the job is considered servile and the person doing it is considered "inferior" to those who don't have to do it, then this psychological burden makes the task much heavier. This attitude was a serious social issue in Benedict's day. Kardong points out that a "worker" was a slave. Since slavery was still in practice in Benedict's time, the connotation of a term such as "slave labor" to refer to the work a monastic is expected to do would have been very strong to his contemporaries. Benedict, however, did not accept the distinction between slaves and free persons. Everybody is free and everybody is a slave to everybody else and to Christ (RB 2:20, Gal. 3:28). As a result, everybody has to do the work that is normally performed by slaves in other households. This is why Benedict emphasizes the importance of *each* member taking a regular turn at serving at meals with only the seriously infirm and those already assigned other heavy jobs excused from it (RB 35:1). Even today, we are apt to consider a "house maid" a lower status than that of a business executive. A humble person, however, cares not about the status of the job, but about the job itself and the benefit the work can confer on other people. This is the lowest place, the place of Christ.

Benedict grinds us deeper into the dust of this sixth step of humility by saying that, after doing what has been commanded of us, we should each regard ourselves as "a poor and worthless worker" (RB 49:49, Lk. 7–10). What Jesus is saying here is that, at the end of the day, the exhausted servant should consider himself worthless. To use this verse to denigrate another is clearly unacceptable, but the parable and its apparent application here is useful for checking the swelling of our own egos. Kardong points out that "although competent monks need not imagine themselves incompetent, they should not imagine that their performance of the important tasks thereby confers on them an exalted place in the ... community."[15] We also need to remember that Jesus himself acts out the role of the "worthless servant" and not the role of the master who orders an exhausted servant about.

This concern with claiming a high status for ourselves on account of the work we do is elaborated in chapter 57: "On the Skilled Workers of the Monastery." Here, Benedict explicitly encourages artisans to practice their crafts. Such encouragement was not taken for granted in the early monastic movement and it is noteworthy that Benedict carves out a place for such activity in his monastery. However, Benedict cautions the artisans to do their work with humility. If anyone becomes "so proud of his expertise that he thinks he is a great gift to the monastery, he should be removed from his work" (RB 57:2). What is crucial here is that we must avoid using any skill we have as a power base or a means of putting ourselves above others in the community. Kardong admits candidly that "if any group of people has had more trouble with holy obedience through the centuries of monastic history than the intellectuals, it is the artists."[16] We have all seen some of the most talented people in the world, from athletes to artists, act as if they are entitled to freedom from the moral restraints appropriate for everybody else. Such is quite the opposite attitude to what is acceptable to Benedict.

We need to pause here and note how we use the word "pride." We usually think we should take pride in our work, and failure to take pride in our work suggests laziness and indifference to the work and a like indifference to the people for whom the work is done. Since the heart of humility is truth, any work we do must involve accurate evaluation of the work's quality. In the case of writing, for example, the writer must be willing to be aware of any flaws that crop up so as to correct them. However, once the work is up to standard, this truth should also be acknowledged so that the writing can be circulated among its intended readers. There is nothing puffed up about taking satisfaction in a job well done. What Benedict is concerned about is the danger of being distracted from our work by competitive relationships with other people. This is why Benedict rings the alarm bell if the artisan claims to be "a great gift," literally, one who "is bestowing a boon" on the community. Benedict's worry is that a monastic might claim a higher status in the community by virtue of the work and the talent that went into it. This flies into the teeth of the sixth step of humility that would have us renounce all claims to higher status on account of what we do, no matter how talented we are. "The point is, of course," Kardong says, "that if one is a member of a community, all one's talents and energies belong to the community by right."[17] That is, one is only doing one's duty by contributing to the whole community. Even the most talented artist is a "worthless worker."

It happens that the best route toward creating a good piece of work is to concentrate on the *work* and not on oneself. This also happens to be the best route toward humility. By concentrating on the *work,* we keep the work separate from ourselves, no matter how much of ourselves we put into it. It is by collapsing our identify into our work that we become proud of *ourselves* rather than proud of the *work* that we have done. If our identity collapses in this way, then we use our work to raise the status of *ourselves* and we do not give God the opportunity to place us where we belong. The radical surgery of separating an artisan from that person's work is a last-ditch effort to show a person that the self and one's work are not the same thing.

The sixth step of humility concludes with a quote from Psalm 73: "*I was reduced to impotence and ignorance; I was like a brute beast before you, and I am also with you*" (RB 7:50). This psalm takes us through the whole journey of the sixth step. Throughout the first half of the Psalm, the psalmist complains that wicked people are "winning" and good people such as himself are "losing." While complaining in this vein, he expresses a deep envy of the wicked on account of the good things they have in life while the righteous, such as himself, are denied them. Then the psalmist comes to discover that he isn't as righteous as he thought. He realizes that his mimetic rivalry has slipped down to the level of the wicked, and he is just as grasping of the good things in life as they are. Just past the half-way mark, the psalmist cheers up only because he realizes that the wicked don't have it so good after all. He has quite a good gloat over their falling to ruin and "being swept away utterly by terrors." Finally, after all this display of bad temper, we come to the verses Benedict quotes to illustrate the sixth step of humility. Suddenly the psalmist sees himself as a "brute beast" rather than a righteous person suffering while the wicked triumph. More important, he begins to realize that he is with God, who holds his right hand and "there is nothing on earth" that he desires more than God. It is important to realize that God hasn't taken riches away from the wicked and dumped them into the lap of the psalmist to make him feel better. God has given the psalmist nothing but God's self. The breakthrough for the psalmist comes in renouncing his mimetic grasping after all the good things the wicked have and giving up their game altogether. It is this renunciation that has made him as content as a child on its mother's breast.

If there is anything harder than the fourth step or sixth step of humility, it's the seventh. In the fourth step, we are ignominiously *put* in the lowest place. In the sixth step, we *act* in the lowest place. In this seventh step of humility we become convinced in our hearts that we are "lower and less honorable than all the rest" (RB 7:51). Just as obedience is not really obedience unless the inner attitude fuels the obedient deed, humility is not humility unless our hearts are in the low-est place. We must be careful here. This seventh step has more booby traps than any other. Believe it or not, being trapped by cripplingly low self-esteem is not the *greatest* danger. The greatest danger is moving into the lowest place and then using it as a power base that helps us swell with pride. Casey explains it well:

> There is a bias in religious life which rewards those who are comfortable in subordinate positions, who are open to guidance and correction and who con-form to the standards and expectations of the group. Passivity and compliance are tacitly inculcated while the original, the outspoken and those with initia-tive are subject to an inordinate level of official criticism and bureaucratic blocking. The result is to advance as the model of a "good monk" one who is loyal to the status quo and submissive to the powers that be. In some people such abasement represents heroic sacrifice; in others it is merely a necessary outcome of their own psychological needs. For them it makes for a compatible and unchallenging life, but they often stagnate, especially if superiors are happy to play the game with them.[18]

Casey would have us see that, as with the other steps of humility, we must be sure to place our hearts on the *truth*. A bad self-image is an image and a false one at that. It is just as false as a self-image swelled with one's own ego. A bad self-image inclines us to compensate for it by creating the false images Casey enu-merates, such as being a "good monk" or a "company man." Casey is also cau-tioning us here that false humility can be a cloak for envy. Envy fueled by pride can destroy both our own genuine talents and the talents of others. Kardong reminds us that the sixth and seventh steps of humility depend on faith where we are "totally dependent on grace and therefore without personal merit." Then Kar-dong goes on to warn us that "from the psychological point of view this convic-tion can slip into low self-esteem and even self-loathing,"[19] which, again, are false images.

Kardong puts a different complexion on this step when he notes that Bene-dict's wording here alludes to Philippians 2:3: "Do nothing from selfish ambition or conceit, but in humility regard others as better than yourselves." This verse moves us away from self-images, that is, images of *self*, and directs our attention to how we look at other people. Paul elaborates on this point with a verse that Benedict quotes in chapter 72, near the end of the Rule: "Let each of you look not to your own interest, but to the interests of others" (Phil. 2:4). What Paul and Benedict would have us understand is, if we act from selfish ambition or con-ceit, we are struggling to climb to a higher place. When we struggle in this way, we are trying to make ourselves stronger than others; we are denying our own vulnerability. To believe in our hearts that we are "lower and less honorable than all the rest" not only makes us vulnerable to others, but this belief *embraces* that vulnerability. De Waal suggests that if we are willing to accept the truth of our own vulnerability so as to act gently with ourselves, then we can deal gently with others. Otherwise, we try to protect ourselves by growing a thicker skin that makes us insensitive both to ourselves and to others. "But if I accept myself as ordinary, weak, frail, in other words, totally human and totally dependent upon God, then I am stripped of any sense of being in some way set apart, different, superior. It is then that the genuine, real self may begin to emerge."[20] Chittester reflects along the same lines: "Aware of our own meager virtues, conscious of our own massive failures despite all our great efforts, all our fine desires, we have in this degree of humility, this acceptance of ourselves, the chance to understand the failures of others. We have here the opportunity to be kind."[21] This step of humility, then, urges us to drop out of the rat race where we are trying to outdo everybody else and come out on top. If we succeed in dropping out, we will see the rat race for what it is: a downward-moving spiral. Once we've dropped out, those still in the game will get "ahead" of us and we will be left behind, behind in the lowest place, where Christ is waiting for us.

The outcry *"I, though, am a worm, not a man. I am the object of curses and rejection"* is a quote from Psalm 22 (RB 7:52). This is the outcry of a victim who has been stripped of all human dignity. If we drop out of the mimetic rat race, we may well experience the same dehumanization as a result. Like many other psalm quotes in this chapter, this was considered a prophecy of Christ's Passion in Benedict's day. This brings us back to the Paschal Mystery as the Christological base of humility. The two verses from Philippians lead into the Christological hymn that celebrates the humility of Christ, who accepted death on the cross. This is where putting ourselves below everybody else leads us. Once again, the crucified Christ is presented as our model: Christ is the one who had everything, but gave up everything because he put *everybody's* interest ahead of his own. Should we do less? More importantly, Benedict is showing us that it is the suffering of Christ that gives us the ability to see other people truly and so see the best way to put their true interests ahead of our own.

There is another level of potential misunderstanding of this seventh step of humility that is as easily overlooked as it is serious. The kenotic model of divesting oneself as Christ divested himself as attested in Philippians 2 tends to speak to those who are in a position of power. Those in power are then asked to renounce the power they have. Such renunciation is of the greatest importance, but it overlooks the inner experience of *the victim.* We see this problem in our legal system even today. Although there is much pastoral outreach to victims of abuse, the law is mainly concerned with punishing the perpetrators. That is, the emphasis is on disempowering the those who have abused power with little emphasis on *empowering* their victims. Rebecca Adams sees this same problem in Girard's exposition of mimetic theory and she offers us some important correctives:

> If we consider the perspective of historically victimized peoples, we begin to see the indispensable need for an adequate understanding of nonviolent empowerment rather than a dichotomous choice between violent power on the one hand and a nonviolent "resignation" or vague acquiescence to the will (desire) of God on the other. Neither option effectively speaks to and has the capacity of liberating actual victims from real violence.[22]

Adams goes on to say that "those with relatively less power do not exactly need to give up their desire to agency and subjectivity. Instead, they need to give up their *lack of will* to *appropriate* subjectivity, desire, and agency as those made in the Image of God."[23] There is no question that Benedict shows a *lot* more anxiety over monastics trying to exert *too much* personal agency rather than not enough. But Adams' point here, coupled with Casey's cautions about the allegedly "good monk," leads us to a deeper understanding of Benedict's teaching that the abbot should adapt his pastoral approach to each monastic in a way appropriate to each one. That is, there are times when the abbot needs to encourage a monastic to develop a stronger sense of agency, even "self-will," than the monastic has succeeded in cultivating. A battered person who has been violently robbed of a legitimate sense of selfhood doesn't have much self-will to renounce.

This consideration raises the question: What is involved in giving another person a sense of agency? Adams reviews Girardian triangles that map out mimetic desire in ways that lead to conflictual mimesis. She argues that in these models, the rival is treated as an object. That is, the rival's subjectivity is denied. No wonder a victim feels more like a worm than a human being! At this point, Adams raises the question: What if the two rivals of a triangle desired, instead of the disputed object, the subjectivity of the other? That is, instead of imitating each other's desire for what they are fighting over, each imitates the desire of the other for the subjectivity of the other? Phrased this way, the question sounds convoluted. What it boils down to is asking the following: What happens if each rival desires the good of the other instead of the object they were fighting over? If that were to happen, the scenario would collapse the mimetic triangle into a straight line of mutual imitation. We have Benedict's vision of mutual obedience. "No rivalry ensues from this act of mimetic desire, since the object of desire by definition is that which cannot be appropriated by (reduced to the subjectivity of) the mediator."[24] That is, if one desires the subjectivity of the other, it is not possible to victimize the other by destroying that person's inner life. This positive mimetic relationship "generates between subjects an escalating circle of desire, but not a vicious one, as once again no rivalry ensues." Adams goes on to say that such positive mimetic desire is *"creative,* not only in the sense that it is capable of generating new forms (which Girard claims of the scapegoat mechanism) but also in the sense that it is theoretically capable of doing so without violence."[25] Affirming the practicing of crafts in the monastery when done with humility is a model of desiring the subjectivity of the other so as to encourage creativity.

Affirming creativity calls to mind the non-rivalrous creativity of God, who desires the being of all creatures. It is this generous creative thrust of God that gives us the model for living a life radically different from that which requires victims. At the same time, Jesus, by accepting the role of a victim, models the giving up of self, even to death. The models of willing the subjectivity of the other and renunciation of self might seem to be at cross-purposes. Alison, however, brings the two together by grounding both in Jesus' participation in creation, a creation that is fulfilled, not on the seventh day, but on the day Jesus rose from the dead:

> God's graciousness, which brings what is not into existence from nothing, is exactly the same thing as Jesus' death-less self-giving out of love which enables him to break the human culture of death and is a self-giving which is entirely fixed on bringing into being a radiantly living and exuberant culture. It is not as though creation were a different act, something which happened alongside the salvation worked by Jesus, but rather that the salvation which Jesus was working was, at the same time, the fulfillment of creation.[26]

Put this way, the unpalatable seventh step of humility becomes the path to the glory of the ever-creating God who is a God, not of the dead, but of the living. What we come to see is that we do not experience the deepest level of humility in this seventh step even by a total emptying of self so as to share the sufferings of Christ by suffering ill-treatment as Jesus did. We reach the greatest depth of this step only when we actively hand over the life of Christ to those who have been emptied of this life through their sufferings.

The last five steps of humility are anticlimactic. Or so they seem. After the journey into the Paschal Mystery of steps four, six, and seven, we come to baby steps that deal with small and trivial matters. But that is precisely their significance. When we delve into deep issues and understand them, or think we do, it is easy to think we have mastered them. Unfortunately, the broad sweep of understanding can blind us to what we must actually do in everyday situations. It is the small matters that give the game away. If we have *really* plumbed the depths of the seventh step of humility, it will show in the small gestures we make and in our small talk. These baby steps are bigger than we think.

The eighth step of humility brings the communal dimension of obedience down to a practical level by telling us that we should do "nothing except what is encouraged by the common rule of the monastery and the example of the veteran members of the community" (RB 7:55). One of the ways in which mimetic rivalry has been known to show itself in monastic communities is by practicing competitive asceticism. Instead of renouncing an earthly good for the sake of God, we renounce earthly goods for the sake of outdoing others in renunciation. A uniform diet and practice of prayer, then, is an important step toward curbing mimetic rivalry in a community. If everybody eats the same thing in the same amount and prays together at set times, there is no room for competing in these matters. Several times in the Rule, Benedict admits that some people may need special consideration, usually for health reasons, but it is important not to interpret special treatment as a cause for pride. It is amazing how special some people feel if they are given a special plate at a common meal, even if that special plate isn't really *better* than what everybody else gets. Anything will do as long as it's special!

Steps nine through eleven make Benedict look like a sourpuss. First, Benedict asks us to refrain from speaking "out of love for silence" and to speak only when asked a question by another (RB 7:56). Worse, the tenth step "consists in not being quick to laugh at the slightest provocation" (RB 7:59). Worst of all, in the eleventh step of humility we are told to speak only "gently and without laughter, humbly and seriously, with few and careful words" (RB 7:60). What we have here is a reprise of chapter 6, "On Silence." The implication is that if our words rise from our participation in the Paschal Mystery of Christ, then our words will emerge from the silence of the Logos.

Before we can understand these three steps of humility, we must look at the positive side of laughter and humor. Benedict himself shows a rather tart humor upon occasion, such as his suggestion that his monastics "should gently encourage each other to offset the excuses of the drowsy" when they rise in the morning (RB 22:8). It seems, then, that Benedict did not intend to banish all humor from the monastery but only a particular brand of humor that is destructive. G. K. Chesterton gives us a seemingly contrary point of view to Benedict's by equating humility with laughter and pride with glum seriousness: "Pride is a weakness in the character; it dries up laughter, it dries up wonder, it dries up chivalry and energy."[27] Chesterton also asserted that "pride cannot rise to levity or levitation. Pride is the downward drag of all things into an easy solemnity.... Solemnity flows out of men naturally; but laughter is a leap. It is easy to be heavy: hard to be light. Satan fell by the force of gravity."[28] We also do well to listen to the anonymous Mother Superior whose discernment of vocation for a novice is based on three questions: Does she eat? Does she sleep? Does she laugh? The implication is that if any of these signs are missing, the prognosis for a solid monastic vocation is poor.

We understand Benedict better when we note that there is something strained, even heavy, about loud laughter and rough humor. When we act in this way, we are putting on an act and thrusting ourselves out on center stage. Putting on an act draws us away from the truth of ourselves and is hardly conducive to remembering God's presence. Such acting out is an attempt to flee from the lowest place. Moreover, when our talk becomes loquacious, it becomes thoughtless and insensitive. Boisterous humor is usually made at the expense of other people and it quickly leads to cutting other people down, especially those who are perceived to be our competitors. It is a sobering realization to take note of how many of our jokes make fun of people for their race, sex, physical shape, awkward mannerisms, or their brainpower. The common suggestion that people who "can't take a joke" need to "grow a thicker skin" acknowledges the violent thrust of humor. There is a fine line between this destructive humor and a gentle, teasing humor that we use to urge each other to grow up. The reason, I think, that the Mother Superior requires laughter on the part of a novice is because we all *must* learn to laugh at ourselves. I would add that only those who know how to laugh at themselves can teach others to do the same without being hurtful. Chesterton reminds us that this is a skill we have to learn when he says that "it is really a natural trend to lapse into taking one's self gravely, because it is the easiest thing to do."[29]

Once we reach the twelfth step of humility, Benedict tells us that this virtue becomes apparent in our "very body." No matter where we are or what we are doing, "whether sitting, walking, or standing," our gaze is "fixed on the earth" (RB 7:62–63). This final step isn't a matter of actually looking down all the time; that could well be mere posing. What matters is whether or not we are genuine. If we have a true perception of our self in the remembrance of God, there is no more playacting. Our words and actions come straight from a heart centered on God, and there is nothing contrived about them. It is in such small moments, when we are engaged in casual conversation or sitting, walking, or standing, that we reveal most candidly what is inside of us. Casey also notes the naturalness of humility when he suggests that this virtue "becomes the total and undisputed determinant of attitudes and actions. The superficial self has almost disappeared. The authentic, inner self has become paramount and, as a result, disorder is banished and truth and love have proportionately more influence on outlook and behavior."[30]

Here, Casey has zeroed in on a matter that this whole chapter has been dancing around: the true human self. As I have noted many times, mimetic theory does not accept the notion of a human self as an autonomous center of a personality that calls the shots. The attempt to forge such a self results in the delusions examined in Benedict's chapter on humility. The more we try to have a self, the less of a self we have. The desires of others and our grasping after those desires make us mere puppets of those desires. In short, when we rush for the highest places, there is no true place where we belong. The true self that De Waal hinted at above and Casey hints at here is a true self that emerges when we don't try to project a self to the world. Paradoxically, the true self emerges only when we stop thinking of ourselves. The true self emerges when we think of other people, about the work that we do for them and, most of all, when we are mindful of God.

What kind of self is this? Obviously the true self is not some kind of lump that is *me*. The white stone that has a new name written on it that "no one knows except the one who receives it" (Rev. 2:17) is still in God's hands where I cannot cling to it. Clinging to myself is a sure way to lose myself. That is to say, trying to save one's life is a sure way to lose it. A "true self" is a set of relationships, as mimetic theory would have it. What makes such a set of relationships constitute a self true is the self's grounding in God, from which the self reaches out to others with God's creative love. If we lose our life, we will find it. The true self is a gift from God planted within us, like a mustard seed (Mt. 13:31–32). This seed is much less impressive than the dreams of grandeur that mimetic rivalry gives us, but it is a seed that will grow inexorably into a great plant if we let it. This growth will be free since a living being can grow in any number of ways from its seed. And as the seed within us grows into a flourishing true self, many other people will expand the self by resting in our branches. The more one wills one's own true self, the more one will also will the true self of other people. Willing our true selves, then, is the key to willing the subjectivity of others, which is the path to Glory that the seventh step of humility offers us.

The end result of the steps of humility is to reach the *"perfect love which drives out fear"* (RB 7:67, 1 Jn. 4:18). This love allows us to "accomplish effortlessly, as if spontaneously" everything that we "previously did out of fear" (RB 7:68).

Mimetic rivalry makes us afraid of other people because it makes us afraid they will win the game of life at our expense. As long as we are caught in that bind, we will project this same fear onto God and treat God as yet another opponent. Perfect fear casts out love. The steps of humility remove this fear so that we act instead "out of the love of Christ" (RB 7:69). Far from conceding defeat, humility helps us realize that we haven't lost out on life because there never was a contest. What began as a journey that looked grim and promised nothing more than abasement has turned out to be a journey into love, love of a God who does not will that anybody "lose," but wills instead that everybody "win." De Waal says that this coda reveals that the ladder of humility is not a "progression into human perfection; it is growth into a relationship of love."[31] Where is this love that frees us from fear? In the lowest place, with Christ.

CHAPTER 11

▼

THE WORK OF GOD: THE DIVINE OFFICE AND INTERIOR PRAYER

The chapters of Benedict's Rule covered so far deal with the inner virtues that form the Christian life. These are tools of the heart. Benedict consistently portrays these inner virtues as dynamic movements that culminate in right actions. Kardong points out that the three "essentially passive" virtues: Obedience, silence, and humility demand an attitude of "ready, attentive listening before the word and will of God." Throughout the rest of the Rule, Benedict focuses on the things we must *do* in order to cultivate these inner virtues, even as these inner virtues spur us on to these actions. And yet these are gentle virtues. They give the chapters on monastic practices a "contemplative tone."[1] De Waal adds that the preceding chapters have helped to form in us "the attitude that is to underlie the art of praying: the fear of the Lord, the total dependence on God, the constant awareness of God's presence and patience, and, above all, the motivation of love."[2]

The Divine Office, what Benedict calls the *opus Dei*, "the Work of God," is the most important of all practices. It is the first practice that he discusses, and he discusses it at greater length than any other. In English, the word "work" gives the strongest indication of the exertion that worship requires. We often think of an office as a place where one sits at a desk. A service is a church service where nothing much happens. It shows us how easily we slacken our efforts by forgetting that the term "service" means just that: *serving*. And "serving" is what the Latin word *officium* means. The Work of God is the *activity* by which we serve God. Benedict impresses upon us the prime importance of this practice by telling us that "nothing should be put ahead of the Work of God" (RB 43:3).

The Divine Office grew out of the early Church's practice of praying at set times of the day. In the monastic tradition, this practice mushroomed into an elaborate structure of seven canonical hours plus a night office, which forms the backbone of a monastic's day. Benedict quotes the Psalm verse *"Seven times a day I have praised you"* (RB 16:3, Ps. 119:64) to justify the sevenfold office, but Kardong thinks it likely that the practice came first and the biblical justification second.[3] These hours, as they became known in the liturgical tradition, are Lauds (praise, done at sunrise), Prime (the first hour of the day), Terce (the third hour), Sext (the sixth hour), None (the ninth hour), Vespers (evening prayer), and Compline (prayer at bedtime). Since "the Prophet likewise says regarding the night Vigils: *'In the middle of the night I rose to praise you'*" (RB 16:4, Ps. 119:62), Benedict prescribes this office, also known today as Matins, to be done before sunrise. The office of Prime has been dropped almost everywhere, even in monasteries that keep the rest of these canonical hours. Monasteries with large apostolates, such as running a school, usually have three to five offices a day. Many non-monastics today have rediscovered the value of the Divine Office and do anywhere from two to seven offices a day, depending on the circumstances in life. The exact number of offices is not important as long as prayer is a fabric woven into the whole day, to make the whole day prayerful.

The Office is scriptural. Most of the text comes straight out of the Bible with the Psalter holding pride of place. In Benedict's scheme for the Divine Office, all 150 psalms are performed at least once in a week, while a few are done every day. Although Benedict allowed other abbots to arrange the psalmody for the Divine Office differently, he insisted that, "despite our tepidity," we should perform the whole Psalter in the course of a week. (This in contrast to early monks who prayed the whole Psalter *every day!*) At first glance, Benedict's chapters on the Divine Office look like little more than laundry lists of what psalms to perform at which offices. These lists are interesting for liturgical historians, but not for anybody else. But we also will find buried in these chapters concise, but powerful, statements about prayer where Benedict has planted small explosive seeds that generate endless reflection.

Cultivating the constant remembrance of God, the first step of humility, does not happen automatically; it has to be nurtured by disciplined practices. Praying the Divine Office at set times is the most important practice to this most important step of humility. When we examine ourselves, we realize that it is not likely that we will think of God very often if we do not attend to God during times of worship. Benedict tells us that "God is present everywhere," but we should "be totally convinced that this is so when we are present at the Divine Office" (RB 19:1–2). Although God cannot really be present in one place more in than another, God is *particularly* present when we are gathered for worship. Not only is God present, but Benedict quotes from Psalm 138 to remind us that we sing in the presence of the angels as well! It is these same angels who also report to God everything that God already knows about us (RB 7:28). By widening the worshiping body to include the angels, Benedict adds solemnity to the importance of worship and reminds us that the invisible presence around us when we pray is at least as significant as the presence of other people whom we do see.

De Waal writes perceptively that, in the Divine Office, "prayer is never taken out of the natural flow of life itself. It is firmly inserted with the rhythm of the changing seasons, of winter and summer, of day and night, and not least of the rhythm of my own body."[4] With today's technology, we are likely to overlook the ways Benedict dovetails the Office with the times of day and the seasons. Since most of us are not dependent on natural light, we can more easily use the same timetable all year. The daily rhythm of the body, however, is still the same, and here Benedict shows himself to be startlingly practical. Allowing his monastics to rest "a little more than half the night" is more lenient than it seems when we remember that the community retired for the night at sundown (RB 8:2), thus allowing for roughly eight to twelve hours of sleep, depending on the time of year. This leniency is in strong contrast with St. Columban, who demanded "that his monks 'come tired to bed, asleep on their feet, and be forced to get up before their sleep is complete.'"[5] All this presupposes that monastics don't spend their evenings in night clubs or at the bowling alley. Benedict goes on to say that, after sleeping for this generous amount of time, they should "rise with their food digested" (RB 8:2). During the winter, monastics are expected to learn the Psalms, most likely by heart. (Lenses for presbyopia were not available in Benedict's day and, by about the age of forty, many people could no longer read the liturgical texts.) During the warmer months, when the days are longer, the morning office of Lauds should follow the night office immediately, but "with a very short interval in between, when the brothers can go out for the demands of nature" (RB 8:4). This verse is a fine example of Benedict's awareness of the need to provide for our physiological needs as well as our spiritual needs. De Waal observes, "Benedict respects our total humanity—body, mind, and spirit—and recognizes that balance here: praying is disassociated neither from a gentle handling of bodily needs, nor from intellectual demand."[6]

Benedict insists that a monastic respond to the signal for the Divine Office with the same alacrity as to the call of a superior. In both instances, this alacrity is tantamount to responding to Christ. Benedict says that when the signal is given, we should drop whatever we are doing and rush to the church "with the greatest haste," although with dignity "so as not to provide occasion for silliness" (RB 43:1–2). Likewise, upon rising for early morning worship, monastics should "hasten to beat one another to the Work of God—of course with all decorum and modesty" (RB 22:6). Here, Benedict notes both the competitive edge that encourages the members of the community to arrive for worship ahead of the others and the restraint needed to curb any such competition. What should motivate monastics to hasten to worship is the desire to be with God. Moreover, the desire to respond to the call of worship should also be accompanied with concern for the others so that, early in the morning, monastics will "gently encourage each other to offset the excuses of the drowsy" (RB 22:8).

In other ways Benedict relies on social pressure to give us an incentive to be punctual at the Divine Office. Benedict shows his typical awareness of human weakness when he humorously gives potential latecomers a little bit of slack before he lowers the boom. A monastic is not late for the night office until the *Gloria* of Psalm 95 has been concluded, for which reason, he says this psalm should be "said very slowly and with pauses" (43:4). Benedict prescribes similar allowances for the day hours as well. However, those who *are* late in spite of this leniency become the objects of serious displeasure and public embarrassment. The penalty for tardiness is to lose one's normal place in choir and take, instead, the last place, or a place set apart "for those who err in this way" (RB 43:5). This may not seem like much of a punishment, but when one has an assigned place, it is unpleasant to have to give it up through one's own carelessness. Moreover, through this process, the latecomer is made conspicuous, "seen by … everyone." Benedict goes on to express the hope that latecomers "will change their ways under the shame of being seen by all" (43:5–7). Benedict insists that latecomers should still come into the church as otherwise they might return to bed or gossip outside with a second latecomer, in which case they would lose *all* of the Office instead of just the beginning of it, and on top of that, would be *"giving the devil an opening"* (RB 43:8, Eph. 4:27). Chittester notes how something is lost through tardiness by reminding us that "tardiness, the attempt to cut corners on everything in life, denies the soul the full experience of anything."[7]

In fussing about punctuality at the Work of God as he does, Benedict is challenging us to show a greater concern for the communal activity of prayer than for our private projects. It is often easier to be absorbed in an individual task than in a group activity. This is just as true of work that benefits the whole community as it is of our pet projects. No matter how devoted to prayer we are, it seems easier to leave the church when the office is ended to return to our work and pet projects than it is to leave these individual activities for the sake of corporate worship. One of the reasons that this is so is because, although solitary tasks do not necessarily give us a competitive edge over other members of the community, there is always the chance that they could. Moreover, tasks that we do for the common good can easily become a personal power base, even if it is nothing more than a well-mopped floor. Any personal accomplishment, no matter how modest, is something that we can hold over/against the rest of the community. The Divine Office, on the other hand, is a cooperative work by the community. There is no way any one of us can appropriate this corporate activity for ourselves. Any hint of competitiveness during worship destroys the Office.

So it is that a monastic timetable punctuates the day with interruptions of our personal activities. Of course, if we are already mindful of God and are caring primarily about that, then a signal to go and be mindful of God is not an interruption after all. But when our mindfulness of God falters, our work can slip into idolatry where we think we *are* the work we do. The signal to the Work of God, however, tells us loud and clear that we are *not* the work we do. We are children of God and we should stop what we are doing from time to time to remember that. This is why Benedict admonishes us to put nothing "ahead of the Work of God" (RB 43:3). Nothing. Do not prefer to finish a letter that will make somebody see the light. Do not prefer to cut another slice of bread for the next meal. Don't linger to add a bit more to a book on Benedictine spirituality. All of our activities that can tempt us to place ourselves in a higher place than is rightfully ours must be put aside several times a day for the sake of a communal activity in which we are each parts of a greater whole. Chittester tells us,

> There is nothing more important in our own list of important things to do in life than to stop at regular times, in regular ways to remember what life is really about, where it came from, why we have it, what we are to do with it, and for whom we are to live it. No matter how tired we are or how busy we are or how impossible we think it is to do it, Benedictine spirituality says,

Stop. Now. A spiritual life without a regular prayer life and an integrated community consciousness is pure illusion.[8]

Not surprisingly, Benedict insists that we continue to give the Divine Office top priority once we are there by giving it our best attention. Benedict knows that, even with our best efforts, mistakes happen, but when they do, the person who makes the mistake must "make humble satisfaction right then and there before all" (RB 45:1). Again, Benedict is relying on social pressure to motivate us to do our best. We don't know what specific act Benedict required for "humble satisfaction." The traditional act in monastic practice is to genuflect, but this practice has become rather rare. Even if there is not a public gesture of apology, it is quite embarrassing to cause a breakdown in the Office by committing a serious error such as coming in on the wrong psalm verse. On the other hand, it is important that we not allow ourselves to get unduly upset over mistakes committed during the Office. The smallest show of temper, frustration, or embarrassment will seriously upset the spirit of prayer that the Office is meant to foster. We need to be patient with ourselves and with others.

To do the Divine Office well and give it our top priority, we have to exert ourselves to ward off distractions. Some distractions are innocent in the sense that they are not malicious thoughts. But when these distractions consist of idle thoughts about our pet projects, we are letting our private projects take priority over our lives just as much as if we had ignored the signal for worship or come late for the Office because of them. More serious are the distracting thoughts that dwell on how we can get the better of somebody else in an argument, or figure out the best way to reform somebody *else's* life. Most serious are distracting thoughts of lust and anger that ensnare us in obsessive fantasies of harmful dominance over other people. These more dangerous distractions seduce us into playing God and making ourselves the object of worship. It is no wonder that a monastery can be a breeding ground for quite a tangle of mutual grudges and resentments if attention to prayer collapses in this way. These are the same *logismoi* that destroy silence and humility and embroil us in the mimetic rivalry that God would relieve us from. Since God is beyond the world, yet the sustainer of the world, God is not part of the mimetic webs in which we catch ourselves. That is why prayer provides a space where we can move, free of the petty tensions we humans are addicted to. What a relief this prayer space should be for us! Unfortunately, we keep slipping out of this space. Somehow, we often prefer to go over the same quarrels in our minds that plagued us before the signal for worship was given than to pray the Office. When we try, even half-heartedly, to resist these distractions and concentrate on worship, we discover how deeply ingrained these mimetic tensions are. This discovery is half the battle. When we have a better idea of what we are up against, we are better equipped to handle these tensions with God's help. The other half of the battle is learning to persevere in redirecting our attention back to God when we become distracted.

Attention to the Divine Office is essential for doing it well, but attention, of itself, is not enough. Competence is also necessary. "As regards singing and reading, no one should presume to carry out these functions unless he is capable of edifying the listeners" (RB 47:3). Note that Benedict is not setting impossibly high standards for us. Rather, Benedict urges us to accept realistically both our strengths and weaknesses in our ability to edify the listeners. In short, we should do what we can and not what we cannot. For example, we should not try to sing liturgical music that is beyond our capabilities. On the other hand, competence is an acquired trait. Surely we should stretch ourselves so that we sing and read as well as we possibly can.

Benedict's glowing advocacy of the Divine Office is a strong contrast to the role of ritual in the primitive sacred as Girard sees it. For Girard, ritual is one of the three pillars of culture, along with myth and prohibition, that is founded on collective violence:

> I believe that the key to the mystery [of the function of ritual] lies in the decisive reordering that occurs at the end of the ritual performance, normally through the mediation of sacrifice. Sacrifice stands in the same relationship to the ritual crisis that precedes it as the death or expulsion of the hero to the undifferentiated chaos that prevails at the beginning of many myths. Real or symbolic, sacrifice is primarily a collective action of the entire community, which purifies itself of its own disorder through the unanimous immolation of a victim, but this can happen only at the paroxysm of the ritual crisis.[9]

So far, I have not found any liturgist who shows any awareness of this dark side of ritual. Liturgists who say anything at all about primitive worship make vague remarks to the effect that these rituals were a benign tuning in to the Absolute. But the well-documented worldwide phenomenon of human sacrifice should be enough to tip us off that the real roots of ritual lie in sacrificial violence, as Girard suggests.[10] We need to remember that ritual in the primitive sacred did have the virtue of binding a community together in such a way as to minimize the amount of violence required to sustain this binding. Benedict also sees ritual as a means of holding a community together, but in a way that does not require even the minimal violence of the primitive sacred. We can best grasp Benedict's vision of the Divine Office as a constructive practice by looking further into the contrast with ritual in the primitive sacred. What I have already said about distractions and how they can fuel mimetic passions should be enough to give warning that the primitive sacred retains a shadowy presence when we pray the Divine Office, much as the Divine Office moves us in the opposite direction.

For Girard, ritual is an ordering imposed on the chaos that overwhelms a society when the prohibitions that normally prevent mimetic disturbances fail. When a mimetic crisis comes to a boil, people ask one another: "How can our society be saved the way it was saved the last time this happened?" Girard says, in this kind of situation, the community reverses its tactic. "Instead of trying to roll back mimetic violence, it tries to get rid of it by encouraging it and by bringing it to a climax that triggers the happy solution of ritual sacrifice with the help of a substitute victim."[11] Afterward, as the people reflect on the strange events that saved them, they suggest to one another that "if the whole process unfolded as it did, it was without doubt because the mysterious victim wanted it that way."[12] If the deified victim wanted it once, the deified victim will want it again under the same circumstances. So it is that the same collective violence is repeated when the same crisis occurs again. At a later stage of development, the community regularizes this process with rituals containing repetitious sacrificial acts that are universally believed to have been taught by the deity who is honored, even nourished, by the rituals. In order to do everything "right," "the communities proceed to copy their experience of violent unanimity in a fashion as exact and complete as possible. In the case of uncertainty, better to do too much than not enough."[13] Girard goes on to explain how primitive ritual flirts with danger because it has to. That is, the ritual must draw on the mimetic contagion of violence so as to achieve the unanimity without which the ritual will fail and the community will be destroyed. "This is the source of the idea, universal in origin, that ritual activity is extremely dangerous. To diminish the risk, the community would try to reproduce the model as exactly and meticulously as possible."[14] It is like trying to swallow poison in just the right amounts to build up an immunity to it. Girard then rebukes the psychoanalysts who make fun of the "neurotic" behavior of primitive people. These psychologists fail to understand "the real action that the people offering sacrifice reproduced: the violence that is reconciling because it is spontaneously unanimous."[15] This reconciliation, however, is necessarily unstable because it is poisoned by the death of the victim. There is need for a cure that won't kill a society with every overdose.

Jacques Attali, drawing on Girard, argues that the function of music in primitive societies was sacrificial. This codification "gives music a meaning, an operationality beyond its own syntax, because it inscribes music within the very power that produces society."[16] In its ritual function, music "creates political order because it is a minor form of sacrifice ... it symbolically signifies the channeling of violence and the imaginary, the ritualization of a murder substituted for the general violence, the affirmation that a society is possible if the imaginary of individuals is sublimated."[17] The trajectory that Attali outlines for music is precisely the trajectory that Girard outlines for sacrificial ritual. Just as the sacrificial ritual seeks to take control of violence and channel it into an order that restores peace, albeit at the expense of the victim, so music "constitutes communication with this primordial, threatening noise—*prayer*. In addition, it has the explicit function of *reassuring*: the whole of traditional musicology analyzes music as the organization of controlled panic, the transformation of anxiety into joy, and of dissonance into harmony."[18] The sweeping musicological claims are debatable to say the least, but there is no question that some music does precisely what Attali says it does. When these qualities are narrowed into a funnel by the sacrificial social structure, it "rebounds in the field of sound like an echo of the sacrificial channelization of violence: dissonances are eliminated from it to keep noise from spreading. It mimics, in this way, the space of sound, the ritualization of murder."[19] In light of Attali's remarks, the third chapter of Daniel is an interesting example of how music can be made a channel of sacrifice. Nebuchadnezzar demands that Shadrach, Meshach, and Abednego bow before the golden statue at "the sound of the horn, pipe, lyre, trigon, harp, drum and entire musical ensemble" (Dan. 3:15). Attali goes on to argue that in the subsequent social stages of music's societal function, music continued to be caught in society's power structure until the present, which is sufficiently chaotic to allow music to free itself from these shackles. Music lovers, myself included, who have experienced many wonders in music will rightly protest the reductionism of Attali's thesis. Even so, it is important to realize that music has been hijacked by sacrificial structures and it can happen again.

A major aspect of ritual is the synchronized movement that takes place among the worshippers. In light of mimetic theory, one would think that this mimetic behavior in ritual would be of great importance for understanding both Girard and Benedict. Curiously, I cannot find anything in any book on liturgy and ritual that notes this phenomenon. It has been left to the fine historian William McNeill to examine anthropologically the mimetic process that takes place in corporate worship. In his stimulating book *Keeping Together in Time: Dance and Drill in Human History*, McNeill analyzes a mimetic phenomenon that he calls "muscular bonding." "Muscular bonding" takes place in such events as military parades, dances, football games, and worship. McNeill recounts how the Prussians discovered that military drills were a practical way of making an army act as a unit so as to increase its effectiveness in battle, given the practical difficulties at the time of loading and firing muskets. Even more important, the Prussians realized that "the emotional resonance of daily and prolonged close-order drill created such a lively *esprit de corps* among the poverty-stricken peasant recruits and urban outcasts ... that other social ties faded to insignificance among them."[20]

Then McNeill brings his analysis of "muscular bonding" to our topic in his chapter, "Religious Ceremonies." After noting that "words define religious meanings," McNeill notes that "public worship always involves muscular gestures and ritualized performances as well."[21] First, McNeill discusses "muscular bonding" in various instances of corporate religious enthusiasm. Among the ecstatics is Saul. He came across a group of prophets engaged in a group ecstasy and joined them in their mimetic activity (1 Sam. 10:9–13). At approximately the same time that Saul was made king of Israel, ecstatic Dionysian celebrations were sweeping across the Hellenistic world. In his play *The Bacchae,* Euripides portrayed the out-of-control sacrificial violence this cult engendered.[22] The Dionysian ritual noted by McNeill would be an example of a late development of this phenomenon where the borderline between ordered ritual and spontaneous violence tended to be blurred. McNeill goes on to say that both ecstatic groups evolved into literary traditions where the verbal embodiment of spontaneous ecstasy came to dominate. The literary results of this process have come down to posterity in the form of the Greek plays and the Hebrew books of the prophets. McNeill explains that "both descend from religious inspiration generated by keeping together in time. In both instances, moreover, it is worth pointing out that the supersession of muscular by literary inspiration recapitulated the way I believe that muscularly generated emotional bonding had been superseded by linguistic communication in the evolution of humanity."[23]

For McNeill, it is "literary inspiration" that directs "muscular bonding" in a constructive direction away from "religious enthusiasm," the kind of frenzy that Girard sees in sacred violence. The Hebrew Bible offers many examples of this phenomenon. The narrative of Saul deconstructs the king's ecstatic prophesying by showing it to be of no religious or moral value whatever. Furthermore, although Samuel seems to claim that Saul's prophetic frenzy was a sign that God was with him, the narrative casts doubt on this claim by showing how this ecstatic king constantly embroiled himself in intense, even murderous, mimetic rivalry with Samuel, David, and even his son, Jonathan. Saul isn't the only bad guy in this story. Both Samuel and David, though considered prophets by

Benedict, were at least as rivalrous as Saul. Samuel put Saul in double-bind situations and David committed worse crimes than Saul ever did. Only Jonathan comes off well, but not only did he not inherit the crown, he was never considered by the biblical narrator to be a "man after God's own heart." Neither has Church tradition designated Jonathan as a figure of Christ, and yet he was more Christlike than either his father, Saul, or his friend, David. In contrast to the enthusiastic prophetic bands of which Saul was a member, the "literary inspiration" in the Hebrew Bible forged a prophetic tradition sharply honed to social and ethical issues, beginning with Nathan's denunciation of David's adultery and continuing on through the teachings of Isaiah, Jeremiah, and the other late prophets. This prophetic tradition is then given an even sharper focus in the teaching and life of Jesus of Nazareth. In Girard's view, it is this "literary tradition" of the prophets, culminating in the passion narratives, that clears away the mystification of sacrificial rituals that were fueled by myths that obscured the truth of collective violence.

When McNeill discusses the tension between enthusiastic "muscular bonding" and the more restrained liturgical worship in the early Christian centuries, which were heavily subjected to "literary inspiration," he throws out some tantalizing hints from early Christian literature that suggest that in early Christian worship, dancing was a widespread activity. The monastic writer St. Basil of Caesarea "approved of imitating the dance of Heaven by dancing in circles on earth."[24] Likewise, Ambrose of Milan "believed that suitably holy dancing in church helped to carry souls to Heaven, since, in his own words, 'He who dances the spiritual dance, always moving in the ecstasy of the faith, acquires the right to dance in the ring of all Creation,' that is, in Heaven."[25] It seems, though, that the mimetic power of dance raised anxieties among the bishops, including Ambrose himself. They feared that the enthusiasm dance can foster could become detached from the "literary inspiration" on which Christian worship depends. The unregulated enthusiasm of some early monks and hermits raised similar anxieties.

To remedy this problem, the Church's leadership turned to communal monasticism as a means of controlling the individual enthusiasm of the early monks. "Eventually, duly constituted authorities constrained nearly all Christian monks to live together in monasteries and conform to rules, thus ending public outbreaks of the sort that had occasionally turned Egyptian hermits into leaders of riotous crowds."[26] It was in order to control the frenetic group activity of ecstatic prophets and dancing congregations that the Emperor Theodosius decreed that Church leaders "standardize their chant and song, together with processionals and other ritual gestures."[27] Ecstatic worship, however, could not be stifled so easily, as the numerous examples that McNeill traces through the Christian centuries attest.

McNeill's reference to "riotous crowds" shows that the problem of overenthusiastic behavior was not limited to unbridled liturgical dance. The problematic Egyptian monks often stirred up mob action in favor of one side or the other in doctrinal disputes. These incidents show how frenzied mob violence and "literary inspiration" can be tangled up with each other in destructive ways. On the one hand, the bishops were seeking to articulate the Church's "literary inspiration" so as to witness to fundamental truths about the Trinity and the Personhood of Christ. These articulations were, in turn, drawn from the "literary inspiration" of the Church's liturgy. On the other hand, there was constant wrangling for prominence between the most powerful cities in the Roman world, with the result that theological truths were obscured by disputants who, in their behavior, had become indistinguishable mimetic doubles.

The movie *O Brother, Where Art Thou?* is a particularly interesting study of various instances of "muscular bonding" that can help us further examine the relationship between "enthusiasm" and "literary inspiration." From start to finish, the three escaped convicts experience music and ritual as embedded in mimetic processes. In the film's central episode, these three men make a record with a black guitarist they met on the road. Unknown to the escaped convicts, who were busy fleeing the sheriff and his men, this record touched off a mimetic reaction throughout the state by becoming a smash hit. The act of making music together is, in itself, a constructive activity, one that helps make the three fugitives more sympathetic characters than the lawmen who chase them. Moreover, unknown even to the racist blind man in the studio, not to mention the wider public enmeshed in racist hatred, the ensemble included a black man.

The two moral extremes of musical ritual are shown in the baptism in the river and a conclave of the Ku Klux Klan. At the river baptism, two of the convicts, Pete and Delmar, suddenly jump into the river to join the congregation and receive baptism. They seem to have done this impulsive act just because the other people are doing it; that is, they are mindlessly caught up in the mimetic process of the ritual. Their understanding of baptism doesn't seem to get much past the notion that their deliverance from sin means they shouldn't have to go back to prison. The "literary inspiration" that informed the baptismal liturgy to the other worshippers has not yet reached these two men. The "liturgy" of the Ku Klux Klan is a reversion to sacred violence, but with a difference. Ironically, the members of the Klan seem to be more aware of what they are doing than Pete and Delmar were when they plunged into the water to be baptized. The centerpiece of the Klan's "ritual" is to hang Tommy Johnson, the guitar player who helped make the record. Fortunately, Tommy is rescued by his companions, and the sacrificial liturgy is spoiled.

At the end of the movie, the song sung by the three escaped convicts and their guitar player is used by the corrupt governor to swing a mimetic process away from his reforming challenger, who was unmasked as equally corrupt. The "literary inspiration" of the song "I Am a Man of Constant Sorrow" was lost on its listeners, however. There is no sign that anybody in the movie became more socially sensitive from buying the record or listening to it on the radio, although the "literary inspiration" of the song's lyrics proclaim freedom from the sacrificial restraints society places on the poor. The escaped prisoners never seem to understand the political use that is made of them, not even when they are "pardoned" by the governor, who, nevertheless, fails to protect them from the lawmen who still haven't given up the chase.

This movie helps us to see that the moral and constructive uses of "muscular bonding" do not fall neatly in McNeill's categories of enthusiasm and "literary inspiration." The "liturgy" of the Ku Klux Klan, in perverting the Christian symbol of the cross, shows about as much "literary inspiration" as the baptizing congregation at the river. The chanting of the Klan is cold and deliberate in contrast to the ecstatic singing of the baptizing congregation. These examples indicate that the level of intensity does not necessarily determine the direction that "muscular bonding" takes. Although the literary prophets are credited by McNeill with giving "muscular bonding" a "literary inspiration," most of them were about as wild as the ecstatic band that attracted Saul, but in their case, their raving had moral content. They articulated a challenge to the people to move away from sacred violence and redirect the mimetic process of worship toward a vision where the wolf lives peacefully with the lamb and Lady Wisdom hosts a banquet that feeds all comers (Is. 11:6, 55:1–5). McNeill held up Teresa of Avila, who danced while keeping time with a tambourine, as an example of a Dionysian mystic.[28] What McNeill missed is the clear focus of "literary inspiration" grounded on Christ that guided the fervor of this great mystic. The drilling techniques of the Prussian army had as much "literary inspiration" behind them as the prayer of monastics, and they were just as disciplined as monastic chanting. Neither activity can be considered "enthusiastic." Yet the directions of these two mimetic processes are very different. One is directed toward killing human beings efficiently while the other is directed toward praying to God.

Although "literary inspiration" does not automatically give a mimetic process of "muscular bonding" a constructive direction as McNeill thinks, Girard's theory of collective violence suggests that without "literary inspiration," ritual is doomed to perpetuating the cycle of periodic cleansing of a society via sacrificial reenactments of the original collective violence. The mimetic process that leads to collective violence that is then institutionalized in repetitive sacrificial rituals is an unconscious process. It has to be, or it will not "work" to reestablish peace. Rituals deriving from sacred violence depend on "muscular bonding," both for their sustenance and for keeping the reality of sacred violence below a conscious level. Girard has demonstrated how the myths that accompany sacrificial rites obscure the truth behind them so that they serve instead to keep the participants in these rituals unconscious of what they are really doing. That is why myths fail to serve as "literary inspiration" for these rituals. Girard also says that it is no longer possible to perform sacrificial rituals in a culture that has been the least bit touched by the Judeo-Christian tradition. The "literary inspiration" of the Bible makes it impossible to be sufficiently unconscious of what one is doing. The examples in the movie *Brother, Where Art Thou?* bear this out. The ritual of the Ku Klux Klan is just as inconceivable to the primitive sacred as the baptism at the river.

Although the Divine Office as prescribed by Benedict fosters "muscular bonding," "literary inspiration" predominates. As far as I know, there is nothing remotely like the Divine Office in the primitive sacred. If Girard is right about the primitive sacred, there could not have been. It is telling that not only did the "literary inspiration" of the Hebrew Bible combat the sacrificial rites of the surrounding nations, but it could not help but undermine the sacrificial rites of Judaism itself. So it was that synagogue worship became the backbone of Jewish piety after the Temple was destroyed in Jerusalem. So powerful is the "literary inspiration" of the Hebrew Bible and the Psalter in particular that most of the content of the Benedictine office is furnished by this tradition. It is significant that devotional practices similar to the Divine Office have developed in other religious traditions precisely insofar as they eschew sacrifice. Islamic worship is centered on recitation of the Koran, and Buddhist monastics chant sutras.

The Eucharist, on the other hand, may appear to be a throwback to a sacrificial ritual, but a closer look at it shows it to be as contrary to sacrificial rites as the Gospels are to mythology. That is to say, the "literary inspiration" of the Gospels transforms what would have been a sacrificial rite to something radically different. To begin with, "literary inspiration" plays an important part in the Eucharist in that the actions at the altar are preceded by the liturgy of the Word, which tells the anti-mythical Story that the ritual at the altar acts out. The Eucharistic prayer is itself shaped by the "literary inspiration" of Jesus' life, death, and Resurrection. Although sacrificial language has at times been used of the Eucharist, the sacramental presence of Christ precludes the Eucharist from being a sacrifice in the sense of presenting fresh victims of any kind. The rite focuses on the sacrifice Christ made of himself by his own free will and his subsequent Resurrection. The risen victim has put an end to all sacrifices.

The Eucharist did not play a major role in early monastic worship, including that in Benedict's monastery. Monasticism's origins as primarily a lay movement is one factor in this tendency. Another factor, though, is that the Eucharist was not normally a daily ritual in the early Christian centuries. Rather, Sunday, the day of Resurrection, was the day for this celebration. There was, however, among some Christians, a daily reception of the Eucharist as it was usual for the head of a household to take consecrated elements home after Sunday worship to distribute to his household each day. In line with this practice, The Rule of the Master describes a daily reception of pre-consecrated bread and wine that the abbot distributed from the reserved sacrament. As he did so often, the Master expressed his Eucharistic piety in a negative way by concentrating on the brother who is haughty about receiving Communion. "And if afterwards he wants to receive Communion, let him not be permitted to do so for a time. As long as he is puffed up without reason, so long will the abbot or the dean be angry with him for good reason."[29] The Rule of Benedict gives one hint, and a vague one at that, of a possible daily reception of Communion at his monastery when he allows the reader at table to "receive some doctored wine before he reads" because of the Holy Communion (RB 38:10). Since the Master gives many more details of daily life in his Rule than does Benedict, it is very possible that Benedict's monastery followed the same practice. We have noted that there are times when Benedict uses only few words in important matters. This is one of them. We have already seen examples of Benedict's Christological understanding of the Psalms and the sacramental dimension of his spirituality that indicate a profound reverence for what the Eucharist represents on Benedict's part. We shall see further examples of these traits below. Benedict's Eucharistic sentiments have long since led to the establishment of a daily Eucharist as a major part of worship in Benedictine communities.

With the stress on "literary inspiration" in the Divine Office, one would expect that the "muscular bonding" in this form of worship would be as much on the restrained side as Church legislators hoped it would be. That indeed is the case, but the restraint in the monastic office has more to do with the internal needs of monastics than the agendas of emperors and bishops. When monastic communities spend two to four hours a day in worship, a low temperature of decorum is required. Otherwise, monastics could easily burnout from overdoses of overwrought prayer. It is liturgical restraint that keeps the flame of the Spirit alive and strong in a community over a long period of time. Even so, much "muscular bonding" occurs through the common recitation and chanting as well as such gestures as standing and bowing in unison. Given the power of the mimetic behavior that Girard has analyzed, it is quite important that the large doses of mimetic behavior involved in monastic liturgical prayer be maintained at a calm level.

Plainchant is particularly well-suited for fostering "muscular bonding" at a low but ardent level. In his historical survey of hymns, Erik Routley pointed out that plainchant was developed primarily in monastic communities because its fluidity of musical line made it suitable for a small group of people who were used to singing together over a long period of time. In the absence of a beat that drives later Western music, plainchant requires that all singers listen carefully to each other to stay together and develop an instinctive feel for what the whole choir is doing. Everybody has to both lead and follow the choir at the same time.[30] It is perhaps these very qualities that has made plainchant surprisingly popular in the present era when neither monastics nor their spirituality are known or valued. Other styles of singing the Psalms have emerged in recent years to accommodate the change from a Latin office to a community's local language. The liturgical music of monastic communities has shown over the centuries that "muscular bonding" through music can, contrary to Attali's strictures, bring people together without need of a sacrifice.

One effect of the fairly low temperatures of "muscular bonding" in the Divine Office is that the "literary inspiration" receives prime importance. Benedict makes it clear that the Divine Office is intended to teach us about ourselves, God, and our relationship with God. There is a very particular direction in which Benedict wishes the "muscular bonding" in the Divine Office to go. It is important to remember, however, that this didactic element does not make the Divine Office an intellectual exercise. One is taught not only by the words, but by the corporate gestures and the practice of saying or chanting the words with others. That is, the "muscular bonding" is part of the teaching of the Divine Office.

Since the bulk of the Divine Office consists of the Psalter, with each of the Psalms being done at least once a week, the Psalms are the principal vehicle of the "literary inspiration" in the Office. The Psalms encapsulate spontaneous responses to God that guide us in understanding our relationship with God and how we should live. Heim suggests that the Divine Office and the Psalms in particular fleshed out the attempt of monastics to live without sacrifice and instead "live a new form of community centered on the crucified one."[31] Heim goes on to say that "those who live in intense proximity, seeking to overcome divisions and maintain unity without recourse to violence and sacrifice, find the Psalms a road map of the emotions and dangers that must be overcome." [32]

The quotes from the Psalms in the Rule highlight certain verses that Benedict considers especially important. Benedict established the custom, still followed today, of reading the Rule three times a year. These readings constantly remind its listeners of these highlighted psalm verses. Then, when these verses come up during the Office, the monastics are reminded of the passage in the Rule where the verse was quoted. This back-and-forth movement between Rule and Psalter greatly enhances the teaching function of the Office and clarifies the direction in which the mimetic process of "muscular bonding" should go.

In his call to conversion in the prologue, Benedict poses this fundamental question from Psalm 34: "Which of you desires life and longs to see good days?" (RB Pr. 15). This verse causes us to ask ourselves, Do we desire life, or do we prefer death? Do we long for good days? Do we even have any idea of what "good days" really are? Benedict's call to conversion is most powerfully expressed in Psalm 95: "Today, if you hear his voice, do not harden your hearts" (RB Pr. 10, Ps. 95:7–8). We have already noted how this verse recalls the people's murmuring against Moses and against God in the desert. This urgent daily call to turn away from hardening our hearts is intensified when we recall that the peoples' murmuring led to threats of collective violence against Moses. With Benedict's repeated warnings against murmuring in the Rule, it is clear that he intends that this psalm reinforce his teaching on this insidious vice.

The frequent complaints of collective violence voiced in the Psalter make this phenomenon a nearly ubiquitous presence in the Divine Office. Schwager estimates that roughly one-hundred of the 150 psalms explicitly complain of collective attacks from enemies. [33] Psalm 3, which is coupled with Psalm 95 to form the introduction to the Office on a daily basis, starts the morning with a cry for help: "How many are my foes! Many are rising against me; many are saying of me; there is no help for him in God." The distraught psalmist goes on to ask God to "break the teeth of the wicked" (Ps. 3:7). To get some idea of what curses such as this meant to Benedict and his monastics, we have to note the tendency in Benedict's day and long afterward to give these problematically violent verses figurative interpretations that yield edifying lessons in spirituality. A particularly telling example is the final verse of Psalm 137, where the psalmist blesses those who take the "little ones" of the Babylonians and "dash them against the rock" (Ps. 137:9). Twice in his Rule, Benedict invokes the stock interpretation of his time that the "little ones" are "incipient thoughts," that is, bad thoughts in their infancy that must be smashed against the "rock" that is "Christ" (RB Pr. 28, 4:50). The rock of Psalm 137 is identified with Christ via Paul's identification of the rock that yielded water in the desert with Christ (1 Cor. 10:4). Such figurative interpretations were a salutary development in that they were motivated by a desire to follow the New Testament teachings on nonviolence, but mimetic theory encourages us not to lose sight of the real violence boiling over in these psalms. The amount of violence in the texts of the Psalms gives one more reason for balancing this violence with a restrained manner of "muscular bonding."

We noted earlier that Benedict, in his chapter on humility, quotes from the persecution psalms to help us understand the need to deal constructively with victimization. Here, we will take a closer look at Benedict's use of the Psalter in that chapter to examine how the Divine Office interacts with the teachings in the Rule. In the fourth step of humility, on the need to embrace harsh and unjust treatment, Benedict tells us to "bear such things without flagging or fleeing, as Scripture says: *Let your heart be strengthened and endure the trials of the Lord*" (RB 7:36, Ps. 27:14). Worse, "To show that the faithful person ought to endure all adversities for the Lord's sake, the Prophet says on behalf of the suffering: *All day long we are put to death on your account; we are considered as sheep for the slaughter*" (RB 7:38, Ps. 44:22). In the seventh step, where we are expected to consider ourselves the lowest of the low, Benedict quotes the "Passion" Psalm—"I, though, am a worm, not a man. I am the object of curses and rejection" (Ps. 22:7)—and then plunges to the darkest of psalms: "I was raised up, but now I am humiliated and covered with confusion" (Ps. 88:16). These psalms, however, do not leave us in the depths of despair, neither do they remain stuck in their cries for vengeance, blood-curdling as some of them are. With very few exceptions, the psalmist moves from a complaint about persecution to an expression of confidence in God's deliverance. Even the "Passion" Psalm moves from its heart-rending outcries to joyous outcries of thanksgiving: "The poor shall eat and be satisfied; whose who seek him shall praise the Lord. May your hearts lives forever" (Ps. 22:26). That is to say, the Psalms prefigure not only the suffering of Christ but also Christ's vindication through his Resurrection. Benedict captures this same rhythm when, in the fourth step of humility, he follows the chilling quote from Psalm 44 by encouraging his monastics to be "so hopeful of divine vindication that they joyfully stay their course, saying, "In all these things we triumph because of him who loved us" (RB 7:39, Rom. 8:37).

The "literary inspiration" of the Psalms, particularly when they are recited or sung in light of the Gospel, maps out quite clearly the collective violence toward which "muscular bonding" inevitably moves when it is not accompanied by a "literary inspiration" that firmly leads in the opposite direction. By demonstrating the mimetic process gone bad time after time, the Psalms increase our consciousness of this process and the part we play in it. The "muscular bonding" in the mimetic activity of corporate prayer guides us by texts that follow the mimetic process through collective violence to God's deliverance of both victims and perpetrators from this violence. We must remember that the consciousness fostered by the Divine Office is not automatic. The mimetic process that leads to violence *is*. Every morning, we must renew our repentance from grumbling as the Israelites did in the desert and turn back to God. If we do not consciously reorient ourselves to God time and time again, we will inevitably slip back into unconscious mimetic processes by default. Benedict's use of the "persecution" psalms in his chapter on humility with his own progression from pain to praise makes it clear that, for all of the explosive fury uttered in the Psalms, it is Benedict's intention that we follow Christ through the pain Christ suffered so that we may reach, with Christ, God's vindication as proclaimed in these psalms and fulfilled in the Resurrection of Christ.

Two biblical texts that hold prominent places in the Divine Office on a daily basis are the *Benedictus* at Lauds and the *Magnificat* at Vespers. Benedict never quotes either of these canticles in the Rule, so we don't have any of his reflections on them as we do with key texts such as Psalm 95. However, it is inconceivable that they could have failed to influence Benedict's outlook on spirituality. Both texts look forward to the New Covenant in Christ with hope, first with the Forerunner John the Baptist and then Jesus' birth of Mary. That in itself puts the preceding psalms into a Christian context. I also cannot help but think that the exaltation of the lowly in the *Magnificat* inspired Benedict's constant concern for the weak and the poor. These same lines would almost certainly have been coupled in Benedict's mind with the words he quoted from Luke at the beginning of his chapter on humility: "Whoever is self-promoting will be humbled, and whoever is humble will be promoted" (Lk. 14:11, 18:14). Regardless of what crossed Benedict's mind while chanting this canticle, we can readily see its formative value for increasing sympathy for society's victims and linking that sympathy with our deepest hopes in Christ.

Benedict's most powerful statement on the pedagogical thrust of the Divine Office through "literary inspiration" comes in chapter 13, where he tells us that "the celebration of Matins and Vespers must certainly never transpire without the superior concluding with the complete Lord's Prayer while all the rest listen" (RB 13:12). Benedict's use of the phrase "certainly never" suggests a strongly held opinion. Kardong thinks that the "curious custom" of the superior saying the prayer aloud except for the conclusion might be explained by Augustine's remark that some people seem to think that omitting the petition for forgiveness relieves them of the obligation to forgive! To prevent people from taking themselves off the hook, everyone is required to say these words.[34] In any case, it is precisely this petition that Benedict underscores as supremely important. He says that the reason the whole prayer should be said aloud is "because of the thorns of quarreling that often spring up" (13:12).

The Latin phrase translated here as "thorns of quarreling" is *scandalorum spinas*, which literally means "thorns of scandal," that is, stumbling blocks. This expression, straight from the heart of Girardian theory, suggests that members of a community can easily become mimetic doubles, stumbling blocks to each other. Kardong notes that the word means "obstacle," but it could mean "quarreling," which he thinks is likely in this instance. Kardong goes on to comment on how effective this image is because "it puts emphasis on the constant potential for strife in a small, closed community, and the need for quick reconciliation."[35] *Scandalorum* is not a word native to Latin; it is a direct import from the Greek New Testament. Benedict would have known the word well from its use in key places in the New Testament, most emphatically the instance Jesus calls Peter a *skandalon* when Peter protests Jesus' prediction of his imminent death (Mt. 16:23), and also when Jesus laments the woeful fate of those who scandalize any of his "little ones" (Mt. 18:6). This latter verse especially notes how *skandala* are obstacles to faith. In various other places in his Rule as well as here, Benedict shows that he was well aware that when we quarrel, we become stumbling blocks to each other and so become obstacles that hinder the spiritual growth of one another.

The image invoked by the phrase "thorns of scandal" is deeply suggestive. People who are quarreling become entangled in the same way that thorn branches are entangled with each other. The end result of our "thorns of scandal" is the crown of thorns placed on Jesus' head. Girard notes that, just before his Passion, Jesus had warned his followers that he was "about to become a scandal to them."[36] Girard goes on to note that although the disciples' participation in the Passion is mainly passive, this word applies to them nonetheless. "Now we see that the word also applies to the participation in the mimetic consensus against Jesus."[37] It is precisely this mimetic contagion that caused the disciples to quarrel among themselves and that causes Jesus' monastic followers to do the same. Benedict shows that he clearly wishes the recitation of the Lord's Prayer to redirect the mimetic entanglements of the "thorns of quarreling" when he goes on to say, "When [we] respond to the prayer: 'Forgive as we forgive,' [we] make a solemn pact to purge this vice from [ourselves]" (RB 13:13).

For Benedict, "muscular bonding" and "literary inspiration" are one indivisible package. The gestures help us internalize the words that we speak. Benedict sums up his underlying attitude to liturgical prayer by telling us, "Let us be careful how we behave in the sight of God and his angels. And let us "stand to sing in such a way that our mind is in harmony with our voices" (RB 19:7). Chittester says that prayer "is not an exercise done for the sake of quantity or penance or the garnering of spiritual merit," neither is it "an excursion into a prayer-wheel spirituality." Rather, "if done in the spirit of these chapters," prayer "becomes a furnace in which every act of our lives is submitted to the heat and purifying process of the smelter's fire so that our minds and our hearts, our ideas and our lives, come to be in sync so that we are what we say we are, so that the prayers that pass our lips change our lives, so that God's presence becomes palpable to us."[38] Words alone do not move the heart in the right direction, but the words spoken during worship put us in a position to let God soften our hearts until we embody "great humility and total devotion" (RB 20:2). It is hard to say words such as those in the Our Father without realizing the claim they make on our lives. They force us to take personal responsibility both for forgiving and accepting forgiveness, a responsibility that De Waal says entails "admitting that things have gone wrong and that I am involved in all the muddle and mess." De Waal goes on to return to the image of the prodigal son hinted at in the prologue, assuring us that if the return of the prodigal to a loving father is "the way of Benedict," then the father awaits us "with unconditional love and unconditional forgiveness."[39]

Other brief comments interspersed in the chapters on the Divine Office indicate that the external actions in corporate worship should cultivate a deep inner respect for God. When the Gloria is sung, Benedict tells us to "rise from [our] seats out of respect and reverence for the Holy Trinity" (RB 9:7). Although Benedict does not state it explicitly, Kardong believes that the custom of bowing for the Gloria after standing was almost certainly followed in Benedict's day.[40] Here we have an energetic gesture done in common that builds up "muscular bonding," but this gesture is done while words are recited that direct it to the Triune God. This act of standing and bowing both embodies and fosters the attitude of reverence. Kardong warns us that simplifying the liturgy to the point of leaving no role for our bodies can turn us into "talking heads, as sometimes happens on the TV screen."[41] Near the end of Sunday Vigils, Benedict prescribes that the abbot should read from the Gospel while everybody stands "out of respect and reverential awe" (RB 11:9). Again, the posture of standing for the Gospel reminds us of the importance of this text. This posture also increases the chances that we will pay attention to what is read. The outward gesture is not a substitute for the inward disposition, but it helps make it happen. Likewise, the reader of scripture should edify the hearers, not through self-centered histrionics, but through reading with "humility, sobriety, and reverence" (RB 47:4).

In his brief chapter on interior prayer, Benedict uses even stronger language to enjoin reverence and respect toward God: "When we wish to propose something to powerful people, we do not presume to do so without humility and reverence" (RB 20:1). The continuum from deference to a human being to deference to God could hardly be more explicit. Kardong says that this attitude of respect "excludes all attempts by the suppliant to lecture, cajole or manipulate the superior."[42] "How much more," Benedict goes on to say, "should we approach the Lord God of the universe with great humility and total devotion" (RB 20:2). In our more egalitarian society, we resent being expected to grovel before one who presumes to have authority over us. As mimetic theory so powerfully shows us, however, if we knock those in authority off their pedestals, we set off a mimetic chain reaction where authority figures become indistinguishable from one another as they knock each other off the pedestal. In this scenario, the bond of respect between human beings dissolves and society falls apart. Respect, however, is not meant to be a one-way street. As the chapters on the abbot of the monastery show, an abbot should show all the respect for the those under his authority as these people should show to him. In the end, Benedict would have every person show equal respect for every other person.

Even so, the image of approaching an oriental potentate is a daunting analogy for prayer. Should we not seek more intimacy with God than that when we pray? Jesus himself said that he calls us servants no longer, but friends (Jn. 15:12). But Benedict goes on to balance this daunting perspective. He says that it is not because of our many words that God hears our prayer, but because of our "purity of heart and tearful compunction" (RB 20:3). Purity of heart is a particularly important phrase in monastic tradition. In a Girardian approach, we would strive for the purity of heart that directs our desires away from our mimetic entanglements and directs them toward God. "Compunction of tears" has nothing to do with clinging to a bad self-image. Kardong says that the literal meaning of *compunctio* is "a sharp jab at arousing a torpid animal or person."[43] That is to say, compunction should awaken us from the "inertia of disobedience" cited in the prologue and prod us into running to "accomplish now what will profit us for eternity" (Pr. 44). When we direct our desires to God, the hardness in our hearts caused by our mimetic desires softens. Softening the heart brings on tears, sometimes interiorly, sometimes in our eyes. Prayer is not a meek petition to an aloof ruler; prayer is a heartfelt reaching out to the radically transcendent God who is closer to us than our heartbeats. Benedict says further that the monastic who goes into the church to pray alone should "pray, not in a loud voice but with tears and full attention of heart" (RB 52:4). Not only is this inward prayer deeper than ostentatious prayer that makes a commotion, but exterior quiet allows another person to pray without being disturbed. When we bear in mind that the steps of humility urge us to eschew loud and boisterous laughter, we realize that making a loud display of ourselves in prayer could be a sign of pride rather than the work of the Holy Spirit.

We find in Benedict's few words echoes of what John Cassian wrote on interior prayer. About the deepest levels of compunction, Cassian writes the following:

> For frequently the fruit of a very beneficial compunction emerges from an ineffable joy and gladness of spirit, such that it even breaks forth into shouts of joy that is too vast to be repressed, and the heart's delight and the great exultation reach the cell of one's neighbor. But sometimes the mind is hidden by such silence within the bounds of a profound speechlessness that the stupor brought on by a sudden illumination completely prevents the forming of words, and the stunned spirit either keeps every expression within or releases and pours out its desires to God in unutterable groans. Sometimes, however, it is filled with such an abundance of compunction and with such sorrow that it cannot deal with it except by an outpouring of tears.[44]

The possibility that compunction might cause the outcries of a praying monastic to reach what would have been a distant cell of a neighbor would not have amused Benedict, but what Benedict, like Cassian, most cared about was authenticity in prayer, so maybe Benedict would have been understanding of an occasional shout. However, again like Cassian, Benedict expects either a profound silence or tears to be the more likely outcome of deep prayer. Cassian says that it is occasionally possible that the understanding be suspended so that "it gushes forth as from a most abundant fountain and speaks ineffably to God, producing more in that very brief moment than the self-conscious mind is able to articulate easily or reflect upon."[45]

The relationship between this level of deep prayer and mimetic theory is still largely unexplored territory. We can see readily enough that prayer, from the recitation of the Divine Office to silent "purity of heart and tearful compunction," is the primary means of living out the first step of humility where we ground ourselves in the awareness of God. In their essays in *Violence Renounced*, Willard Swartley and Jim Fodor break much of the same kind of new ground as Rebecca Adams in conceptualizing a deep positive mimesis grounded in God's generous love. Swartley analyzes the "imitation" texts in the New Testament to demonstrate the various levels of imitation that Christian discipleship calls for. Not only must the disciple imitate the virtues of Jesus and the apostles in exterior actions, but this imitation must sink deeply into interior levels as well. After noting how the lists of vices and virtues in the Pauline letters are corroborated by Girard's analysis of mimetic desire, Swartley goes on to say that "not only is the believer's life to be modeled ethically after virtues that flow from the new life in Christ, but the destiny of believers is interconnected to a process of change."[46] Swartley illustrates his point with a quote from 2 Corinthians 3:18: "And all of us, with unveiled faces, seeing the glory of the Lord as though reflected in a mirror, are being transformed into the same image from one degree of glory to another." Swartley says of this verse: "Here the image that functions as the object of desire is the exalted Lord Jesus who significantly (see 1 Cor. 4) is never unhooked from the suffering Jesus Christ. But this also means that the model of mimetic desire in the new creation is not only the Jesus of suffering, forgiving, and humble service, but also the exalted, vindicated Jesus, victorious over the powers of evil."[47] This is precisely what John Cassian and Benedict are talking about when they urge us to pray with "purity of heart and tearful compunction." Such prayer internalizes the Paschal Mystery so that it sinks into the depths of each person who turns to Christ with this level of commitment. Swartley says that "if there is mysticism here, it is moral and mimetic at its core. It is linked to *desire* and assumes that thought, conduct and aspiration are governed by new *desires*."[48] Here we have an important corrective to any notion that mysticism is amoral and detached from the real responsibilities of life.

In his response to Swartley's essay, Fodor elaborates these points further. While expressing amazement that we are called to be *friends* with God (John 15:12), Fodor says that our lives "must mirror the self-dispossessive features which characterize the Trinitarian relations of the Godhead."[49] Fodor calls for an "epiphanic quality" of discipleship that, in the end, is "not about obedience or submission but rather about manifestation and witness—disclosing, making visible, making palpable, making present the purposes of God in the world."[50] Fodor calls this visible embodying of Christ's desires "participative imitation." It is by "participative imitation" that our smallest gestures and our smallest words truly reflect God in the ways Benedict describes in the twelfth step of humility. The words and the gestures of corporate worship coupled with the quiet moments spent in tears and compunction are the path to "participative imitation." A story I heard about René Girard suggests that the vision of spirituality called for here by Swartley, Fodor, Benedict, and John Cassian is very close to Girard's heart. When asked, after a presentation of his ideas, how one could live out his theory, Girard paused and then said, "We should begin with personal sanctity."[51]

A small chapter that is easily overlooked gives us one last powerful indication that, for all the restraint Benedict prefers in the performance of the Divine Office, he expects that it will lead to fervent prayer that breaks open in praise. Today we take the exclamation "Alleluia" so much for granted that we think nothing of it when we come across chapter 15, which is called "The Seasons for Alleluia." This little chapter does nothing but specify the times when the word should be said or sung. Kardong tells us, however, that the liturgical use of "Alleluia" outside the Easter season seems not to have been a universal custom in the Western Church in Benedict's time. For that reason, Benedict had to go out of his way to impress on his monastics the importance of this word of praise.[52] Since this word is used in the celestial liturgy in Revelation 19, use of it in the Divine Office reminds worshippers that praying together on earth is meant to be an anticipation of praying together in heaven. Many psalms take us through our mimetic struggles and the pain that these struggles cause. The climax of the Psalter, however, is the final triad of Psalms 148–150. They are called the *Laudate* Psalms because they are filled with praise. These three psalms are done every day in Benedict's arrangement at the climax of the morning office of *Lauds* (which thus gets its name from these three psalms). Praise of God is well on the far side of our mimetic entanglements. When we praise God, there is no room in our hearts for "the thorns of quarreling." This word, then, springs from the human heart to the depths of God, where the "thorns of quarreling" are dissolved.

CHAPTER 12

▼

HEALING A BROKEN COMMUNITY: DISRUPTION AND RECONCILIATION

The subject of punishment is as difficult as it is painful. The mimetic quality of human nature ensures that disruptive behavior will always pose a dilemma to a community. Misbehavior on the part of one person can easily start a chain reaction that spreads to the whole community if it is not checked by somebody who has the authority to do so. Unfortunately, opposing misbehavior with force can cause as many problems as it solves. Discipline easily degenerates into a contest of wills between authority figures and delinquents until they become mirror images of each other. The more people behave in destructive ways, the harder it is for people in authority to respond in a rational and constructive way. The more irrational and destructive the response of authority, the more authority loses credibility. Given these difficulties, any attempt to grapple with offenses and their punishments are likely to have as many problems as helpful insights. The chapters in the Rule of Benedict on punishment are no exception, and it is understandable that many people today prefer not to deal with these chapters. I have found, however, that even among the problematic suggestions in these chapters, there are some most powerful affirmations of the Gospel that can inspire us in our own handling of these difficult issues.

When faced with the need to correct misbehavior, we must be as aware as possible of the pitfalls that mimetic theory shows us. To begin with, we must remember that those who participate in collective violence to solve a society's mimetic crisis are totally certain of the victim's guilt. From our vantage point today, it is easy enough to see these acts of collective violence as unjust. With our rational court systems of justice, we assure ourselves that if we all agree that a particular person is guilty, this person is indeed guilty and must be punished for the betterment of society. What Girard has told us about the dynamics of collective violence, however, should make us wary of *any* scenario where everyone has agreed that one person is the guilty one. We certainly should be suspicious of any attempt to build such a consensus as a means of unifying a social body. There is the danger that the mimetic process is strong enough to hijack a rational judicial system and lead it to collective violence. Perhaps Oedipus would not have a fair trial even today. The Dreyfus case is an example where the rational judicial system was powerless to prevent injustice resulting from mimetic contagion. On the contrary, "mimetic contagion maintained a contagion so kindled by anti-Semitic prejudice that no disclosure of the real facts of the case during these years succeeded in shaking it."[1]

Bailie quotes an article by the journalist Janny Scott, who suggests that "execution is a brutal act, but it is one carried out in the name of civilization." Bailie goes on to assert, "Clearly, after the shaky justifications based on deterrence or retribution have fallen away, this is the stubborn fact that remains: a brutal act is done in the name of civilization."[2] Bailie then follows Scott's reference to Louis West, a UCLA professor of psychiatry, who charges that "society uses its occasional legal victim of the gas, the rope or the electric chair as a lightning rod to focus divine wrath upon a single offender, while at the same time magically insinuating the survivors into the good graces of the gods by the blood sacrifice." Bailie finds it telling that "the ancient language of blood sacrifice goes more directly to the heart of the issue than does the more conventional language of modern social science."[3]

These reflections suggest that definitively proving that a person is guilty and worthy of punishment does not mean the prosecution of that person is untainted by the same mimetic contagion that leads to miscarriages of justice such as the Dreyfus case. All too often, the punishments meted out to certain individuals seem to represent the crimes of many more people who go unpunished precisely because these punishments are deemed sufficient to solve the social problem they represent. That is to say, it is not necessary to imprison or execute every rapist as long as *some* rapists are punished. The story of Achan in Joshua, chapter 7, referred to earlier is a case in point. Only Achan and his family were stoned for looting, although Achan was almost certainly not the only one guilty of this crime. There is a real possibility that all, or nearly all, of the Israelite families were in fact guilty. This problem of representative punishment is shown explicitly in the story of Phinehas. "The people" had sexual relations with the women of Moab and then attended sacrifices of their gods. In response to this apostasy, God ordered Moses to "take all the chiefs of the people, and impale them in the sun." Carrying out this order would likely have wiped out half of "the people" and maybe a lot more! But then Phinehas "rose up and intervened" to kill one Israelite and his Midianite woman, after which the plague, supposedly caused by God to punish "the people," was lifted. Apparently God was satisfied with the death of one couple after all (Num. 25:1–15). This kind of story is repeated time and time again in our judicial system today. One troubling aspect about capital punishment, besides the executions themselves, is the tendency to execute just one person for the homicide although several more were involved in it and convicted of complicity. Helen Prejean documents two cases like this in *Dead Man Walking* that were conflated into one crime in the famous movie of that name. More troubling is the fact that only a small percentage of people committing homicide are executed and that all of these convicts are poor and most of them are Afro-Americans. It seems that much of the American public both craves the death penalty and is satisfied with few instances of its use, roughly 1 percent as it happens.[4] In her more recent book *The Death of Innocents*, Prejean analyzes in detail two court cases for murder that ended up in the execution of the defendant. Not surprisingly from the standpoint of mimetic theory, in both cases, she shows how desperate the law enforcers and prosecutors were to pin the blame for a horrible crime on *somebody*, and once they had such a person, they worked with a tunnel vision that assumed guilt and shaped all of the "evidence" in that direction.[5]

This arbitrary application of the death penalty gives it the same underlying dynamic as the collective violence of the primitive sacred. There is, however, a major difference: the collective violence of execution no longer "works." Bailie explains it this way:

> Whether it is a public hanging, a war, or a televised glorification of violence, a culture's righteous violence will fascinate its onlookers. It will be a spectacle.... When, however, the violence loses its religious aura, the fascina-

tion that the spectacle of violence arouses will not lead to a reverence for the sacred institution that unleashed it. Rather, the spectacle of violence will become a model for similar violence, and those who were its most entranced spectators will replicate it—beginning with the youngest and most mimetic in society.[6]

At the end of this quote, Bailie refers to a poem dealing with a crowd's reaction to a public hanging written by Coventry Patmore. First the crowd watched the hanging, standing "agape with horrid thirst." After the hanging, the people went off to perpetuate their own delinquent behavior, including the thief "with ample spoil." Among the young imitators of the violence were two children who "caught and hanged a cat."[7]

When Timothy McVeigh was executed for destroying the Oklahoma City Federal Building, I was struck by the pervasive tone in the press that the execution had not brought the sense of closure that many people expected. The execution did not "work." I suspect that this failure is partly due to the realization that with a crime of such magnitude, no conceivable punishment is equal to the horror committed. Vengeance was exacted, but it was not enough. Much the same thing happened in the rural community where my monastery is located. We were all shaken some years ago by the murder of a woman in our area, one that our monastic community knew well, and whose friendship we valued. Several weeks went by before the body was discovered. The uncertainty of the woman's fate was an emotional strain for all of us. When the body was discovered, it was impossible not to hope that the perpetrator would be found and prosecuted. Yet, when a man was arrested for the crime, tried, and convicted to a life sentence (Michigan does not have the death penalty), uneasiness remained, partly because the rightness of the verdict was not certain and partly because the sentencing didn't really resolve the loss the crime inflicted on us. I have to admit, though, that this experience helps me understand the frantic efforts to find a culprit, any culprit, that Prejean analyzes in such excruciating detail.

Meting out punishment for deviant behavior gives the illusion of control, but it is just that: an illusion. A community might feel better because of the punishment. It might feel that things have been set to rights. But the community has not really been healed by the punishment. Girard's mimetic theory, of course, predicts this sort of unsettled outcome to the collective punishment of criminals. In a lecture by Bailie that I attended, he said that one would have expected the crucifixion of Jesus of Nazareth to have sent everybody home rejoicing and singing the National Anthem. But Luke said, "And when all the crowds who had gathered there for this spectacle saw what had taken place, they returned home, beating their breasts" (Lk. 23:48). That is to say, the crucifixion of Jesus didn't "work." Luke goes on to note that a group of women "stood at a distance, watching these things." The disciples had fled, and Peter had denied that he knew Jesus. Only these women remained as the first visible dissenters to the execution of Jesus. But once you get dissenters, no matter how few, collective killing of a victim no longer "works."

Unfortunately, some versions of atonement theology lead us to overrate the efficacy of punishment. If we consider punishment, in itself efficacious to the point that human sin *requires* punishment to restore our relationship with God, then it ceases to matter *who* is punished as long as *somebody* is, even if Jesus takes the rap that *we* deserved. Christopher D. Marshall questions this penal model of the Atonement by suggesting that "such is the emphasis on law in the penal model that God's own freedom is constrained by it. God *cannot* forgive until the punishment demanded by the law is exacted."[8] Marshall goes on to explain why punishment fails both in theology and in real life. A "penal theory of atonement ascribes too much potency to punishment and too little to sin." However, "sin is not merely an affront to God's dignity requiring reparation, or a breaking of God's rules requiring correction; it is a state of volitional-moral enslavement and relational distortion that requires deliverance and reconciliation."[9] When it comes to dealing with real human beings who are disruptive in their behavior, punishment may have to play some role in dealing with the problem. But even when punishment is a legitimate means to the end of restoring and maintaining order, it must not become an end in itself. What Marshall is getting at is that the important thing is to restore relationships. A preoccupation with punishment could very well thwart the desired restoration.

One particularly serious drawback to a retaliatory model of justice is that it is almost always blind to the reality of the offender. We use phrases such as "He needs a thrashing" or "He needs a few years in the pen," but the truth is, it is *we* who feel the need to thrash a person or put him in the pen. The immediate rejoinder is that the "needs" of a serious offender are not worthy of consideration because the offender doesn't deserve it. However, catering to the "needs" of the person meting out punishment is a sure recipe for injustice. Benedict shows this awareness as an everyday pitfall when he says that children should be disciplined by all, *but* "even this ought to be done in a moderate and reasonable way" (RB 70:5). Anyone who "flares up wildly at the children" will be subject to discipline in turn (RB 70:6). When anger and fear govern the punishments we give out, the unfortunate result is that a weaker person often gets punished for what somebody *else* did to the one dealing out punishment.

If a vindictive spirit governs punishment, it is very hard to root out this bad spirit because it seems so righteous. It is *right* that somebody should *pay* for the wrong that has been done. It is only justice. This attitude, however, is a swift path to injustice. Punishment administered in a vindictive spirit naturally draws a vindictive response. This, in turn, sets off a spiral of retaliatory violence. I do not for a minute want to give the impression that renouncing vengeance is easy when one is directly affected by a serious crime. Prejean's portraits of the bereaved victims' parents show how real and powerful the need for vengeance can be when one's life has been devastated by the murder of a child. It also shows how understandable this need for vengeance is. In discussing the seventh step of humility, we examined the genuine needs of victims that require much healing. Although attempts to rush victims of heinous crimes into forgiveness almost always backfire, a gradual move toward forgiveness consistently proves to be a deep-seated need of a victim in order for the victim to be freed of the trauma. In any case, we have to remember that a vindictive approach, however understandable, often results in a further multiplication of victims. An extreme example referred to earlier is the vengeance enacted by David against Saul's family on behalf of the Gibeonites (2 Sam. 21:1–6). The question we must ask is, must the needs of those who were wronged and the needs of those who committed the wrong always be at cross-purposes? Benedict's handling of delinquency and punishment suggests that the answer is no. It is worth noting that, although Benedict expresses much exasperation over the bad behavior of some monastics, he never caters to anyone's emotional need for vengeance. Neither does Benedict suggest restoring a delinquent monastic to full communal life who has not "made satisfaction" (RB 24:4, 7). Most important, Benedict has already told us that forgiving as we are forgiven is indispensable to untwisting "the thorns of scandal" (RB 13:12–13).

Vindictive punishment and reformation of character almost always work at cross-purposes. Putting a drug user into prison because that person is deemed wicked and deserving of punishment makes it unlikely that the prisoner's drug problem will be cured. Putting that person in a rehabilitation program lets an undeserving criminal get off without *paying* for the crimes committed, but there is a good chance the person will be cured. It is worth noting that there is some built-in "punishment" that an offender experiences in the course of a reforming program. Anyone who has struggled to overcome chemical addiction or deep-rooted behavior patterns knows how painful an effort it takes to change for the better. Arguably, a person who undertakes a rehabilitation program suffers much more emotional stress than does a person who spends many years in prison but makes no effort to change. For a person in authority, going the way of reformation requires eating humble pie. Punishing an offender in a vindictive spirit makes one feel powerful. Helping the offender reform not only feels weak; it *is* weak. Instead of wielding a big stick, the authority becomes a suppliant begging for a change of heart. When the superior takes this approach, a community may feel that the situation is out of control if the perpetrator has not undergone enough suffering to satisfy everybody, even if disruptive activity has been brought to a halt. On the other hand, the more retaliatory violence plays a part in the punishment meted out in a community, the greater the danger that violence will escalate, even to the point of destroying the community.

Benedict shows concern that the abbot treat each person in a way appropriate to his or her temperament when it comes to dealing with offenses and punishment: "Every age and mentality should have an appropriate regimen" (RB 30:1). He thinks that children or youths being raised in the monastery might not appreciate the gravity of excommunication (to be examined in detail below), and so they should "be deprived of food or pressured with sharp blows to correct them" (RB 30:3). Corporal punishment is questioned today much more than it was in Benedict's time. It would take us too far afield to debate the issue here. Benedict's concern that the children not be treated unreasonably makes it clear that Benedict does not want children to be beaten for the frustrations of their elders. It is also worth noting that, as in so many other instances, Benedict's advocacy of corporal punishment, rough as it may seem to modern readers, was considerably less harsh than other known monastic rules of his time. Moreover, Kardong suggests that Benedict misjudged a young person's ability to understand the gravity of excommunication when he asks, "What could be more painful for a ten-year-old than to be cut off from the gang, and for a fifteen-year-old to be separated from peers?"[10] Monastics today routinely note that although monks and nuns or even their young students are no longer beaten with rods, all too often, they are beaten with words and contemptuous treatment. Benedict's admonitions concerning control of the tongue suggest that it is important to be alert to this danger and not assume that sparing the rod automatically makes us more humane than our forebears. The Latin phrase *ut sanentur*, translated as "correction," has the primary meaning of "healing." Kardong sees this as an important reminder that "Christian discipline is strictly aimed at salvation, not vindication."[11] In any case, Benedict clearly put the focus on the needs of the offender and what it takes to make the offenses stop.

In acting appropriately to the offender, Benedict takes into account the offender's inner dispositions insofar as they can be read. Punishment should be inflicted on one who is "defiant or disobedient or arrogant or a murmurer" (RB 23:1). These attitudes are highly destructive to communal life. Time and time again, Benedict enjoins punishment for those who manifest pride, such as artists who take inordinate pride in their work (RB 57) or priests who take too much pride in their ordained status (RB 62). Benedict's response to offenses such as damaging communal property and tardiness at meals or worship varies considerably, based on whether or not the offender shows humility in confessing a fault or shows pride and defiance. An emphasis on inner disposition has the merit of avoiding a legalistic approach to discipline, and it draws attention to the importance of cultivating virtues of the heart. The problem is that it is hard to judge a person's motives. There are few worse social problems in a community than a tendency to assume bad motives on the part of others for their behavior. Benedict does, however, note some outward signs that are usually reliable clues to a person's inward disposition concerning faults committed. If a person minimizes the fault, claims exemption from the rules governing the rest of the community, or, worse, treats the fault as a virtue, then there is pride and defiance that must be curbed. When a person is willing to own up to the fault, apologize for it, and take steps to avoid committing that fault in the future, then there is humility. Chittester catches the relationship between interior disposition and its communal consequences very well when she says that "Benedict does not punish severely for everything. He does not punish for incompetence or lack of spiritual intensity or ignorance or weaknesses of the flesh. No, Benedict punishes harshly only for the grumbling that undermines authority in a community and the rebellion that paralyzes it. Benedict punishes severely only for the destruction of the sense of community itself."[12]

Benedict first lays out the hope that a person will take the initiative by confessing a fault to the community. Any monastic who, while "working in the kitchen, the cellar, in serving, in the bakery, the garden or at any craft or any other place—and if he commits some mistake, or breaks or loses something, or errs in any other way in any place" must immediately confess the fault (RB 46:1–2). Benedict goes on to say that if the fault is discovered by somebody else, the delinquent monastic must suffer a more severe penalty than would have been the case if the careless monastic had confessed the fault. Kardong notes that in the convoluted syntax of these verses, Benedict "lapses into a paroxysm of frantic concern to close up all possible loopholes to his legislation."[13] Benedict comes across here as inordinately fretful over the possibility that somebody might escape from doing penance for any fault. The intensity we see in this passage reminds us that

Benedict was a human being like the rest of us, and his teachings about punishment and reconciliation were forged through deep inner struggle.

Benedict tailors the punishment of each offense to what is appropriate for each occasion by outlining different degrees of excommunication for different faults. The term "excommunication," as Benedict uses it, should not be confused with its ecclesiastical meaning of excommunication from the sacraments. In the Rule, excommunication is restricted to exclusions from certain aspects of community life. For "minor faults" (chapter 24), a monastic is excluded from common meals. The monastic still joins the community for worship but is not allowed to read or intone a psalm. For "a more serious fault" (chapter 25), the monastic is excluded from both table and oratory. De Waal notes that, as so often in the Rule, table and oratory are linked. "Faults in ordinary daily life are no less serious than faults of a more strictly spiritual nature."[14] Looking at it more positively, we could say that healing is holistic, affecting both daily life and prayer in equal measure.

To create space for healing and reconciliation, Benedict follows the progression listed in Matthew 18:15 for dealing with offenses: "Let him be admonished privately once and a second time by his seniors," and "if he does not change his ways, let him be publically upbraided before in the presence of all." If these admonitions do not bring about amended behavior, then the offender should be excommunicated (RB 23:2–3). There is nothing like delinquent behavior to make one lose patience. The Gospel process outlined here by Benedict forces the abbot to deal with offenses with restraint and patience. Even a gentle rebuke will be painful to some people, and that is all it will take to improve that person's behavior. Other people never understand what is said, no matter how clearly and how long it is explained to them. It will be necessary to take some sort of action with such a person. In any case, making private admonitions the first step gives that person a chance to reform and avoid public embarrassment. But if a private admonition has no effect, a public rebuke becomes necessary. One hopes that the embarrassment and its concomitant social pressure will motivate the rebuked person to change for the better. At this stage, it is also important that the abbot show the community that he is holding a firm line against the bad behavior and not ignoring the problem.

In dealing with these faults, Benedict shows that he knows very well how the actions of one person are the business of everybody who has to live with these actions and their consequences. The process of excommunication in the Rule treats these offenses on a communal level. Excommunication cuts the social bonds for a time with the hope, stated by Paul in 1 Corinthians 5:5 and quoted in RB 25:4, that the end result will be healing for both individual and community. Excommunication, then, is not an action that cuts an intact social fabric; excommunication states the *real* state of affairs. The abbot is not breaking the community; he is announcing the fact that the community is broken. Monastics routinely note that an abbot doesn't excommunicate a member of the community; the offending monastic excommunicates himself or herself. Given the denial that dysfunctional behavior usually spawns in a community, the importance of facing the reality of social alienation can hardly be overstated. Healing does not take place as long as nobody acknowledges that there is a problem. Once the situation is faced, something constructive can be done about it.

Benedict strictly forbids anyone not specifically authorized by the abbot to associate with the excommunicated member "in any fashion" (RB 25:2). Anyone who disobeys this order is also excommunicated (RB 26). Behind this stern order is Benedict's concern that the excommunicated monastic have the opportunity, however painful, of "maintaining all the while a penitential sorrow" (RB 25:3). In this way, Benedict creates an ample space for the estranged person to reflect on the behavior and attitudes that brought things to such a pass. This space allows one to break out of the pattern of reflex actions born of pride and contempt, reflex actions that may have become so habitual that the offender was not even aware of them. In such a case, the offender might really need this opportunity, hard as it is, to become aware of what he or she was really doing. Flatfootedly filling this space with well-meant but distracting chatter would defeat the purpose of this whole process. Another reason for forbidding contact with an excommunicated member is the danger of contagion. Girard would call it mimetic contagion, where the dysfunctional behavior of one person is imitated by others until everybody catches the "plague" of this behavior and acts in the same dysfunctional way. Benedict did not need to read Girard to realize that "one sick sheep should not be allowed to infect the whole flock" (RB 28:8). The second thing, then, that excommunication accomplishes is that it quarantines the sick person to prevent the spread of infection. Associating with the excommunicated person without authorization leaves one open to catching the infection from the offender. That is why this person, too, must be excommunicated.

Benedict says that the abbot must proceed "like a wise physician," and administer "poultices, the oil of encouragement, the medicine of Holy Scripture, and finally, the cautery of excommunication" (RB 28:3). These are medical terms, some of which face the real pain that may be a necessary part of healing of a wayward member whose disruptive actions have upset the community. Even if treatment for bad behavior is painful, the pain is never sought as a good in itself, any more than a doctor tries to hurt a patient for the sake of inflicting pain. The medical analogy has its limitations, as we shall see, and Benedict moves past it quite quickly. If all of the effort put into admonitions, excommunication, and wise counsel fail, the abbot should try "a still greater thing: he and all the brothers should pray" (RB 28:4). When read in isolation, this chapter makes prayer seem like a last resort or even an afterthought. There is no question that whenever offenses are dealt with in a vindictive way, prayer is reduced to that role at best. We need to remember, though, that back in chapter 25, when Benedict first raises the possibility that excommunication might be necessary, Benedict prescribes communal prayer for the offender. Clearly, then, this "still greater thing," prayer, is the *first* resort as well as the *last*. Prayer must support the beginning of the process and then sustain all further attempts to effect healing. However, if even the prayers of the community fail to turn a bad situation around, the physician must "use the amputating knife ... for one sick sheep should not be allowed to infect the whole flock" (RB 28:6–7). In other chapters in the Rule where Benedict suggests that a monastic might need to be sent away, the suggestion seems to be driven more by exasperation with a disobedient priest or rebellious prior than by good sense. However, in this chapter, the "amputating knife" is clearly used reluctantly when all else has failed. That the medical terminology should be used even here also demonstrates the importance of not relinquishing concern for the monastic who is asked to depart.

The medical terminology Benedict uses for discipline and excommunication alerts us to its problems. The Greek word *pharmakos* means "medicine," but it also means "poison." There is no denying that medical intervention is violent. Cauterization and amputation are openly violent, even when necessary. We need to remember that pretty pink pills also impose some violence on the body. Sometimes, side effects end up causing more problems than the medicine solves. Indeed, Girard notes that the city of Athens maintained at public expense a group of people called *pharmekoi* whose job was to be sacrificed whenever anything went wrong. The cure for social ills was a poison.[15] Mimetic theory warns us, then, that focusing on one person as the focus of discipline, especially if it leads to temporary or permanent expulsion, may be a necessary medicine, but it is also a poison. Great care must be taken to make sure that delinquent behavior that poisons a community is not cured by an even worse poison. Girard is warning us here that the greater poison might be a communal act of scapegoating. If this should be what is really happening, then the scenario of excommunication as outlined by Benedict will feed a dysfunctional process in the community rather than help an individual achieve amendment of life.

Edwin Friedman's Family Systems Theory can help us examine this problem. One of Friedman's basic concepts is the "identified patient." The "identified patient" is the individual within a system who appears to be the sickest. Friedman warns us, however, that the "identified patient" is "the one in whom the family's stress or pathology has surfaced."[16] That is to say, the "identified patient" bears the tensions of the whole community. "The 'identified patient' enables the rest of the family to 'purify' itself by locating the source of its 'disease' in the disease of the 'identified patient.'"[17] Girard tells us that purification, catharsis, is precisely what the scapegoating mechanism accomplishes to resolve a community's mimetic crisis. Likewise, Friedman warns us that focusing a community's tensions on one person allows that community to "deny the very issues that contributed to making one of its members symptomatic."[18]

An excommunicated member of a community has all the markings of what Family Systems Theory calls the "identified patient." As long as this one person is sick or in trouble, nobody else has to deal with the other social tensions abounding in the community. An "identified patient" is not necessarily innocent of wrongdoing. More likely, this person really does act badly, *but* the "identified patient" is usually getting the message from the rest of the family that it is his or her "job" to act out and absorb the hostility that circulates through the family system. If the system "needs" an "identified patient" to maintain the unstable equilibrium its members are addicted to, then it becomes important to the system that the "identified patient" not get better. If that should happen ("heaven" forbid!), then somebody else must assume that role without delay. Quite clearly, the "identified patient" is the sacrificial lamb who preserves the system. In such a scenario, punishment of the "identified patient" will only sustain that person's dysfunctional behavior, and the family system will sabotage any possibility of healing.

Friedman admits that this phenomenon resembles scapegoating, but he thinks there are a couple of differences. He suggests that scapegoating on a large social scale, such as the scapegoating of Afro-Americans, results from a conscious awareness of what is happening, but "the creation of an identified patient is often as mindless as the body's rejection of one of its own parts."[19] We have seen, however, that Girard argues that the collective violence that produces a scapegoat is as unconscious as the family process analyzed by Friedman. It is, of course, precisely the unconscious element of scapegoating that requires vigilance to this danger. Friedman's second reason for not accepting the category of the scapegoat is that the "identified patient" might be "a strikingly high achiever," possibly an "overly responsible sister," perhaps the one who has exercised leadership in the family.[20]

Such an overachiever, in his or her overachieving, can easily bear the tensions of the community just as much as an "identified patient" could. Girard, as we have already seen, is well aware of how a community's leader or most talented achiever can indeed be the communal scapegoat; hence the community's "identified patient." It is worth noting that Friedman also explores ways in which the "identified patient" may bear the community's tensions in his or her body so that these tensions become visible in the form of physical illness. This does not mean that the illness is psychosomatic. The illness is very real as a physical illness. What Friedman is noting here is how closely our bodies are related to our emotional processes.[21]

Such considerations may tempt an abbot to back off from disciplining a delinquent monastic for fear of scapegoating that person. The problem is, if the abbot holds back, then it is certain that the delinquent member will control the community by bending it to his or her own dysfunction. There has probably never been a monastery, or any other community, that has not had at least one member who refused to take responsibility for his or her actions and so shifted all blame for all personal problems to the community. Such a person uses real or alleged causes for grievance as excuses for exemption from the normal round of duties and a license for hurtful behavior. One monk, commenting on such a scenario, said that he felt that one member was "holding the whole community for ransom." Allowing this sort of thing to happen puts a community into the hands of its least mature and humane members.

When there is serious dysfunction within a community and/or on the part of a member of it, the result is misdirection that makes it increasingly difficult for anybody in the community to see *what is actually going on*. The upsetting behavior of a member can be magnified in the minds of others many times over, especially when several people agree on seeing this person as monstrous. Likewise, a member who feels wronged will exaggerate these wrongs to the exclusion of all else and so reach a highly distorted view of the community. Accompanying these distortions is denial that prevents a community from seeing the dysfunction. Denial leads a community to a level of homeostasis where the mutual distortions settle into an unstable truce. It seems easier to keep the situation as it is rather than take a chance of upsetting the apple cart, however rotten the apples. In such a state, both the disruptive members and their victims have a stake in keeping things the way they are. Unfortunately, homeostasis can be maintained only by systematically avoiding the truth. We need to remember that Satan is a liar and the father of lies (Jn. 8:44).

It follows that getting in touch with the *facts* of what is *really* happening is essential, both to make a beginning toward healing the dysfunction and to avoid sabotage through scapegoating activity. It is well-known that if an intervention is deemed necessary, such as is often the case with chemical addiction, the disruptive person must be confronted with *facts* and not vague accusations or name-calling. While spelling out that the things a person is *doing* is unacceptable, it is equally important to stress love and concern for the *person*. When a community settles into a state of homeostasis with an "identified patient," outside help is needed to help everybody in the community get a grip on the reality they are facing. Benedict suggested calling in the local bishop in such cases to help untangle a communal problem. Today, we also have other available resources such as pastoral counselors, facilitators, and therapists. Such people can give a community valuable assistance in spelling out the facts of what is actually going on. A powerful moment of truth can then help a community move forward out of a state of homeostasis that perpetuates a bad situation and toward the Promised Land of renewal. Such a process is necessary to discern rightly if severing one person's ties with the community is the right thing to do.

Monastic experience over the centuries has confirmed that expulsion, however sad, is the only realistic alternative in some circumstances. Benedict's image of contagion shows an awareness of human mimesis that makes it necessary to guard against allowing one disobedient person to become the model for some or possibly all of the community. More important, experience has shown that care and concern for the disciplined member has to take into account the possibility that the monastic life is not suited to that person after all. Unfortunately, disruptive behavior is sometimes the way a person trapped in an unsuitable situation will cry for help, thus forcing other people to take the initiative in extracting him or her from the situation. In such cases, it is important to make the delinquent member a *participant* in the discernment process for leaving the community. If the decision is made for a person to leave the community, it is also essential that the community be vigilant to the possibility of developing a pattern of needing an "identified patient." If, time after time, a person is either expelled from the community or is healed of dysfunctional behavior only to have somebody else become the target of discipline, then chances are the community is in what Girard calls a "sacrificial crisis." Such a community is caught in a cycle of gaining temporary relief for its deepest problems by scapegoating one person after another. On the other hand, if nobody else emerges as the "goat" in the community after a delinquent person leaves, there is a chance that the action taken was sound.

For all of the anger and fear that Benedict expresses over various offenses, he never fails to place the emphasis squarely on the side of restoration of the offender when it comes to detailing how punishment should be administered. It is precisely this goal that makes it possible for a community to handle a delinquent member without falling into scapegoating. Benedict clearly hopes that the social deprivation of excommunication will help the offender reflect on the attitudes that caused social discourse to break down so badly. Even in isolation, the excommunicated monastic's ongoing membership in the community is affirmed by giving that person work to do that can be done in solitude (RB 25:3). During this time, Benedict recommends that the offender meditate on 1 Corinthians 5:5 where Paul says, "A man like that has been given over to fleshly destruction so that his soul might be saved on the day of the Lord." Kardong points out that even though Paul's "language is very strong, he still wants to bring the person to conversion."[22] By emphasizing this verse where he does, Benedict gives a loud and clear signal that the punishment of excommunication is intended to be remedial and not vindictive. Benedict is not trying to solve a problem by just getting rid of somebody. A sharp student of scripture might notice that Benedict omitted Paul's reference to Satan as the one to whom the outcast's flesh is consigned. Kardong says that Benedict might have used a text that omitted that verse, but he is inclined to think that "the whole idea of 'abandonment' is downplayed because in fact the excommunicated monk is *not* simply gotten out of the way."[23]

Benedict goes on to make it crystal clear that he intends to avoid imprisoning a delinquent member in the role of "identified patient" by the way he treats the offender. "The abbot should focus all his attention on the care of wayward brothers, for *it is not the healthy but the sick who need a physician*" (RB 27:1, Mt. 9:12). The abbot is instructed to "use all the means that a wise physician would" (RB 27:2). First, the "wise physician" should send "wise, elderly brothers who know how to comfort the wavering brother" (RB 27:3). Kardong suggests that right after issuing a "stiff prohibition against fraternization with the excommunicated," Benedict subverts that order by sending a couple of monks "to do just that … thereby jeopardizing the whole system."[24] The implication is that Jesus himself jeopardizes all human penal systems. Benedict sends "wise, elderly brothers" to comfort the "wavering brother" to "urge him to make humble satisfaction and also *console him so that he be not devoured by too much sorrow*" (RB 27:3, 2 Cor. 2:7). Sending "wise elderly brothers" to the excommunicated member is a good practical move on the part of the abbot, because the abbot, when required to play the role of the heavy, is not in as good a position to console a monastic under discipline as somebody else who is unencumbered with juridical authority. Although only a few monastics are delegated to console the excommunicated member, Benedict affirms the need for the whole community to support that person when he says, "As the Apostle likewise says, *let love for him be reaffirmed and let everyone pray for him*" (RB 27:3–4, 2 Cor. 2:7–8). These verses in Second Corinthians are commonly believed to refer to the man in First Corinthians whose flesh was "consigned to Satan" in the first Epistle. Even if that is not the case, the principle is the same. The person who has offended the community should be prayed for and loved in the hope that the person will be restored to the community.

Benedict intensifies his concern with the offender by invoking the shepherd who must "hasten with all keenness and energy to prevent any of the sheep … from being lost" (RB 27:5). This image, of course, refers to Christ and thus adds a Christological depth to the ministry of the abbot and the other community members who assist him. De Waal reminds us that it is "quite possible to cure without compassion, but this can be no more than a shortcut. If Benedict points us all the time to Christ, then in the exercise of his ministry of healing we can see an example of true compassion."[25] The abbot must "understand that he has undertaken to care for the weak and not to dominate the strong" (RB 27:6). With this reference to Ezekiel 34, Benedict impresses upon us once again his concern for the weak. The abbot's concern for the wayward members of the community should lead him to "imitate the good shepherd's devoted example: He left the ninety-nine sheep in the hills to go looking for the one that had strayed. He was so filled with sympathy at its weakness that *he* mercifully *placed it on his* sacred *shoulders* and carried it back to the flock" (RB 27:8–9). With this paraphrase of Luke 15:4–5, Benedict cuts to the heart of the Gospel. If a community preserves its dysfunction by maintaining an "identified patient," then the community is following the famous counsel of Caiaphas, that it is better that one person suffer than that the system should perish. The scapegoat, the "identified patient," becomes the dispensable person who maintains the dysfunctional system. Luke's parable of the shepherd and the lost sheep illustrates the opposite position. Far from being dispensable, the lost sheep is entitled to the greatest energy and concern on the part of everybody else, including the ninety-nine sheep who have not strayed.

This parable is as clear and complete a repudiation of sacred violence as we could possibly have. In using this parable, Benedict makes it clear that when it comes to healing a community, nobody is dispensable and *everybody* must be treated with full human dignity. This also means that nobody may be considered dispensable by allowing a dysfunctional person to bully somebody because it is easier for the community as a whole to put up with that. Here, Benedict captures the inner spirit of the Gospel by picturing the abbot throwing off any sense of abbatial dignity in much the same way as the father of the prodigal son throws off his dignity by running out to greet the son he sees from afar. When we note the words not italicized in the above quote, we see that Benedict added some tender touches by saying that the shepherd was "filled with sympathy"; he "mercifully" placed the lost sheep on his shoulders and "carried" the sheep back to the flock. Kardong points out that we must remember that from the standpoint of common sense, "this behavior is at best risky and at worst, irrational," but "the parables of Jesus judge common sense and are not judged by it."[26]

Speaking of the ninety-nine sheep who did not stray, Kardong says that it isn't the case that the abbot should pay attention to a troubled member of the community at the expense of the others but that "every member is a forgiven sinner in more or less need of assistance on the way to salvation. The abbot should not complain if his time is taken up with the concerns of the troubled and wounded rather than with great works of religion and culture."[27] De Waal picks up this important principle very well when she says that staying with the Rule of Benedict causes her to appreciate how "it provides for the whole range of human weakness and inadequacy, yet with a complete absence of cynicism or pessimism. This is what the human condition is, and this is where God's grace is encountered and the paschal mystery happens."[28] Chittester chimes in by saying, "The idea that the spiritual life is only for the strong, for those who don't need it anyway, is completely dispelled in the Rule of Benedict. Spiritual athletes need not apply. Monasticism is for human beings only."[29] All this is a radical reversal of mimetic rivalry that would have us strive for a higher and stronger position over other people and retain that position at their expense by keeping them as weak as possible. For Christ and for Benedict, it is the stronger person who should embody the weakness of the shepherd who does everything possible to strengthen the weak.

There is a hiatus in Benedict's code of discipline after chapter 30 before he eases back toward this subject. Between these two sets of chapters, Benedict deals with stewardship of material possessions and acts of service in the community. The result of this ordering of chapters is that Benedict's teaching on satisfaction and reconciliation of the excommunicated member is separated from the chapters on excommunication by a large gap. It seems likely that this arrangement of chapters is mere happenstance and not the result of careful architectural planning. But regardless of Benedict's intentions (if any) in arranging his chapters the way he does, Kardong points out that "the effect of separating fault and excommunication from reconciliation is to create considerable tension."[30] It is like being left hanging by an unresolved cadence during a long stretch of music before it finally reaches a resolution. If Benedict was carefully placing his chapters here and not being haphazard, then it is quite likely that he intended "to indicate that there should be no premature solution to these problem."[31] Premature solutions to problems are "solutions" that depend on scapegoating mechanisms.

In chapter 44, Benedict lists several stations in the process of "making satisfaction" that have a liturgical quality. First, the excommunicated member "should lie prostrate and silent outside the entrance to the oratory at the time when the celebration of the Divine Office is complete" (RB 44:1). This station seems likely to last for several days, but the time frame is not specified. In any case, the time allotted for this step is left to the discretion of the abbot, who is expected to decide the length of time on an individual basis and not by an abstract code of punishment. Second, "when bidden by the abbot," the monastic comes and lies "prostrate at the feet of the abbot himself and then of all, that they might pray for him" (RB 44:4). Once again, prayer for the offending person is given prominence. After this point, the abbot readmits the monastic to choir at a time that seems right. Later, again at a suitable time, the abbot allows the monastic to perform liturgical functions once again. Even after readmission to choir and participation in the liturgy, the monastic is required to lie prostrate after the Office until the abbot "again orders that he cease doing so" (RB 44:8).

In comparison with earlier monastic writings, Benedict not only prolongs the ritual of reconciliation but also belabors the process. Although this style of presentation "can wear down the reader," Kardong suggests that the slow pace of the writing and of the process itself may be for the purpose of emphasizing "that reconciliation takes time and cannot be rushed. If we are talking about genuine healing, then it is a truism to say that any attempt to force premature closure will have just the opposite effect."[32] It often happens that when reconciliation happens too quickly, the reconciliation has not penetrated the hearts of those who were estranged, and the grudges that caused the trouble continue to smolder. But when the healing is real, forgiveness comes naturally. As with wounds of the body, wounds of the soul heal at their own pace, a pace that will not be hastened by wishes to the contrary. The actual ritual suggested here is not one that monastics today find helpful, but the reasoning behind it, to give structure for a slow process of healing, is sound. The method is best worked out with each individual case. What matters is that healing be given its proper space and time to occur. What Benedict gives us is a scenario of exile and return, precisely the scenario in the parables of the lost sheep and the prodigal son. Even though Benedict's scheme of excommunication is not appropriate in many social settings, the basic pattern happens quite naturally, such as when a fractious child is sent away from the dinner table and sent to his or her room but then is reinstated to the dinner table once the painful separation has allowed the family to heal the disruption. Whenever we experience difficulty in dealing with one another, we drift apart. The sting of the separation will sometimes motivate us to seek a means of reconciliation—sometimes, but not always. Sometimes, in spite of our best efforts, we end up living with the wounds caused by a separation all our lives.

This model of exile and return is a repudiation of a penal approach to delinquency. That does not mean that there might not be punishment in some cases. In this model, punishment is built into the scenario more than an action purposely done. It is not just the offender but everybody in the community who feels the pain of exile. *Everybody* feels this built-in punishment. Most fundamentally, what the model of exile and return shows us is that, given the reality of exile, the *only* thing that matters is return. We need to do everything it takes to make return possible—but no more. That is, we do not punish another unless we are sure it really is necessary for the sake of return. In the parables of the lost sheep and the prodigal son, there is no punishment; there is only rejoicing that the sheep and the son that were lost have been found.

These chapters on discipline deal primarily with crises rather than with daily life. We must remember, though, that the way life is lived on a daily basis has a lot to do with how effectively a family or any other community handles a crisis when it comes. A well-regulated life significantly decreases the chances of a disciplinary crisis developing. If a disciplinary crisis does develop, the habitual discipline of the community will help contain it. We noted how Benedict, at a dramatic moment, invoked the power of prayer as the most powerful remedy for such a crisis. The truth is, of course, that prayer sustains a community to begin with, and it provides the community a focus for its life. Given the dangers that disciplinary action might degenerate into scapegoating behavior, it is essential that prayer centered on the One who was made a victim of collective violence be the first resort, the middle resort, and the last resort in dealing with brokenness in the community.

▼

CHAPTER 13

MIMETIC STEWARDSHIP
OF MATERIAL GOODS

Benedict insists sternly that the vice of monastics considering anything their own "must be torn up by the roots" (RB 33:1). Benedict seems to be trying to solve the problem of acquisitive mimesis by taking away every object that could become a bone of contention between two or more people. If no monastic possesses a thing that could inflame the desire of another, then there will be no mimetic rivalry. Girard has demonstrated, however, that the real problem is not the objects themselves; it is the mimetic *process* around the objects. We have already noted how a contested object tends to dissolve in the heat of mimetic rivalry. With this being the case, removal of a contested object, such as Benedict is proposing, does not resolve the tension; it escalates the tension. Girard says, "If the object is excluded there can no longer be any acquisitive mimesis as we have defined it. There is no longer any support for mimesis but the antagonists themselves. What will occur at the heart of the crisis will therefore be the mimetic substitution of antagonists."[1] If we are going to find our way to a constructive outcome to the rivalry that results from acquisitive mimesis, we must examine more closely the communal process that occurs around material objects rather than assume that removal of the material objects themselves will solve the problem.

The title of chapter 33 as Terence Kardong understands it shows us right away that Benedict also places his focus on the *process* around material objects. Kardong translates the title as "Whether monastics should *consider* anything their own," *not*, as some translations have rendered it, "Whether monastics should *have* anything of their own." Kardong explains that the Latin verb *habere* does not mean "to have"; it means "to hold in mind" or "to consider." The issue, then, "is not whether one actually has the use of an item, but whether one thinks of it possessively."[2] That is to say, Benedict is much more concerned with the *attitude* toward material things than with the things themselves. De Waal also picks up on this understanding of the word *habere* by saying that Benedict's "interest is not, therefore, on external behavior, but on purity of intention, so that once again it is the disposition of the heart that is the real issue."[3] De Waal goes on to suggest that it is not the presence of material goods that troubles Benedict but "the danger that they are, or can become, the vehicles for relations between people."[4] Chittester zeros in on the same social dimension of ownership when she insists that "common ownership and personal dependence are the foundations of mutual respect."[5] That is, acquisitive mimesis of material goods isolates us from others, while sharing material goods connects us to others in mutual dependence. Benedict's concern, then, is to follow the Gospel so as to redefine our relationship to the material world in a way that is the opposite of acquisitive mimesis.

Benedict further clarifies his contention that poverty is not the absence of material goods, but rather our manner relating to material objects, when he specifies that a monastic should not "presume to give or receive anything without the abbot's permission" (RB 33:2). Fundamental to a right relationship to material goods is relinquishing the initiative for possessing a material object to another person. It is not that monastics are forbidden to have use of a book, writing tablet, or stylus. What is forbidden is that a monastic should make a unilateral decision to acquire any of these things. That decision is put into the hands of the abbot.

When Benedict returns to this subject in chapter 55, he again says that the vice of personal ownership must be "rooted out" (RB 55:18), but he immediately explains that the way the abbot should root out this vice is by providing generously all things that are needed so as to "remove all pretext and want" (RB 55:19). It is significant that the material objects the abbot is expected to furnish are all things needed for personal use. It would not be practical for a monastic to have to borrow a writing tablet or a pad of paper from a common store every time there is a need to write something down. In order to perform our duties for the sake of the common life, we need the constant availability of certain pencils and pens and, nowadays, computers. What Benedict has done here is create a whole different process around material objects to replace the process of acquisitive mimesis that leads to mimetic rivalry.

Benedict puts added stress on the importance of the abbot being the community's provider by forbidding monastics to receive gifts from "relatives or other people" or to "exchange them among themselves" (RB 54:1). Even here, it is not a matter of having no gifts at all, but a matter of permission. Theoretically, an abbot could give a blanket permission to the members of the community to receive small gifts from family or friends, as is usually the case today. Benedict further stresses the communal dimension of the reception of gifts by giving the abbot the power to give a gift received by one monastic to another monastic. The potential abuse of this provision is obvious enough, and it is known to have happened. I once heard about an abbot who took a typewriter given to a monk as a Christmas present and kept it for himself, while generously giving that monk his old typewriter. In such a case, one cannot help but doubt that this abbot was motivated by devotion to the common life! Kardong observes that "the abbot is not a Medici prince but rather a steward of the Lord's justice to the needy and the poor."[6] As we shall see, the main concern here is that the abbot see to the real and legitimate needs of all members of the community and provide for them.

In terms of mimetic theory, one could characterize the presumption condemned by Benedict as the lust to seize an object for oneself. It is this proprietary seizure of an object that is apt to inflame the desire of other people for the same object. However, gaining possession of that same object from the hands of another is not presumption; it is receiving a gift. As the provider of the monastery, the abbot gives his monastics what they need as gifts. This is another way in which the abbot holds the place of Christ in the monastery. Ultimately, all things that humans have are gifts from God. When the abbot distributes material things to his monastics, he is distributing God's gifts. In order to receive gifts graciously, we must receive them in humility and gratitude. It is in receiving materials as gifts that we reverse the process of acquisitive mimesis. Striving to possess objects is not compatible with receiving them as gifts. We are never grateful for what we seize for ourselves. We are only grateful for what we receive as free gifts.

The process around material objects envisioned in the Rule, then, is rooted in obedience. If property is held in common, then the use each person makes of that property is made in connection with everybody else in the community. Benedict shows how deep this dispossession of the process must go when he says that monastics have "neither their bodies nor their own wills at their own disposal" (RB 33:4). Material objects or no material objects, we fall into acquisitive mimesis when we presume to take a proprietary relationship to our own desires. That is, if we insist that our desires belong to us and we are going to hang on to them, we are hoarding desires in just the same way that we hoard material possessions. Such hoarding is presumption, and it destroys community.

An often-noted paradox about monastic poverty is that, although the individual monastic has no legal title to property, the institution often has considerable property and resources. This situation is more in line with Benedict's intentions than against it. It is not the case that Benedict wants monastics to have nothing at all but rather that they receive what they have as a bounty from communal resources. Penury does not help a monastery fulfill its mission; it only hinders it. There must be sufficient material resources to create choir books and have reading material for personal study. Otherwise, monastics will not be able to worship and reflect on the Word of God. Likewise, ministry to guests becomes impossible if there are not the resources to feed and house them. Monasteries today need automobiles, for example, not only for communal errands but also to provide transportation for guests to and from buses, trains, and airplanes. A monastery will have many more books in its library than an individual person has personal resources to collect. However, there is also a great difference between having a sense of ownership over books that fill one or two bookcases and having no sense of ownership whatever over books that fill a hundred bookcases. The books are available as gifts to be *borrowed* by both monks and guests; they are not owned by any one individual. Such a situation reminds us of these words that float around the churches and turn up in retreat addresses: Everything that we have, we have received as a loan from God.

When material goods are received as gifts, the usual relationship between labor and material goods is turned on its head. We usually consider labor a means of earning the buying power to possess certain objects of desire. When work is so entangled with mimetic desire, one works in order to possess objects that are desirable because other people want them, which in turn drives one to work all the harder so as to earn these objects before somebody else gets them. In a monastic setting, the community takes responsibility for providing sustenance to each member, and the community assigns tasks to each member. Labor has no earning power, and bread is provided for free. When life is structured in this way, the worker is free to focus on the intrinsic value of the work itself. More important, work done and services rendered are gifts to others just as much as material goods are gifts.

Lewis Hyde has offered some helpful insights into the anthropology of gift-giving in his book *The Gift: Imagination and the Erotic Life of Property.* Hyde suggests that gifts have transformative power at all times. The exchange of gifts at threshold events such as births, marriages, and funerals highlights this phenomenon. Such a gift may be a marker of change, but "it is also the case that a gift may be the actual agent of change, the bearer of new life."[7] A wedding gift, for example, is a sign of the change taking place in the lives of the newlyweds, but it is also an object that makes the couple's future married life possible by giving them tools they need for their life together. Hyde goes on to say that something much more profound is at stake in the receiving of gifts: "In the simplest examples, gifts carry an identity with them, and to accept the gift amounts to incorporating the new identity. It is as if such a gift passes through the body and leaves us altered."[8] This line of thought gives us a whole new dimension to Benedict's insistence that monastics have "neither their bodies nor their own wills at their own disposal" (RB 33:4). When making a life profession, a monastic relinquishes all legal title to property. Giving of oneself in this way transforms that person body and soul. Since everything the impoverished monastic has from that day on is a gift to be received in gratitude, he or she is transformed daily. Hyde speaks of gratitude "as a labor undertaken by the soul to effect the transformation after a gift has been received." When a gift has worked in us so that "we have come up to its level," we can then pass the gift on to somebody else. "Passing the gift along is the act of gratitude that finishes the labor."[9] Among the examples Hyde gives is Alcoholics Anonymous. Assistance is freely given to those who need help to attain sobriety. Once sober, the grateful person in recovery freely gives the same assistance to others who need it.

So it is that gifts have the power to forge social bonds. In one simple example that Hyde found in the writings of Claude Lévi-Strauss, a group of men come to a French restaurant, each with a small bottle of wine. Each man pours "his" wine into the glass of his neighbor. Economically, nothing has changed, but socially, everything has changed.[10] Out of many more possible examples of social bonding he could have used, Hyde cites the custom of marriage gifts in New Caledonia, where the youth first asks a woman of his choice if she will accept his gifts. She will accept *only* if she desires to establish a personal relationship with that youth.[11] Hyde goes on to say that "gifts of peace have the same synthetic character. Gifts have always constituted peace overtures among tribal groups and they still signify the close of war in the modern world."[12]

In contrast to this view of gifts, some modern anthropologists have portrayed gift-giving as uncontrolled mimetic rivalry. There is ample evidence to support this view. The civic leaders in Rome were aggressive gift-givers of this type. They would give lavish gifts to the city, such as a racecourse, not so much for the sake of being generous but to enhance their own social prestige. Some civic gift-giving today smacks of this quality. The most notorious example of aggressive mimetic gift-giving is the potlatch of the Kwakiutl Indians as portrayed by Franz Boas. Hyde, however, presents a convincing argument that the potlatch as witnessed by Boas was seriously skewed by the Kwakiutl's interaction with Western capitalist economy. That is to say, the modern potlatch is not an example of gift-giving but a descent into a frenzied exchange of commodities.[13]

A commodity, in contrast to a gift, does not establish a connection between people. "A commodity has value and a gift does not." Hyde draws a distinction here between "value" and "worth."[14] Something that has "worth" is priceless. Value is a price. By its very nature, a price limits the "worth" of the item to a negotiated quantity. Placing a value on goods and services brings us into the realm of mimetic rivalry where we struggle over their relative values so as to get the "better deal." This is why a commodity cannot establish a social bond. In a potlatch, material goods are not treated as gifts; a value is placed upon them, a value that the recipient must equal or top in the "gift" that is given in return. That is why a potlatch shows a society in a state of disintegration. Hyde imagines an exchange of objects across a boundary established by two groups of people: "A gift, when it moves across the boundary, either stops being a gift or else abolishes the boundary. A commodity can cross the line without any change in its nature; moreover, its exchange will often establish a boundary where none previously existed."[15] Commodities, then, necessarily create boundaries between people. One could say that a commodity is a *skandalon,* a stumbling block.

The agonistic quality of commodities touched on by Hyde is explicitly analyzed in light of mimetic theory by Cesáreo Bandera. He outlines Karl Marx's analysis of the commodity as a substitute for real human beings, human beings filled with mimetic rivalry. Bandera explains that "the elementary form of value" is "more like an adversarial relationship between individual A and individual B. Each one wants what the other has but neither will abandon what it has because its possession is made valuable by the other's desire, thus becoming a measure of value for the other, the only one."[16] Here, mimetic desire drives the whole concept of the commodity until it turns into full-fledged mimetic rivalry. Even more suggestive from the standpoint of mimetic theory is the fact that in order for a standard of value to stabilize a system, namely money as the medium of exchange, that value must be expelled "from the community of commodities" so that "this particular commodity" becomes "different from all the rest."[17] As if this were not sacrificial enough, Marx was convinced that such a system "cannot possibly function without human victims. In order to work properly it must work for some at the expense of others."[18] Of course, this is the problem with commodities in the first place. Unfortunately, Marx's solution, a Communist revolution, is also driven by the logic "of the sacrificial mechanism." Marx thought that the new society was imprisoned in capitalism, from which it had to be liberated. "Peel the capitalism cover away and the new society will rise from the throbbing carcass of the freshly sacrificed victim."[19] Bandera's analysis of Marx leads us to the conclusion that we must be freed from treating material goods as commodities before we can be freed of mimetic rivalry over these material goods and the sacrificial violence that results from this rivalry.

In radical contrast to a commodity-driven economy, Benedict hearkens back to the collective pooling of resources in the early church as described in Acts 4:32: "Now the whole group of those who believed were of one heart and soul, and no one claimed private ownership of any possessions, but everything they owned was held in common." Kardong points out that Benedict reversed the two elements by saying first, "*Let all things be common to all*, as scripture says," and then going on to say "*that no one may* presume *to call* anything his own" (RB 33:6, Acts 4:32). Kardong says that this reversal "moves the discussion from the biblical realm of practical charity to that of individual asceticism where the great concern is to keep the mind pure from greedy thoughts (avarice)."[20] The inner attitude toward material goods is what concerns Benedict the most, a concern heightened by his addition of the word "presume" to his quote from Acts, the very word that plays a key role in the title of this chapter. There is, however, a communal dimension to this inner attitude, because it sets up a monastic economy where the exchange of goods and services is all gift. Benedict would abolish all commodities from the monastery.

Hyde probes the religious underpinnings of a gift economy when he notes that not only do gifts connect us to other people, "gifts may connect us to the gods as well." Humans, of course, often give gifts to a deity to foster a connection to the divine, but there are also "compassionate deities who approach us with gifts." What Hyde is particularly thinking of are "gods who become incarnate and then offer their own bodies as the gift that establishes the bond between man and the spiritual state."[21] Not surprisingly, Hyde refers to the Christian story where "in the Crucifixion or in the 'Take, eat: this is my body,' Christ's body becomes the gift, the vehicle of atonement, which establishes a new covenant between man and God." In a footnote, Hyde adds that atonement and forgiveness are complementary acts. "In forgiving a sin, he who has been sinned against initiates the exchange that reestablishes the bond. We forgive once we give up attachment to our wounds."[22] The gift of himself that Christ gives us sets up the exchange wherein we give of ourselves to Christ.

Although it is possible to see how a gift economy might possibly work on the scale of a monastery, family, and maybe even a parish community, it does not seem possible on a larger social scale. In any case, it hasn't been done, not even in Communist societies. The early church could more or less work with a gift economy, but it was a struggle even then, as Paul's rebuke to the Corinthians for bringing lawsuits against each other attests (1 Cor. 6:1–11). Once the Church became the centerpiece of an empire, a gift economy became quite problematic, with usury becoming a cause célèbre. Hyde cites Ambrose of Milan as one of the first to deal with this problem. Ambrose invoked the double standard that Moses established which allowed charging interest against non-Israelites. Such a double standard requires, of course, the erection of a barrier between "us" and "them." Theoretically, the New Testament destroyed this barrier. The Church is a New Israel, and everybody is a member of that commonwealth. Ambrose, however, managed to reestablish the barrier by allowing a Christian to charge usury to a foreigner who was "an enemy of the church." Significantly, Ambrose said, "From him exact usury whom it would not be a crime to kill. He fights without a weapon who demands usury; without a sword he revenges himself upon an enemy, who is an interest collector from his foe. Therefore where there is the right of war, there is also the right of usury."[23] Ambrose shows just as clearly as Karl Marx the connection between commodities and violence. The most troubling thing about this Ambrosian "solution" is that it assumes that some people will forever remain outside of the commonwealth established by the Gospel. The Gospel ceases to be Good News for everybody. The Gospel ceases to be the Gospel.

Lewis Hyde goes on to cite a less unsatisfactory compromise between gift and commodity devised by John Calvin in his concept of "equity": "In equable dealings, neither side gains nor loses and there is no enduring social feeling, neither good nor bad will."[24] Equitable transactions do not bind people together, but they don't tear people apart either. It also has the advantage of not necessarily requiring the exile of a group of people in order to work. Given contemporary reality, this uneasy middle ground seems unavoidable. Not even a monastery can avoid it when dealing with the world outside it. It is important, however, that this middle ground be uneasy. It falls way short of the Gospel ideal, and mimetic rivalry destroys equity in an instant. With one spark of mimetic rivalry, the draw that equity establishes becomes indistinguishable from "losing." On the other hand, if we allow the ideal of a gift economy to govern our attitude to money and material goods, we can, little by little, erode the barriers that we have set up, barriers that create mimetic conflict between people. Stewardship, as envisioned in the Rule and in scripture, would have us focus on the notion that everything we have, no matter how hard we worked to "earn" it, is a gift from God, and that we are stewards of God's bounty.

In creating a gift economy that sets up the right social process of distribution and reception that surrounds these material goods, Benedict, as he usually does, calls for flexibility with this quote from Acts: "It was distributed to each one according to need" (RB 43:1, Acts 4:34). The emphasis is not on what anybody has *earned* or on what a person is capable of grasping but rather on discerning what the community needs and what each member truly needs. Benedict approaches this matter with his usual moderation and flexibility: "Each person is endowed by God with a special gift, some this, some that." He goes on to say that it is "with some uneasiness that we lay down rules for the consumption of others" (RB 40:1–2, 1 Cor. 7:7). Kardong observes, "Benedict does not expect anyone to transcend their natural endowment to exercise heroic virtue."[25]

Provision for individual needs, of course, is not intended to allow favoritism of any kind but rather to show "sympathy for weaknesses" (RB 34:2). What is at stake is discerning what each person genuinely needs and what gifts of abstinence each person has. That is, a gift economy works with the gifts God gives each person. The formula Benedict offers for keeping all members at peace is that "one who needs less should thank God and not be sad. And whoever needs more should be humble about his weaknesses and not gloat over the mercy shown him" (RB 34:3–4). The latter point is especially important, because it is easy for a person who receives even a small variance from the usual fare to feel special. We must be truthful about seeing concessions to weaknesses for what they are. More important, the weaknesses of some people should not be occasions for assuming dominance or scornful attitudes toward them. If members of the community compare their relative benefits with each other, the usual result is the dangerous vice of murmuring. It is important that the abbot not be swayed by murmuring but rather should "pay attention to the weaknesses of the needy and not the bad will of the envious" (RB 55:21). Kardong indicates that "if the monks have what they need, they have no reason to fret about the apparent favoritism being lavished on others."[26] Envy and consequent murmuring are prevented through attention to the actual needs of each person. This attention must be exercised by the abbot, of course, but each member of the community must also remain focused on their genuine personal needs so as to prevent wanting something simply because somebody else has been granted it.

Aware that the ability to abstain is a gift of God that varies from person to person, Benedict seeks to establish a middle ground by suggesting what seems to him a reasonable and moderate food allowance that should be possible for everybody. To avoid one extreme, Benedict sternly warns that gluttony must be avoided since a monastic should never be "surprised by indigestion" (RB 39:7). The abbot must be "constantly vigilant that excess and drunkenness do not creep in." The other extreme Benedict wants to avoid is the subtle problem of monastics competing over their ascetic practice. This phenomenon furnishes impressive confirmation of Girard's notion that the problem of mimetic rivalry lies not in objects but in the anthropological process around the objects. By prescribing a common serving in a monastery as he does in the eighth step of humility, Benedict puts a brake on such mimetic problems. There is no contest in eating habits because everybody eats the same thing. Within this common life, one can seek permission from the abbot to fast beyond the common practice. This is why Benedict insists that each monastic must seek discernment as to whether or not a desire for abstinence is a personal gift from *God*. The quality and quantity of food that each person consumes, then, should be governed not by rivalrous relationships with other people but by each person's relationship with God. That is, one does not limit oneself to one crust of bread a day so as to eat less than one who eats two crusts a day.

Benedict again shows his usual concern for human weaknesses with his suggestions for the daily allowance of food and drink: "Two cooked dishes are enough for the daily meal" (RB 39:1), because of "the weaknesses of various persons." The weaknesses at issue here include a person's unwillingness to eat certain foods as well as health issues. When Benedict goes on to suggest that fruit and vegetables be added when possible and describes the allowance of bread as "generous," it again becomes clear that Benedict is far from advocating an asceticism of starvation. In fact, Benedict says that if the amount of vigorous work that needs to be done is great, such as long hours of harvesting in the fields, then the monastics should be given even more than the normal allowance. Likewise, the abbot may increase the wine allowance "if local circumstances or the workload or the heat of summer demand more" (RB 40:5). This attitude on the part of Benedict drives Joan Chittester to exclaim, "Exceptions. Exceptions. Exceptions. The Rule of Benedict is full of rules that are never kept, always shifting, forever being stretched. Only two Benedictine principles are implied to be without exception: kindness and self-control."[27] Kindness and self-control are indeed the controlling virtues of Benedictine flexibility. Speaking of wine, Benedict makes it clear that he is accommodating a communal weakness when he reminds his monastics that wine has not, in the past, been considered a drink suited for monks, but "since monks in our day cannot be convinced of this, let us at least agree not to drink to excess, but sparingly" (RB 40:6). Abbots today experience much the same thing, not only in regard to wine or beer but also in regard to items such as coffee, candy, and junk foods. In all these things, concessions need to be sufficiently moderate so as to maintain an overall healthy diet without any excess.

The end result of renouncing avarice and envy is contentment. De Waal says:

> If I am content … with what I am given, whether it be my talents and gifts or my material possessions, then I can rejoice in what I have received and look with equal rejoicing on what others have been given. This asks a true mutual concern for one another. Neither the strong nor the weak envy the other. Grumbling is the enemy of this. When I think of those greatest grumblers of all, the Pharisees, who are the prototype of the strong and who are jealous of the mercy show to the weak, I realize that what is being asked of me is a deep, loving openness, which does not judge, which is in fact simply the exercise of unconditional love that is ultimately what Benedict is hoping for in us all.[28]

Just as acquisitive mimesis leads eventually to hatred and violence, contentment with what one receives leads to peace and love.

Jesus' use of the steward figures in many of his parables suggests that Jesus was trying to wean us away from a sense of personal ownership over material goods to a sense that we receive material goods in trust from God. This is the position of a steward, who is a person responsible for the proper use of things that belong to another. In chapter 32, Benedict recommends that the abbot "choose brothers of reliable life and habits" and entrust them with the monastery's tools "to be cared for and collected" (RB 32:1–2). That the monastics entrusted with this responsibility must be "reliable" indicates that personal character is an important element for the right use of material goods. Those entrusted with the monastery's tools must demonstrate that material goods are intended to be "cared for," not fought over. Benedict sternly orders that anyone who "neglects the goods of the monastery or fails to keep them clean" should be reprimanded. If such a one does not improve, that person must be subjected to further punishment (RB 32:4). This discipline of stewardship is essential for the sake of the common life, and it can only be fueled by genuine concern both for the tools themselves and for the other people who use them. We have a greater motivation to take care of personal possessions when the economic impact of poor stewardship is immediate and palpable. Extra car repair bills resulting from poor maintenance translate into less food on the table or fewer recreational items. The resources of an institution such as a monastery are often extensive enough that a member does not usually feel the consequences of poor treatment of tools so sharply. Hence, it is all the more important to be concerned for the material possessions of the community because God cares about them. Likewise, caring for material goods is an imperative imposed on all of us by ecological concerns today. We are easily lulled into thinking that we can take anything we want from the planet, when we want it, as long as we don't feel the pinch ourselves. But, Kardong reminds that we must realize "that the earth's resources are not unlimited and need to be carefully marshaled if future generations are not to live an impoverished existence."[29] Whether we have legal title to certain things or not, we are stewards of God's creation and not the owners of certain things we happen to possess. This truth reminds us that everything we do with the materials given us is done for the sake of others and not ourselves.

Benedict lays out his spirituality of stewardship most systematically in chapter 31, "the Qualities of the Cellarer." The cellarer is a delegate of the abbot who is given responsibility for the distribution, use, and care of all the material goods of the monastery. This position has the potential to diminish the abbot's role as provider for the community, but Benedict speaks to this danger by specifying that the cellarer be appointed by the abbot. More important, the cellarer should "do nothing without the abbot's order" (RB 31:4). In any case, it is imperative that this responsibility be delegated or the abbot will fall into micromanagement, a vice that seriously disrupts the functioning of an institution. Today, the resources requiring management are usually too great for one person to assume responsibility for all of them, and the cellarer's job is parceled out to several members of the community. Added to the practical advantages of this arrangement is the spiritual benefit that *every* person is on the receiving end of receiving provisions from others at one time or another. The abbot, for example, although ultimately responsible for seeing that everything needed is provided, receives the common servings of food prepared by the cooks just like everybody else.

Before enumerating the duties of the cellarer, Benedict provides a long list of personal characteristics required of the person who holds this post. The cellarer "should be a wise person, of mature character and well disciplined," one who will "not be gluttonous, arrogant, violent, unfair, stingy or wasteful" (RB 31:1). Further on, Benedict says that the cellarer "must not hold anything as negligible." He should neither "be controlled by avarice," nor "should he waste or dissipate the goods of the monastery," but he should "take a balanced approach to everything" (RB 31:11–12). What we have here, of course, is a character description for *any* good and responsible person. By hooking these qualities of discipline, maturity, and wisdom to the use of material goods, Benedict demonstrates the importance of developing character through the way we use these goods. The personal qualities that Benedict requires of the cellarer entail renunciation of mimetic desire for objects, desires that are inflamed by being "gluttonous, arrogant, violent, unfair, stingy or wasteful." What Benedict wants in a cellarer, then, is a person who is sufficiently free of mimetic desire as to be able to model proper stewardship of material goods for the community.

This care of material objects extends to care for the people who use these goods. Far from desiring to *possess* anything, the cellarer should want to *provide* for others. "He should give the brothers their established allotment of food without arrogance or delay so as not to scandalize them" (RB 31:16). Benedict then quotes from Matthew 18:16 to remind the cellarer of the fate of those who scandalize Christ's "little ones." Like Christ, Benedict is aiming for a reversal of the mimetic process around objects. When an object is a bone of contention between two people, it becomes a stumbling block, a scandal, between them. The "thorns of scandal" have sprung up. A cellarer who withholds what should be given out or gives it out in a haughty way is using the object in question as a stumbling block. On the contrary, graciously giving out the needed item is the occasion of binding people together, a gift. Kardong suggests that "since the monks are strictly dependent for their physical existence on these rations, the term 'little ones' is fitting. It is cruel and perverse to make them suffer any humiliation in the process."[30]

There is, of course, much more to the right treatment of other people than simply refraining from ill-treatment. The cellarer should be "like the father to the whole community" (RB 31:2), one who "should lavish great care on the sick, the children, the guests and the poor," that is, the most helpless people who present themselves. If a person should engage in mimetic desire over material goods and "demand something from him in an unreasonable way, he should not crush him with a rebuke, but deny the obnoxious petitioner in a reasonable and humble manner" (RB 31:7). Here is a clear instance of Benedict's insistence on the renunciation of retaliatory behavior. Even if a person whose request has just been turned down starts a shouting match, the cellarer must not respond in kind but should attempt to wean the petitioner from a disordered desire with gentleness. Holding off an importunate person requires the humility to swallow an angry response and not try to "win" a row over the improper request. Likewise, it takes humility to admit that, even for a reasonable request, the resources are not always available to meet it. The cellarer who cannot give what is asked for should "at least return a friendly word" (RB 31:13). Kardong goes on to point out that "this is one of those passages that reveal that Benedict knew well the little things that make community life possible and bearable. No matter how poor or affluent a monastery is, if there is widespread gentleness and kindness, it is a rich community."[31]

Benedict adds a theological dimension to the handling of material goods when he says that the cellarer "should consider the pots of the monastery and all its goods as if they were the holy bowls of the altar" (RB 31:10). This explosive verse tells us that worship is the prime teacher of how we should live. The care that we take with the altar vessels is the care that we should take with everything we have occasion to use, because all our tools belongs ultimately to God just as much as the chalice and paten do. This great sentence in Benedict's Rule plunges spirituality into the heart of the material creation, where it penetrates to the smallest and humblest of our acts. For God, nothing is trivial; everything is important. There is a saying that the devil is in the details, but as far as Benedict is concerned, *God* is in the details. It is not only tools that we must treat as if they were the holy vessels of the altar. Benedict's concern for the treatment of people in relation to material goods makes it clear that we must treat also people as if they were the holy vessels of the altar. Benedict says as much when he warns the abbot against being "too vigorous in removing the rust" that "he may break the vessel" (RB 64:12). When we treat people as fragile vessels of the altar, we see Christ in them.

CHAPTER 14

▼

SERVING ONE
ANOTHER
MIMETICALLY

Benedict's admonition that all members of the community "should serve one another" (RB 35:1) could be taken as his definition of community. In this instance, he is referring to table service, but this principle extends to everything in a community's life. Benedict makes exceptions to this rule for those monks who are seriously ill or who already serve the community in heavy jobs, such as the cellarer. Then he intensifies his demand for mutual service by saying that "the others should serve one another in love" (RB 35:6). Table serving is work that has to be done, and its burden needs to be shared as evenly as possible, but the main reason Benedict insists that this work to be done by everybody is because merit is "increased and love built up" (RB 35:2). So it is that in these six verses, service and love are closely linked together. De Waal reminds us that "the figure of Christ the Servant is never far away as Benedict writes about the life of the community."[1] De Waal goes on to suggest that two New Testament scenes that were probably on Benedict's mind were the ordination of the first deacons in Acts 6:5–6 so that they "could wait on tables" and Jesus' washing of the disciples' feet in John, chapter 13. "The earliest cenobitic founders saw that the reality of living the paschal mystery gave them the example of Christ's own total self-giving as the culmination of a life of service. Living in Christ, living the Gospel, means service in humble love."[2] Here, De Waal has picked up on the Christological dimension of service that complements Benedict's Christological basis for obedience. Service is obedience in action. We must serve as Christ served.

Work is important because it has to be done to keep a community going, but Benedict establishes the priority of the spiritual health work fosters with the opening words of his chapter "On the Daily Manual Labor": "Idleness is the soul's enemy" (RB 48:1). Using work as the remedy for idleness is hardly as sublime a teaching as urging everybody to serve one another to build up love, but Benedict would have us remember that serving others in love requires effort. Idleness will not accomplish that. If one worries too much about idleness, however, there is the danger that it will lead to assigning busy work just to keep people occupied, a problem often noted in early monastic literature. Benedict, however, is alert to this danger. More than once, while listing the timetables for different times of the year, he says that monastics should work "at what is necessary" (RB 48:3, 6). The implication is that monastics should not fill the work periods with work that is *not* necessary. Kardong suggests that Benedict rejects the notion that work should be treated as a punishment for Original Sin in favor of a more utilitarian view, noting that Benedict shows "a mentality that values greatly that which is of use to the community."[3] Kardong goes on to say that "work at what is truly useful is not an expression of individual ascetical endeavor, but rather one that feeds into practical charity. By doing what is needed, one responds to the needs of each member of the community, for all depend on certain tasks being accomplished."[4] For Benedict, doing work that is useful to others is part and parcel of serving each other in love. Work that is not genuinely helpful is not conducive to spiritual health.

As with other monastic practices, Benedict points to the inner attitude that must accompany the external acts of service. This inner attitude is of the essence when it comes to caring for the sick, who should be served by an attendant "who is God-fearing, devoted and careful" (RB 36:7). Likewise, the guest quarters should be run by "a brother who is full of the fear of God" (RB 53:21). In greeting guests, one "ought to manifest complete humility" (RB 53:6). The person assigned to read to the community during meals for the week begins this task by asking the community to pray "that God might protect him from the spirit of pride" (RB 38:2). For most employers, professional competence is the first consideration for assigning a job. For Benedict, this consideration takes second place. Benedict does care very much about the competence with which work is done, as we shall see, but his priority is weighted toward the attitude behind one's competence. There are some jobs where no amount of professional competence can make up for the absence of humility. Caring for the sick and the guests are among them. Kardong reminds us that those practicing jobs of service to such people "who are in a position of relative helplessness and need the charity of God shown them" must "be motivated by the considerations of Christian faith rather than worldly wisdom."[5] We have already noticed the importance Benedict attaches to a humble attitude on the part of the artisans in the monastery. A prideful attitude will undermine any amount of skill and competence that is brought to a task.

If we serve people with humility, we steer away from thinking that we are superior to the ones we are serving. Humility makes us conscious of the needs of others. But if we dwell on how much a guest or sick person needs *our* help, help which we are graciously giving, this attitude of pride will make our acts of service humiliating to the person we are serving. Pride transmutes generosity into a quest for power. Insofar as another needs our help, that person is vulnerable. If we take advantage of that vulnerability to get the upper hand over that person, we are serving our pride rather than the other person. People who offer help from a powerful social position are often surprised when their charitable efforts are resented. This resentment, however, is easy enough to understand when we realize that it is a response to the pride that makes so-called generosity oppressive.

Just as there is an art to serving humbly and generously, there is also an art to *being* served in that same spirit. Benedict alerts us to this art when he says that the sick should "keep in mind that they are being served out of respect for God," and therefore "they should not irritate the brothers serving them with excessive demands" (RB 36:4). This principle of showing consideration for those who serve applies to guests and anybody else who is being served in any way. Being served can easily make us feel proud and superior to the ones serving us. Weak persons can fall into the little game of inventing "needs" just because they feel more important if more things are done for them. Pride can just as easily have the opposite effect of making us resent being served. Since it is humiliating to be helpless, it is not surprising if helplessness leads to resentment of the stronger person who serves in our times of weakness.

It is precisely to counter these problems that Benedict insists that everybody should serve the community at table. Not only does everybody have the opportunity to serve, but everybody also has the opportunity to *be* served. Everybody has to learn both skills. Since pride can swell either from serving or from being served, it stands to reason that pride is dealt with more efficaciously if it is attacked from both ends. This way, there is ample opportunity to develop empathy for the other, both for the person we are serving and for the person who serves us. If we are served arrogantly, perhaps we will realize how important it is to be more respectful of those we serve. If somebody we are serving is overly demanding, perhaps that will teach us to be less demanding when we are served.

Benedict extends several special considerations to those serving the community. When kitchen service is assigned, Benedict asks that "help be given to the weak so they do not lose heart in this work" (RB 35:3). Again, we see Benedict's concern for the weak, whether they are sick, infirm, or just not strong enough to do the work that others can do. Benedict also shows concern for the daily hardships of having to prolong one's fast so as to serve at table or read at meals by suggesting that table servers and the reader should be given a bit of refreshment before the meal so that they can do their duties "without grumbling and undue fatigue" (RB 35:13). Benedict shows his concern for his monastics when they have to be pushed harder than he would like by saying that they "should not be sad" if they have to do the harvesting themselves (RB 48:7). Not only that, Benedict understands, for all of his hatred of murmuring, that just causes of murmuring can arise. Rather than lay all of the responsibility on the person suffering the hardship to keep a stiff upper lip and "take it," Benedict stresses the importance of removing these causes of murmuring. Kardong goes on to say that "if people are laboring under unjust conditions they have a right and even a duty to complain; if they do not, things will never improve."[6] It is preferable, of course, that the abbot and others involved in organizing work assignments be sensitive to the burdens they impose on others. At the same time, one must be sufficiently aware of the toll that our burdens take on us and know when to ask for relief. Needless to say, when *everybody* takes turns at serving, including the abbot and others in authority, this degree of understanding is much more likely to be in evidence.

Benedict counters the danger of serving with oppressive pride by grounding service in the service of Christ: "The sick are to be cared for before and above all else, for it is really Christ who is served in them. He himself said: *I was sick and you visited me,* and *Whatever you did to one of these little ones, you did to me*" (RB 36:1–3, Mt. 25:36, 40). "All guests who arrive should be received as Christ, for he himself will say, *I was a stranger and you took me in*" (RB 53:1, Mt. 25:35). The reference to Matthew's parable stresses the vulnerability of the sick and the guest of the monastery. Benedict shows his sensitivity to these vulnerable people by insisting that his monastics "lavish great care on the sick, the children, the guests and the poor" (RB 31:9). As for guests, "the greatest care should be exhibited in the reception of the poor and pilgrims, for Christ is more especially received in them; for the fear of the rich wins them respect" (RB 53:15). We all know how spontaneously we roll out the red carpet for supposedly important persons, but we are not so easily motivated to extend ourselves for the powerless. It is for that very reason that Christ "is more especially received" in the poor, because we are not likely to respect such people on their own merits.

This last thought should bring us up short. If we fail to respect anybody on their own merits, service to these weakest and least important people will be condescending. To avoid this pitfall, we must realize that Christ makes even the most vulnerable people genuinely important. Moreover, when we realize that it is *Christ* who makes people important and not the people themselves, however rich or powerful or competent they may be, we will be more ready to see Christ in everybody who comes our way. The more we learn to value other people as Christ values them, the more we will respect these people for who they are and what they have to offer us. That is, Christ helps us see the merits of other people that we might sometimes overlook. We hardly need Kardong's reminder that "God must be reverenced in the least attractive members of the community, who are likely to be neglected if merely human standards are all that prevail."[7] The abbot does not hold the place of Christ in the monastery so that he can throw his weight around; he demonstrates the presence of Christ in others by expending the greatest care on those who need it most.

The ability to see Christ in others is grounded in the first step of humility, which is to live constantly in the presence of God. The famous verse in Hebrews 13:2 tells us that in welcoming strangers we might "be entertaining angels unknowingly." Kardong, however, says that a "Christian should *expect* to encounter Christ in the stranger."[8] The more we are aware of Christ's abiding presence in our lives, the more we become aware of Christ's presence in other people. The more we look for Christ in order to serve him, the more we will find him. De Waal asks herself, "Do I also find the risen Christ in the face of the one who comes? Is this what is being asked of me in receiving the other as Christ ... If I am to be ready I must remain alert, awake, not stumbling blindly along like those two on the way to Emmaus with eyes that do not really see, ears that do not really hear."[9]

Treating the vulnerable as Christ in a Christlike way makes us vulnerable to their demands and, sometimes, to their serious dysfunctions. The contrast between Benedict's view of guests and the sick and that in The Rule of the Master could hardly be greater. Where Benedict says that guests should be treated as Christ, the Master says they should be treated as crooks by assigning two monks to guard the guests at night to make sure they don't steal anything from the monastery.[10] In similar fashion, where Benedict says that the sick should be treated as

Christ, the Master says they should be treated like cheats. Suspecting that a "sick" monk is probably faking his illness, he orders that he not be fed on the grounds that if he is really sick, he won't be hungry, and if he is faking, he will recover quickly.[11] Benedict shows himself to be much too aware of human nature not to have his own suspicions about people, but comparisons such as these show that Benedict prefers the vulnerability of charity to the safety offered by suspicion. For Benedict, the importance of showing respect for other people trumps our suspicious impulses to protect ourselves against the wrongs we *might* suffer as a result of trusting and helping them.

At the same time, Benedict provides his monastics some protection against the potential intrusions of guests and the compromises that welcoming them entails. He legislates some distance between monastics and guests, even to the extent of serving guests in a separate kitchen and dining room. Moreover, "those who are not assigned to the guests are not to visit or speak with them. But if one meets or sees guests, he should greet them humbly, as we said. One should ask for a blessing and then move on, explaining that it is not permitted to converse with a guest" (RB 53:23–25). De Waal says that Benedict is telling us here "to do two things at once.... There is this wonderfully full and generous reception, but there is also the withdrawal and standing back.... Unless the monastery protects its enclosure ... the warmth and openness of its hospitality ... becomes impossible."[12] One can add that a monastery offers its unique hospitality best when it provides a monastic atmosphere that is supported by silence. Silence and the opportunity this gives for personal prayer and reflection are rare treasures. If monasteries do not provide them, nobody will.

Seeing Christ in other people is not just a mental veneer pasted on them in the pious imagination. Seeing Christ in others is the result of cultivating a deep-seated habit of the heart. This habit is made possible by engaging in a long-term relationship with Christ through worship and prayerful study of the scriptures. These practices cultivate the humility that empowers us to serve in the right spirit and prevent the pride that makes us feel superior to the ones we serve. When prayer intervenes before acts of service, then both the ones being served and the ones doing the serving are put on the same level before God. Benedict drives this point home several times by specifying a liturgical dimension to mundane acts of service that bring them into the context of a monastic community's worship.

Benedict prescribes what amounts to a small liturgy to meet arriving guests and treat them as Christ: "The brothers should hurry to meet him with every mark of love. First they should pray together and then be united in peace" (RB

53:3–4). Benedict draws the liturgical gesture and the right attitude behind it closer together by insisting that "the greeting itself, however, ought to manifest complete humility … by an inclination of the head or by a complete prostration on the ground, one must adore Christ in them, for he is in fact the one who is received" (RB 53:6–7). After feeding the guests and washing their hands and feet, the monastics pray this verse: "We have received, O god, your mercy in the midst of your temple" (RB 53:14, Ps. 48:10). Kardong suggests that the significance of using Psalm 48:10 to greet arriving guests is much deeper than we might think. The key word here is *suscepimus* (we have received). This same verb is they key word in the Psalm verse that a monastic chants at life profession: "Receive me O Lord, according to your promise that I may live; do not disappoint me in my hope" (RB 58:21, Ps. 119:116). In this verse, the newly professed monastic thanks God for the gift of entry into the monastery. That is, first the monastic receives hospitality from God, and then, having been on the receiving end of hospitality, is empowered to be a giver of hospitality. Kardong reminds us that "we are not acting out of the magnanimity that the landowner proffers to the landless traveler," but we are stewards of God's house who merely extend the "merciful hospitality that God has extended to us."[13] Everybody is a guest of God.

Kardong points out that this little liturgy is modeled on Abraham's reception of the three angels in Genesis, chapter 18, a model that was often followed by early monastics.[14] This impromptu liturgy is not practicable today and probably was not practicable in Benedict's monastery. Other passages in the Rule suggest that it was probably more normal for the porter to greet the guests, bring them to the guest quarters, and take care of their material and spiritual needs. The principle remains valid, however. Prayer must be a monastic community's first ministry to guests. The greatest gift a monastery can give to a guest is to maintain a round of prayer that the guest can participate in. Chittester says that when prayer is the primary welcome to guests, "it is understood that our welcome is not based on human measurements alone: we like you, we're impressed with you, you look like our kind, you're clean and scrubbed and minty-breathed and worthy of our attention."[15]

Benedict reinforces the connection between liturgy and work by blessing the table servers and the reader at meals. On Sunday morning, when these assignments are changed, the monastics whose week of service has ended pray the Psalm verse, "Blessed are you, Lord God, for you have aided me and comforted me." Then the monastics whose week of service is beginning say the verse, "God, come to my assistance; Lord, come to my aid" (RB 35:15–18, Ps. 86:17, Ps. 70:2). Then the reader asks for the community's prayers with this psalm verse:

"Lord, open my lips, and my mouth will proclaim your praise" (RB 38:2–3, Ps. 51:17). Using these psalm verses to bring prayer directly into our acts of service reminds us that worship supports our work. Then, when we pray the Divine Office, these same psalm verses remind us of the specific acts of service associated with them. The cry for God's help in Psalm 70:2 is particularly important because Benedict followed the monastic custom of opening each of the day hours with this verse, a liturgical custom that remains in effect today. This verse reminds us that we are fully dependent on God's help, both to worship well and to serve people well. John Cassian said, "This verse should be poured out in unceasing prayer so that we may be delivered in adversity and preserved and not puffed up in prosperity."[16] Psalm 51:17, the verse recited by the table reader, comes from a penitential psalm that was said every morning at Lauds. The whole psalm warns us against the pride that Benedict would have the reader avoid.

The monastic custom of table reading has some important effects for community dynamics that help tie meals with worship at the Divine Office. Normally, community is built up at the table when people share their lives verbally while they share food with one another. That is the ideal. John Cassian noted that monks were forbidden to talk at the table because it gave rise to quarrels. A. R. Gurney gives a modern view of this problem in his perceptive play *The Dining Room*. Through several vignettes involving a wide range of people's experiences in their dining rooms, we are shown the many ways that common meals become the means of alienation rather than fellowship. When Benedict says that "no one should presume to ask questions about the reading or about anything else" but then allows the abbot to choose to "make a brief remark for edification" (RB 38:8–9), he gives the impression that talking at meals can do the community more harm than good. Although the monastic model does not seem workable for families, the danger that talk at the table can be a source of pain needs to be borne in mind if the positive aspects of conversation are to be fostered. It is Augustine of Hippo who offers a more positive reason for table reading: "Not only should your mouths eat food, but your ears should take in the word of God."[17] This sentiment, of course, recalls Jesus' words in Luke 4:4: "One does not live on bread alone but on every word that comes from the mouth of God." The importance of table reading, then, is that we feed both our bodies and our souls when we gather at the table. The purpose of maintaining silence at meals and listening to reading is to allow for all to hear the Word of God. Even though it is not customary in monasteries today to read solely from the Bible at meals, even books of a secular nature can give a praying community occasion to reflect on God's care for the human experience explored in such books. Kardong reminds us that "disciplined charity" is "necessary over the long haul if the common meal is to be a vehicle of love and commitment."[18]

Benedict links manual labor with the Word of God most succinctly in the opening sentence of chapter 48 where he says that one "ought to be occupied with manual labor, *and* again at determined hours in *lectio divina*" (RB 48:1, italics mine). The literal meaning of the phrase *lectio divina* is "reading from God." Today, the term usually refers to the prayerful reading of any material with spiritual value. In Benedict's time, it most probably referred to prayerful study of the Bible, and the Bible remains the most important source of lectio. The point here is that work and lectio are linked so that, together, they make up a life of service. In Benedict's scheme of things, there is no room for mimetic rivalry between contemplation and acts of service. The two strengthen each other, and we cannot weaken one without weakening the other. The fact that Benedict assigns one or two monastics to patrol the monastery during reading times is a strong indication that lectio is *work* (RB 48:17). As with physical work, Benedict is on the lookout for the needs of the weak, realizing that some people might not be up to the full allotment of study time. When that is deemed to be the case, he recommends that such monastics be "assigned a work or craft so that they will be engaged but not so crushed by heavy labor that they will flee" (RB 48:24). It is expected, then, that we should expend serious effort and energy in searching for Christ in the scriptures, the same strenuous effort we should make in searching out Christ in the people whom we serve.

For all of the importance Benedict places on the need for right attitudes to undergird our acts of service, it still remains the case that neither the sick nor guests are served as Christ if the care they receive is sloppy or incompetent. The "god-fearing" attendant of the sick must also be "careful." Likewise, the brother "full of the fear of God" who manages the guest quarters must make sure that "a sufficient number of beds are made up there" (RB 53:22). Benedict demonstrates his habitual attention to details by asking that a separate room be set aside for the sick (RB 36:7). If, as Kardong believes, Benedict's Rule marks the first time such a provision was made in monastic history, then Benedict's practical sense here is particularly impressive.[19] The table servers are admonished, at some length, to wash the towels and utensils they have used at the end of the week and return them to the cellarer "clean and intact" (RB 7:11). The reading at meals should not be done by just anyone "who happens to pick up the book," but the job should be assigned on a weekly basis only to "those who edify the listeners" (RB 38:1, 12). This is the same phrase Benedict uses as a requirement for those assigned to read in church. Benedict's use of this phrase in these two different contexts reinforces his concern that the same care should go into both worship and work.

Benedict would not have us choose between a humble attitude and compe- ✓ tence. Humility and competence reinforce each other. In order to serve others with humility, we must practice our skill with an eye to how others are affected by it. The more we focus on what needs to be done for the other and on how to do the task well and efficiently, the less room we have in our minds and hearts for worries about our superiority or inferiority to others. Likewise, readers at meals should focus on the text and on how best to convey that text to the listeners rather than focus on their own human skill. The artisans should focus on the work they are doing and how that work will affect others rather than on how their work stacks up against that of other people. On the other side of the coin, those being served need to be aware of the needs of those serving and try to be as considerate of their needs as possible. In short, the best way to counter pride and its role in fueling mimetic rivalry is for both the server and the one being served to be attentive not to their respective *positions* at the time but to the needs of the other. This is why Benedict avoids ranking the members of the community by their skill in serving others. Having the jobs of being the guest master or the cellarer, for example, do not, in themselves, give one a higher rank. Being a servant is a great way to advance in the Christian life, but it is not the way to get ahead in life.

Benedict's teaching on work and service is a whole different universe than the nightmare of a society caught up in a mimetic crisis. Far from competing with one another in any way, Benedict expects the members of a community to look out for one another and build each other up. The acts of service examined in this chapter are concrete, practical ways of "willing the subjectivity of others" that Adams urges on us. If, on the contrary, we succumb to mimetic rivalry, our attention to other people is diverted to keeping track of who is "winning" the struggle. In such a situation, our actions receive little or no attention in themselves. Rather, our actions are principally or possibly *only* perceived in terms of whether or not they put us ahead of the other or cause us to lose ground. In such a scenario, the weaker members of a community will feel that the service rendered them is driving them to the bottom of the totem pole. Resenting the service they receive is one of the few defenses they have left. The possibility that mimetic rivalry could become as serious as this is most likely the reason Benedict recommends that a proud artisan not be allowed to practice the craft that has become an occasion of pride. One small detail that Benedict pulls out to keep these principles grounded in mundane reality is found in his instructions as to how monastics should conduct themselves during meals as one of their number is reading to them. Since nobody is allowed to talk, it is necessary for everybody "to serve the needs of one another so that no one need ask for anything" (RB 38:6). In this instance, as in so many others, Benedict directs our attention away from self and redirects it toward the other *and* toward what needs to be done for that person's benefit.

When we consider how the escalation of mimetic rivalry leads either to a total breakdown of society or to collective violence, the acts of service envisioned in these chapters of Benedict's Rule seem small and weak. Surely we can't hold off social catastrophe by passing salt across the table, sweeping a floor, or welcoming a stranger into our lives. As a matter of fact, people do those things all the time, and modern society is still falling apart. However, it is worth noting that mimetic rivalry as outlined by Girard begins with equally simple and trivial matters such as two children fighting over a toy or two adults fighting over a promotion at work. In a monastery, where bones of contention are taken away when they are spotted, this vice can still manifest itself with two monastics fighting over a pencil. The point here is that the kind of social conflagration resulting from the mimetic rivalry that Girard warns us about begins in small matters. Benedict realizes that the transformation of society into God's kingdom begins with equally small matters. Perhaps we are tempted to act like Naaman the Syrian who, when told by Elisha to bathe in the Jordan, walked off in a huff because the prophet didn't engage in an impressive performance of hocus-pocus. Naaman's servants then chided their master by suggesting that since he would have been willing to do something difficult if the prophet had demanded it, he should be willing to do something simple when asked to do that (2 Kings 5:1–19). These simple acts of service done in humility do not make newspaper headlines, but they help turn society in the right direction, away from mimetic rivalry. These simple acts of service can snowball just as much as simple acts of mimetic rivalry can snowball. We can roll one snowball at a time, but many people can roll many snowballs. As Naaman was cured of his leprosy by doing a simple act, our society also can be cured by simple acts.

Unfortunately, this simple prescription for curing society is not as simple as it sounds. To begin with, it is not enough to do a simple act of service once in a while. What Benedict envisions is a life consumed by the dance of serving and being served. Although the renewal of society is made up of small matters, these small matters need constant attention and nurture. We can take a vacation from a job, but we cannot take a vacation from the daily task of serving and being served. The reason humility is such a difficult virtue is that we are constantly being pulled away from humble acts of service by our prideful fantasies. Humility and loving attention to others is not our default mode; mimetic rivalry is the default that kicks in as soon as we stop paying attention to what we are doing. That is why humility requires constant effort. The problem is, if we push ourselves to be humble, we become self-conscious about our humility, and self-consciousness is the opposite of humility. What we need to do is constantly nudge our consciousness away from our fantasies and back to other people, their needs, and what acts we can do for them. Again and again, day by day, we learn that humility is a fragile virtue. Insofar as we focus on other people, we leave ourselves vulnerable to them. At the same time, we depend on others to care for us while we care for others. As soon as others fail to care for us, and they do, we are tempted to switch back to taking care of ourselves. We fall into a chain reaction where our own weaknesses are compounded by the weaknesses of others. Care of self and care of others becomes a competitive balancing act. People who work in the "helping" professions easily run into this difficulty, not least the clergy. The end result of tension between caring for others and caring for self is burnout.

Another factor that makes the prescription of simple acts of service more difficult than it seems is that anger gives us a quick release of energy, but humility does not. When we feel worn down by the demands of others, anger gives us a quick fix. Love gives us no such thing. Since the sick and other helpless people are prone to harboring anger because of their pain and helplessness, the people who serve them are likely to bear the brunt of that anger when *they* need the burst of energy that anger gives them. Being the object of anger from people we are serving, in turn, drains us of what energy we have. The quickest way to recapture the drained energy is to imitate the angry person and fight back. There are two problems with this. One is that this burst of energy is short-lived. The other is that we fail to serve others effectively in love when we give way to anger. Only love can sustain acts of service over the long haul. This is why the cellarer must "deny the obnoxious petitioner in a reasonable and humble manner" (RB 31:7). The difficulties that we experience every day in trying to do simple acts of service go a long way toward accounting for why these acts of service have not yet created a perfect society on earth.

A deeper reason why this simple prescription is not so simple is that Benedict seeks to create a social nexus where the social structure supports a life of mutual service, a structure that is governed by a gift economy. Unfortunately, the broader social structures that surround us tend to work at cross-purposes with this scheme. When we are already locked into social positions of more and less power in relationship with other people, it is very difficult to follow the advice Benedict gives us to serve each other. Even in the sphere of a small community, it is difficult to avoid replicating the social structures of the surrounding society. Although Benedict is remarkably egalitarian in comparison with the Roman society of his time, monastic houses have not had an easy time maintaining that vision. By the Middle Ages, monasteries and convents were saddled with almost all of the social inequalities of the greater culture. Only younger children of the aristocracy were offered the opportunity to live the monastic life. These monastics did not till the fields around the cloister; peasants did that. The pluses and minuses of a liberal democracy are quite different from the feudal system of medieval times. Today, monasteries are not held in a viselike grip of a rigid social structure. The fluidity of modern society is almost enough to make us think that it is not a problem for monastics. However, we need only look at a few commercials on television to see how highly competitive this fluid society is, how swamped it is in mimetic rivalry, and how dominated it is by commodities as opposed to gifts. This competitiveness is currently leading to a widening gulf between rich and poor where the number of the rich is shrinking and the number of the poor is swelling. Far from being considered worthy of being treated like Christ, the poor are considered adversaries who must be defeated by those with economic and social power. Treating people within and without a monastery in a contrary fashion to this trend takes much vigilance and stamina.

Given the toxic social pressures against humble service, the vertical dimension to the relationship between server and the one served through identifying the other with Christ takes on an urgent importance. When we serve others as Christ and accept service in return because Christ is seen in us, we no longer have two people negotiating acts of service as if they were commodities. Christ drives away any competitive aspect of the relationship. The sick "should keep in mind that they are being served out of respect for God" (RB 36:4). The implication is that they are not being served out of any pretensions of their own any more than the abbot is honored as Christ out of any pretensions on his part. When we are served because of Christ's identification with us, then we must realize that this service is a gift of unmerited grace and not something we have earned. When we receive a stranger to serve Christ, it is Christ whom we serve, not just the particular person. This does not mean that the person served is not important compared to Christ; it means that it is Christ who makes *everybody* important. When Christ is served through serving others, then both people in the relationship are put on the same level where Christ is serving Christ. It would be ludicrous in the extreme for anyone to serve Christ in another and believe that person to be inferior! Since Christ is our Lord, Christ can only be served in humility. Being served by Christ does not bring us any lower than we were before, because we are already indebted to Christ for what he has done for us. Even more important, any possible competition between the needs of the server and the one served is nullified in Christ. Not only does Jesus model acts of service that eschew all attempts at self-protection, but Jesus identifies with the needs of everybody, the needs of the one serving as well as the one in need of service.

▼

LENT:
THE GATEWAY TO
EASTER

Benedict's notion that our lifestyle ought always to "have a Lenten quality" seems a bit depressing at first glance. Does he really mean that forty days of misery are not enough, and so we should make ourselves miserable all 365 days of the year? Benedict quickly goes on to admit that "few have that kind of strength." It seems that, just as monastics of his time could not be persuaded to give up drinking wine, monastics could not be persuaded to live out a Lenten discipline the whole year round, either. Perhaps Benedict is grumbling over the failure of his contemporaries to measure up to the heroic monastics of an imagined Golden Age, but I can't help but suspect a bit of wry humor here. As a realist, Benedict realizes that it is normal for people, even dedicated monastics, to become slack in their discipline and thus to need a special season for effacing "the negligences of other times" (RB 49:3).

The practices Benedict prescribes for this holy season are to "restrain ourselves from all evil habits and devote ourselves to tearful prayer, reading, compunction of heart and asceticism" (RB 49:4). These are *Lenten* practices? Elsewhere in the Rule, Benedict prescribes these practices for the *entire liturgical year*. When Benedict goes on to suggest that we deny our bodies "some food, some drink, some sleep, some chatter, some joking," again, he is recommending few sacrifices beyond the norm. Benedict constantly urges us to curb indulgence in more food and drink that we might desire but don't really need. Benedict's reference to the excuses that sleepy monks like to make when the bell rings for Matins reminds us that the monastics renounced sleep every morning. Moreover, in his chapter on humility, Benedict makes it clear that he does not approve of chatter or joking in any season, especially when they lead to self-aggrandizement and injury to other people. It seems, then, that this "increase" in discipline during Lent is intended to bring us up to the level of the Rule itself. In other words, since we don't follow the Rule most of the time, let us at least try to follow the Rule during these forty days!

Joan Chittester tells us that, for Benedict, "Lent is the time to make new efforts to be what we say we want to be.... We know, for instance, that even people who were married years ago have to keep working at that marriage consciously and intently every year thereafter, or the marriage will fail no matter how established it seems. We know that people who own businesses take inventories and evaluations every year or the business fails. We too often fail to realize, however, that people who say that they want to find God in life have to work every day too to bring that Presence into focus."[1] Benedict's chapter on Lent, then, reminds us that our efforts to be attentive to God and neighbor require constant renewal; they will not renew themselves. One way that the entire year can have a Lenten quality is to renew our commitment to God every day. This kind of commitment isn't a matter of wearing hair shirts or starving ourselves; it is a matter of renewing our worship of God so as to strengthen us to look at other people, become aware of their needs, and serve Christ in them.

We often think that renunciation means giving up something we want for the sole purpose of diminishing our happiness. But Benedict tells us that we are given the opportunity to offer God something beyond what is imposed on us of our own free will "with the joy of the Holy Spirit." There is more to this sentiment than Jesus' admonition that we "not look dismal, like the hypocrites" when we are fasting, so as to draw admiration for our ascetical endeavors (Mt. 6:16–18). Brightening our faces while remaining inwardly miserable only earns us the reward of being miserable. The damage that a doom-and-gloom style of asceticism can do extends much farther than the individual who has chosen this path. Focusing on our self-inflicted pain and deprivation is self-regarding at the expense of God and our neighbor. Such self-regard makes it inevitable that we will consider ourselves better than those who aren't fasting as much as we are. Worse, if we should see somebody else fasting better than we are, we will try to outdo them and become either frustrated if we fail or self-congratulatory if we succeed. In this process, God is forgotten and love is driven out of the heart.

But giving up certain things in "the joy of the Spirit" brings us to a deeper renunciation, namely renunciation of self-consciousness. Rather than being focused on what *we* are giving up for *God*, we become focused on what *God* has given up for *us*. Kardong says that "Benedict makes sure that the personal initiative of the monk for Lenten penance does not stem from willfulness or self-delusion. What is necessary is to purify one's motives so that the Spirit can work freely in one's heart."[2] Of course, when the Spirit is given free rein within us, we are free to love other people regardless of how their discipline stacks up against our own. If we don't need their admiration, then we are free to do those things that genuinely merit their admiration.

Benedict stipulates that every Lenten discipline should be done with the abbot's "blessing and approval" (RB 49:8). The danger of falling into a self-centered gloom is surely one reason for seeking the abbot's approval, as is the problem of ascetic rivalry. That is why Benedict is so insistent on putting our individual acts of renunciation into a communal context. Rather than seeking to increase our own spiritual good for ourselves alone, we should seek the spiritual good of the community. Any renunciation, then, is a gift of love for the benefit of others.

Benedict then specifies that "the joy of the Spirit" that should fuel our self-denial of food, drink, sleep, chatter, and joking strengthens us to "await Holy Easter with the joy of spiritual desire" (RB 49:7). This joyful wait for Easter places our renunciations and "tearful prayers" at the heart of the Paschal Mystery. In giving up our self-indulgence, we begin to experience the death to ourselves that opens us up to the risen life of Christ. The pain involved is no longer that of mourning what we gave up; the pain becomes a longing for Christ, whom we do not yet possess in his fullness. This longing is a "joy." For Benedict, Lent is not a time of doom and gloom that we endure for the sake of a deferred happiness; Lent is a time for joyfully looking forward to the coming of the Divine Guest.

De Waal points to a startling element of this chapter when she notes that the two times the word *gaudium* (joy) is used in this chapter are the only times Benedict uses this word in the Rule. Given its emphatic use here and Benedict's promise that "our hearts will swell with unspeakable sweetness" (Pr. 49), Benedict's avoidance of this word does not indicate that he was a sourpuss but rather that *gaudium* should be spoken of only when it is the most real and deepest joy. De Waal goes on to explain that "our joy must be an interior joy, just as the observances should be interior and not exterior.... There is a difference between a true, deep joyousness and the vapid hilarity that passes for joy, the superficial jolly cheerfulness that often covers up an inner hollowness."[3] Many times we have seen indications in the Rule that the deepest joy is found when we hear "the still small voice of God." It is worth recalling here how the boisterous joy that Benedict would have us shun all year round is often a spiteful joy indulged in at the expense of others. The more intensely we are involved in mimetic rivalry, the more intense our "joy" if we "win." This is the sort of "joy" that we snatch up for ourselves. But the deep inner joy that is "the joy of the Holy Spirit" (RB 49:6) is a joy that we *receive* as we look forward to Easter. Since the Holy Spirit gives joy to all comers, receiving this joy does not make us superior to anybody else. More important, we do not receive this joy at the expense of anybody else. On the contrary, this joy is a gift, not only to us but to everybody else we encounter.

De Waal adds further depth to our understanding of Easter joy when she reminds us that "the paradox is that the joy of Lent is necessarily connected with sorrow, that it is a joy that flows from sorrow."[4] The key term here is *compunction*, a term we encountered before. The sorrow of compunction is a sorrow that we have not received as much of the joy in the Holy Spirit as we could, free as this joy is. De Waal explains that "compunction is, therefore, a long way from the negative sort of guilt that can encourage soul-searching, obsessive regrets, and a dwelling on the past. This I know only too well can easily become sterile, a deadening inner monologue, which does not bring me the energy to change and move forward."[5] I noted earlier that compunction is focused on God, not self. Focusing on our regrets is focusing on self. The sorrow of compunction is a deepening awareness of a joy in the Spirit that we have not yet accepted. This sorrow causes us to yearn for more of this joy. If we yearn for it, we will get it.

There is a deeper level to compunction than the personal sorrow we feel over falling short of the Easter joy that is offered us. Given the widespread and ever-increasing poverty in the world while smaller numbers of people hoard greater quantities of wealth, the escalating plunder of the world's natural resources, and violence that spins out of control, we cannot be content with sorrowing over our own personal lack of Easter joy; neither can we be content with any Easter joy we might experience in our own little hearts. There is a connection between each of us and the suffering of our planet, as our personal shortcomings contribute to this suffering through our wayward actions and indifference. The point is, we must be pricked into a deep sorrow over the immense suffering that humans inflict on other humans and on the earth. St. Paul said that not only is creation "groaning in labor pains," but we, too, "who have the first fruits of the Spirit, groan inwardly while we wait for adoption, the redemption of our bodies"

(Rom. 8:22–23). Surely this inward groaning is a major part of the joy in the Spirit that Benedict is talking about in this chapter. This inward groaning gives us hope because it tells us that it is God's will that the massive oppression humans inflict on others and on the planet should be overcome and, in the end, God will not be thwarted.

There is much more to Easter joy than Easter lilies, Easter hymns, and chocolate Easter eggs. Girard says that when he asks the question as to how so small a group, themselves "half-possessed by the violent contagion against Jesus," could suddenly have found the strength to confront the worldwide crowd and the authorities in Jerusalem, he can no longer find a plausible response to this question "within a purely commonsensical and 'anthropological' context.'" In this impasse, Girard says, "This time … *it is impossible.* To break the power of mimetic unanimity, we must postulate a power superior to violent contagion. If we have learned one thing … it is that none exists on this earth. It is precisely because mimetic contagion was all-powerful in human societies, prior to the day of the Resurrection, that archaic religion divinized it."[6] Just as one facet of Easter joy is to groan inwardly over the mimetic contagion that still holds so much of the world in bondage, it is another facet of Easter joy to celebrate the fact that the killing of victims is no longer necessary to hold society together. We groan deeply that none of our present-day victims are necessary as we celebrate the risen Christ who still bears the wounds inflicted on his mortal body as he takes the part of every victim.

Yet another facet of Easter joy is forgiveness: forgiveness of our own sins and the sins of all other people, and most particularly the sins of those who crucified Jesus. I noted earlier how the risen Christ never exacted vengeance on his tormenters, but instead he devoted himself to gathering his people. Easter joy spurs us on to play our part in gathering God's people. Easter joy is the inward groaning we suffer insofar as God's people are scattered time and time again. Easter joy is the freedom to forgive all those who have wronged us and other people made in God's image. Easter joy is groaning inwardly at the anger and anguish that prevents us from forgiving the people who hurt us and those we love. There is nothing complacent about the forgiveness of Easter. Just because God forgives those who use their economic power to keep millions of people in helpless poverty doesn't mean that God accepts this abuse of power. For all of the solicitude and forgiveness offered a disruptive member of the community, Benedict did not for a minute expect a community to allow this disruptive behavior to continue. The oppressed creation groans every day of the year. Every day of the year we must yearn for the forgiveness that overcomes the mimetic hatred that keeps us embroiled in destructive relationships with each other. This yearning for the joy of Easter that Jesus has prepared for us is not something that can be put aside even during Eastertide. This is why the whole year should have a Lenten quality to it so that the whole year can be filled with yearning for the joy of Easter.

▼

MONASTIC MIMETIC CONFLICT: THE PRIOR OF THE MONASTERY

The opening sentence of chapter 65 is as fierce as it is blunt: "All too often it has happened that the installation of a prior has made grave scandals arise in monasteries" (RB 65:1). Benedict cuts straight to the cheese by charging priors with becoming "puffed up with an evil spirit of pride, thinking themselves second abbots and grasping at autonomous power. They nourish disputes and create quarrels in communities" (RB 65:2). Although the term "prior" (*praeposito*) means literally "placed at the head" and was used for the superior of a monastery in some early monastic literature, the term "abbot" had become normative for a monastic superior by Benedict's time. The term "prior" then became the customary term for the monk who was second-in-command after the abbot. This is a position that Benedict finds inherently problematic.

Kardong says that this chapter is "probably the hardest test for an interpreter of the Rule of Benedict." There is no difficulty in understanding what this chapter says. The difficulty is understanding Benedict's "bad temper," a difficulty exacerbated because this chapter directly follows the stirring words about the abbot in the previous chapter.[1] De Waal calls it "the least prayerful chapter in the Rule."[2] When this chapter is read with the help of mimetic theory, however, even the bad temper becomes understandable, if still deplorable. Ignited by the fury of what was likely a real-life event rather than a hypothetical projection, Benedict shows deep insight into how mimetic issues can play out destructively in a community.

From the standpoint of mimetic theory, the phrase "second abbots" is as red a flag as one can get. It shows that Benedict understands that the conflict is caused by mimetic doubling. The prior, puffed up with pride, makes himself a mirror image of the abbot. Kardong notes that Benedict might be making a play on words here, as this phrase is close to the expression "the man second to the abbot," which is what the prior is supposed to be. The distortion of being instead a "second abbot" causes "grave scandals" to arise in the monastery. Again, Benedict uses the Greek word *skandalon* as he does when he admonishes the abbot to say the Our Father aloud at Lauds and Vespers because "thorns of quarreling [*scandalorum*] are likely to spring up" (RB 13:12). That is, the prior and the abbot become stumbling blocks to each other and to the whole community. Kardong acknowledges that the usual meaning of this word is "a thing or situation that undermines faith," but here it means "disputes."[3] A Girardian reading would suggest that when the "abbot and prior are at loggerheads," the faith of the disputants and that of the rest of the community is undermined, thus making the dispute a "danger to their souls" (RB 65:8). Kardong notes that a more literal translation of this verse would suggest that the abbot and prior "see things differently," but this is not strong enough for the context. A mere difference of opinion between abbot and prior should not be a danger to anybody's soul.[4] The results of this antagonism that Benedict lists are "envy, squabbles, backbiting, rivalries, dissensions and disorders" (RB 65:7). When these evils are present in a community, mimetic rivalry has escalated out of control. When things come to such a pass, any differences in outlook are lost in the heat of conflict.

The scope and intensity of conflict portrayed in this chapter is typical of a scenario where the antagonists are both in positions of authority. A dispute between two monastics who are not in responsible positions can cause damage in a community, but the conflict is usually much easier to contain. Such a dispute between two people who are "at loggerheads" will endanger the souls of the two involved, but it is not likely that others will become involved and actively take sides. A novice might be highly disruptive, but the novice is not likely to become "a second abbot" the way the prior could. If a novice is motivated by a lust for power, he will likely compete for a greater influence among his fellow novices.

The closer to the top a subordinate position is, the greater the chance the person holding that position will be tempted by mimetic rivalry for the abbot's position. So it is that when the disputants are the top two authority figures, "their subjects, having to please one or the other, likewise go to ruin" (RB 65:9). Here we have the fratricidal bipolar conflict such as that between Cain and Abel, or between Remus and Romulus. Instead of the chaos of everybody against everybody, the conflict is "ordered" by the two poles, where everybody joins one leader or the other so that the two factions become mimetic doubles as much as their leaders. De Waal reminds us that "a split personality can be as dangerous to the corporate situation as to the individual."[5] Joan Chittester says that such an attempt to "wrest authority away from the center … in order to make ourselves look good" is using "a group for personal gain instead of for the good of the group. It is the story of a Rasputin or a Lucretia Borgia. It is a grasp at power for its own sake."[6]

Bailie explains that "mimetic desire is always kindled in those whose social situations most closely approximate that of the one whom they envy."[7] Scriptural examples include the story of Susanna and the incident of Naboth's vineyard. In Susanna, it is two elders who rank just below Joakin, "the most honored of them all" (Sus. v.4), who try to seduce Susanna, Joakin's wife. In the story of Naboth's vineyard, Jezebel writes the "elders and the nobles who lived with Naboth in his city," ordering them to orchestrate the slander and stoning of Naboth (1 Kings 21:22). Saul and David competed for the kingship of Israel because their social standing put the crown in reach of both of them. Abner and Joab, on the other hand, did not compete for the crown; they competed for the position of chief military officer, with fatal results for Abner. Benedict's fear of conflict between abbot and prior shows that he understood this dynamic very well.

Benedict realizes that the temptation for a prior to consider oneself a "second abbot" is greatly exacerbated if the "prior is installed by the same bishop or abbots who install the abbot," because "at the very moment of installation, the grounds for pride are present" (RB 65:3–4). Here, the mimetic doubling is traced back to the way the appointment is made. In such a case, it is natural for the prior to think that "he has been freed from the abbot's power" precisely because he was installed by the same people who installed the abbot (RB 65:5). By blaming the prior's recalcitrant behavior on the manner of the prior's installation, Benedict indicates that he sees the problem more as one of community structure than personal psychology. That is to say, personal psychology is strongly affected by one's position in the community. Elsewhere, Benedict makes it clear that a community runs best when each person to whom responsibility has been delegated remains obedient to the abbot. The cellarer, for example, is expected to "follow the abbot's orders" (RB 31:12). This principle applies all the more to the prior, whose responsibility is even greater. In order to facilitate the obedience proper for a prior, the prior should be appointed by the abbot himself. If the prior's position is derived from the abbot rather than from the source of the abbot's own appointment or election, then there is less reason for the prior to consider himself the abbot's equal. Benedict drives this point home by going on to say that "this prior must do what he is told by his abbot, without acting against the abbot's will and arrangements" (RB 65:16)

But then Benedict lets it be known that he would rather have no prior at all! He would prefer that "all the affairs of the monastery should be managed by deans under the abbot's supervision" (RB 65:12). Back in chapter 21, Benedict recommends that if the community is a large one, brothers "of good reputation and holy life" should be made deans, each in charge of a deanery consisting of ten monks each. Those chosen for the task should be those with "whom the abbot can confidently share his burdens" (RB 21:1–3). Benedict further defends the deanery system by adding that "when the management is entrusted to many, no one person will grow proud" (RB 65:13). Again, Benedict intends that all authority be delegated by the abbot and that each person with responsibility carry out the abbot's wishes and not one's own. Benedict's clear preference for deans is driven by his conviction that a person's moral disposition is likely to be affected by that person's position in the community. A monastic who is made responsible for ten fellow monastics in a large monastery is not as likely to compete with the abbot as is a prior who is put in charge of the entire monastery, second only to the abbot. An arrangement of deaneries, however, is practicable only in a large monastery. Even then, the need for a prior has shown itself for precisely the reason Benedict wants one person, the abbot, to be in charge of the community. It is inevitable that the abbot be away from the monastery from time to time. At such times, there needs to be one deputy who takes charge in the abbot's absence. The practicality of having the same person in charge each time the abbot is away speaks for itself.

One reason this chapter is so jarring is that Benedict usually shows himself to be trusting of human nature and gentle, if strict, with human weaknesses. Yet here he goes on a tirade that comes close to *assuming* that a prior will be a sower of discord just because he is the prior. We have already noted, however, that Benedict's distrust, bordering on paranoia, is not directed at the *person* holding the position of prior; it is directed at the *position*. Actually, Benedict has much the same fear for the deans and for any monastic ordained to holy orders. The sin that worries Benedict more than any other is pride, and Benedict worries about pride most when a person's position has the potential to inflate pride. The greater the responsibility, the greater the hazard of a moral and spiritual downfall.

The danger of pride that Benedict sees on the part of those holding responsible positions suggests that it is the wisest and the best of monastics who are most susceptible to this vice. After all, it is precisely advancement in holiness that qualifies a person for a position of authority. The monastic chosen to be the cellarer of the monastery should be "a wise person, mature of character and well-disciplined, one who fears God and is like a father to the whole community" (RB 31:1–2). Likewise, the deans of the monastery should be chosen "for the merit of their lives and the wisdom of their teaching" (RB 21:4). Benedict expresses a bit of anxiety that the cellarer might abuse his position and treat a needy person unkindly, but he does not suggest that the cellarer is likely to become prideful and disruptive. When it comes to the deans of the monastery, however, Benedict says that "if it should happen that one of the deans is found to be puffed up with pride and needs to be corrected," he should be corrected up to three times, and if "he refuses to amend, he should be removed from office" (RB 21:5–6). These words are mild compared to what Benedict says about the prior. If the prior "should be found to have serious faults, or if he allows his position to seduce him into pride, or if he is discovered to despise the Holy Rule, he should be admonished up to four times." If the prior proves to be incorrigible, and Benedict seems to assume he will, "then he must be deposed and if even then he is not quiet and obedient in the community, he must be expelled from the monastery" (RB 65:18–21). Clearly, Benedict thinks that a dean is more apt to be puffed up and disobedient than the cellarer, and the prior is more apt to be puffed up and disobedient than a dean. Benedict further betrays his heightened anxiety about the prior by suggesting that a dean might need to be admonished to change his ways up to three times, but a prideful prior may need to be admonished up to *four* times!

Another position of power and authority that Benedict considers dangerous is that of the priesthood. Benedict betrays an automatic distrust of priests when he says, "If one of the priestly order asks to be received into the monastery, do not agree too quickly" (RB 60:1). Benedict justifies the extra obstacles he puts into the way of a priest by quoting the words Jesus said to Judas at Gethsemane: "Friend, what was your purpose in coming?" (RB 60:3, Mt. 26:50). This chilling scripture reference suggests that Benedict fears that a priest is in greater danger of betraying Christ than someone who is not ordained. Benedict allows the abbot to have a monastic ordained if the community has need of priestly services, but the newly ordained priest "must beware of vanity and pride, nor should he presume to do anything but what the abbot has ordered" (RB 62:2–3). In dealing with priests, Benedict insists at length that a priest *must* obey the Rule, thus implying that a priest needs to have this admonition drummed into his head much harder than laypersons do. Benedict clearly fears that a priest will be tempted to put himself above the other monastics because of his position in the Church. To counteract this danger, Benedict stresses not only the stronger need for inner humility on the part of a priest but also the importance of the abbot's not giving a priest a *position* of any authority in the community solely on account of his priesthood. If a priest is given a higher rank, it must *only* be "because of the merit of his life" (RB 62:6). As with priors and deans, Benedict goes on to threaten contumacious priests with admonitions and, if necessary, expulsion. It is quite possible that Benedict's anxiety over priestly pretensions was heightened because of the lay status of most monastics at the time, including most abbots. Benedict himself was almost certainly not a priest. One can see, then, how Benedict might fear that a man who held a higher position in the Church might feel that he ought to hold the same higher position over laypersons in the monastery.

In all fairness to priors, it should be noted that the prior's position can lead to problems not of the prior's own making. A monastic who is at odds with the abbot, but has little power or authority, will often try to enlist the support of somebody who *does* have power and authority. If the monastery has deans, then perhaps a dean will do, but a prior is the best catch of all. Again, it is the *position* of the prior that makes him so vulnerable to any tensions in the monastery. Even if a prior has no ambitions to usurp the abbot's authority, the prior will bear the brunt of any tensions between the abbot and other members of the community for the simple reason that the prior is in the middle. Benedict gives no indication that he sees this nuance in potential conflict with a prior, but his concern with the dangers of the *position* suggests that he may have had some intuition of such ramifications.

On the whole, Benedict shows himself to be very one-sided against the prior. If there is a conflict between the abbot and the prior, it is the fault of the prior, or the fault of those "who created such disorder in the first place" by appointing the prior. Apparently it can't be the abbot's fault. In spite of Benedict's bias here, Benedictine history lists many more abusive abbots than abusive priors. In the end, however, it turns out that Benedict is not totally one-sided in blaming the prior, deans, and priests for all the troubles in a monastery, and he is not convinced that the abbot is beyond reproach. He realizes that, in correcting others, the abbot "must always be wary of his own brittleness" (RB 64:13). In the midst of listing the sublime qualities an abbot should have, Benedict warns the abbot that he "should not be restless and troubled, not extreme and not headstrong, not jealous and oversuspicious; for then he will have no peace" (RB 64:16). Benedict does realize that insecurity over one's authority can lead to paranoia that destroys both the inner peace of the abbot and the peace of the community. If the abbot should fall into such a disorder, it would then become the *duty* of the prior and other leaders of the community to oppose the abbot, not as a personal vendetta but as a loving correction of the abbot's behavior. Although such a rightful intervention could still lead to a shattered community, nobody would be intending to become "a second abbot." Instead, everyone would be trying to restore the abbot to his position of exercising sound leadership. Most telling of all is the final sentence of chapter 65. After ranting about the evils of the prior for twenty-one verses, Benedict shifts gears and reminds the abbot to remember that "he must answer to God for all his decisions," and he must be careful that "the flames of envy and jealousy will not sear his soul" (RB 65:22). Perhaps Benedict had to heed his own admonition during a difficult time in his ministry as abbot.

We have already seen that Benedict gives the abbot an exalted position in the community, but it is in this chapter that Benedict shows just *how* exalted the abbot's position is. Benedict intends the abbot's position to be unassailable, so high above any other position as to be unreachable for anybody else, even for the prior. Benedict has given numerous instances of the dangers arising if anybody else has any proximity to the abbot's authority. This danger is removed if nobody is close enough to the abbot's position for the abbot's authority to be attainable by anybody else. This is why Benedict prefers deans with more limited authority and why, if "local conditions demand it or the community appeals for it with good reasons and humility; and the abbot judges it best, a prior be appointed who will know his place and keep it" (RB 65:14). Then there are no contestants, because there is no contest. Nobody competes with the abbot, and the abbot does not need to establish his power by competing with his monastics and beating them into submission.

Far from grasping after power or exercising tyranny on the community because of his exalted status, the abbot "must profit others rather than precede them" and "should aim more at being loved than feared" (RB 64:8, 15). Throughout the Rule, the abbot is required to make sure that special care is taken for the weak and the vulnerable. This job description is the exact opposite to that of a tyrant. Moreover, the abbot "is believed to hold the place of Christ in the monastery" (RB 2:2). This means that one should not want to compete against the abbot any more than one should want to compete against Christ himself! Another way to say this is as follows: Any monastic who *does* want to compete with the abbot should try to be more Christlike than the abbot. Of course, the more Christlike a monastic becomes, the more that monastic will want to do only the "will of the One who sent me" (RB 4:13, Jn. 6:38). As one who takes the place of Christ, the abbot "ought not to teach, arrange or command anything not in accordance with the law of the Lord" (RB 2:4). That is to say, the abbot must hold to God's orders just as much as the monastics under him must hold to the abbot's orders. If the abbot's position is treated as unassailable so that there is no contest, the abbot is free to act like a shepherd who nurtures the flock with special attention to the weak. If the abbot should come under attack, then regardless of who is at fault, it becomes difficult, if not impossible, for the abbot to nurture anybody.

De Waal says that "if Benedict knows how destructive divergent and centrifugal elements can be, he also knows the importance of accepting the wide range and variety of human nature and human experience. The question is how to hold these elements together and integrate them so that the whole body becomes life-giving rather than life-denying."[8] De Waal is telling us that the primary job of the abbot is to hold the community together, to make it one in Christ. If other members of the community are feuding, there is still a chance that the abbot can be the stable focal point of the community, provided he does not become a participant in the feud. Unfortunately, this is what a person who is igniting a feud wants the abbot to do. But if the abbot himself becomes involved in a feud, then the center is gone. De Waal asks, "Where is the axis on which everything turns?"[9] What this question tells us is that it is not the abbot who is the axis of the community; it is Christ. The abbot holds the place of Christ at the center, at the axis. If the abbot is drawn away from the center, Christ, the true center, is still in place, but no member of the community is with Christ in that place. No wonder De Waal finds this the least prayerful chapter of the Rule. At the very moment when prayer is most needed, it is the least present! More important, since Christ is the center of the community, the abbot does not bear an insuperable burden. Ultimately, it is Christ who bears the burden that the abbot bears. The abbot need not, and must not, make himself the center of the community. Christ has prepared a place for the abbot, and the abbot need only take that place. Then the community will be at peace.

CHAPTER 17

▼

MIMETIC COMMUNITY ORDER

Mimetic theory suggests that we are placed in a double bind as soon as we try to bring order to a group of people. When there are distinct positions that are higher or lower than the others, there are apt to be struggles over the higher positions. In the last chapter, we noted that competition over the highest positions is limited by creating unbridgeable gulfs between social groups. For example, only the second- and third-ranking judges competed for Joakin's top position, while the rest of the town's population did not. Likewise, the prior, a dean, or a priest might try to compete with the abbot, but novices can't. If there are positions of rank at all levels in a monastery, however, there will be competition at each level, just as the sixteenth-chair violinist in an orchestra will compete against the player in the fifteenth chair. But having no order at all creates a state of indifferentiation where mimetic rivalry will infect everybody with the speed of a brush fire and destroy everything. Typically, Benedict addresses this set of problems with practical advice on ordering a community as a means of opening our hearts to a non-rivalrous way of living with one another in Christ.

Benedict opens chapter 63 by saying that all members of the monastery "should keep to their ranks as established by the time of entry, merit of life or the abbot's arrangement" (RB 63:1). As this chapter progresses, Benedict makes it clear that time of entry is far and away the most important consideration, while the other two are exceptional and problematic. Benedict strengthens the importance of date of entry by saying that "in no situation at all shall chronological age have any part in determining or influencing the ordering of the community" (RB 63:5). That is to say, a monastic who enters at the second hour of the day is junior to the monastic who entered at the first hour "no matter what his age or status" (RB 63:8). The great advantage of this method of determining community order is that it has so incontestable an objective basis that it does not give anybody a basis for attempting to supplant the rank of another.

What is so revolutionary here, given the hierarchical structure of Roman society, is that holding a high rank in society before entering the monastic life has no effect whatever on a monastic's rank within the community. If a former slave enters an hour before a patrician, the former slave holds the higher rank. Chittester notes that the wide variety of people entering a monastic community would have been "conditioned to very defined expectations of privilege or oppression," as is the case today as well. Chittester goes on to say that Benedict's scheme "detoxifies the entire environment" of the social rank people bring with them. Benedict's method of rank, then, is "designed to free people from their past castes or demands.... The image of a world unskewed by material values and social definitions is the vision thrust before us in Benedictine spirituality. In a world where sex and race and money mark our spaces on the social ladder it is a picture of human liberation gone outrageously giddy with the freeing power of God as the sign of its sanctity."[1]

That rank should be determined by something as serendipitous as time of entry seems absurd to a society where we expect rank to be earned through a struggle for dominance over others. A high school class is ranked by each student's grade point average. An employee in a business advances by outdoing his or her colleagues. In other social sets, superior ability to handle or manipulate people is decisive for how high one climbs on the social ladder. Over against these struggles for dominance, a person's rank in a monastic community is a gift, a gift that is a reward just for joining the monastery. The position is neither a reward for charming the abbot nor a reward for cooking gourmet meals. Kardong comments that "the eyes of faith see all this as a matter of Divine Providence, for it depends on one's answer to the call of God."[2] Benedict's vision of a community structured by gift rather than commodities is never stronger than it is here.

Perhaps it is our "normal" society that is absurd, and Benedict's method of ranking is an act of genius precisely because each place in the community is an unearned gift. Girard suggests that we "examine what goes on in the sectors of modern life where feverish competition and the pangs of promotion by merit flourish within a context of relative leisure, which favors reciprocal observation: business circles obviously, and especially intellectual circles, where the talk is always of others, by people who pay scant attention to themselves."[3] Girard does not pull any punches in telling us that this situation is seriously sick. His diagnostic term for people caught in this mimetic situation is "a kind of cyclothymia" where people become obsessed by the social signals that surround them, "like a thymic alternation that accompanies it." We reach the point where "it is hard not to be pleased at something that depresses [our] rival and not to be depressed at something that pleases him." Girard strengthens the sense of obsession by his use of the term "cyclothymia," which refers to an advanced state of a manic-depressive syndrome, a psychiatric problem so common today that we almost take it for granted as "normal." Girard goes on to say that "in a society where the place of individuals is not determined in advance and hierarchies have been obliterated, people are endlessly preoccupied with making a destiny for themselves, with 'imposing' themselves on others, 'distinguishing themselves from the common herd—in a word, with 'making a career.'"[4] It is for this reason that there must be an order of some kind, an order where each member has a definite place, but a place that has nothing to do with "making a career."

Kardong admits that "modern sensibility is not attracted to hierarchy."[5] That is quite an understatement for most Americans. A monastery is a hierarchy in the sense that each person has a distinct rank in relation to each other member. However, as we have already seen, this hierarchy is a rather strange animal, an animal so strange that it undermines every instinct to establish hierarchy through mimetic rivalry. The challenge posed by this system is especially hard for any person who has achieved rank or merit in life before joining the monastery. A person who has achieved a high professional standing still enters the community in the lowest place just as much as a younger person who has only graduated from high school or college. The humility it takes to enter a community on this basis is a shock to anybody's system. It's supposed to be. More important, we cannot advance in rank through any of the methods by which we advance in other social groups. The only way to gain a higher rank is to persevere in the monastic life. That is challenge enough. The only thing that a "higher" position offers is personal respect along with a few perquisites such as getting served at meals before those who are lower in the community order. The two things that a higher rank does not, of itself, give are the two things that people most strive for in order to advance in a community: power and responsibility.

When rank is determined by the date of entry, the appointment to an office in the monastery, no matter how important, does not affect one's rank in the community. Not even the cellarer or the guest master, for all the responsibility given them, advance in rank as a result of such appointments. Likewise, with his inveterate suspicion of priests, Benedict insists that any monk who is ordained at the abbot's request "must always keep to the rank of his entrance into the monastery" (RB 62:5) with the problematic rider that a priest can be advanced on account of the merit of his life. This arrangement separates power and responsibility from rank so that an appointment to a responsible position is an act of charity to others and not a stepping-stone to a higher position. This policy also makes it likely that monastics who hold a higher place by virtue of seniority will be required to accept the authority of a monastic with less seniority in the sphere of that monastic's responsibility. Even the most senior monastic has to accept what the cellarer gives out and follow directions regarding the right use of the monastery's tools. With everybody in the community sharing responsibilities, everybody has occasion to both exercise authority and be subject to the authority of others. That is to say, everybody has to be obedient to everybody else.

The other two considerations Benedict gives for establishing rank in a community besides date of entry bristle with so many problems and qualifications as to be unusable. The abbot may give a monastic a higher rank on the basis of merit of life or simply decide to advance somebody. If the abbot raises a monastic's rank for merit of life, the other monastics may feel that they deserve a higher place for the same reason. This sort of judgment is too subjective to be a fair way of ordering the community. Worse, it will lead to the unedifying spectacle of several monastics competing for higher places by trying to outdo each other in achieving greater merit of life! The problem here is that greater merit of life presupposes greater humility, and greater humility presupposes being deeply committed to *not* seeking a higher rank in the community, as ambition is quite contrary to humility. In this case, only a person who does not want a higher rank than that held by time of entry would be worthy of receiving the higher rank. But being advanced in the community as a reward for humility defeats of the purpose of being humble. Clearly, it is better not to take any chances of fostering ambition by advancing monks due to "merit of life." Indeed, this hardly ever happens in Benedictine monasteries today for these very reasons. The notion that a monastic's rank might be raised by "the abbot's arrangement" is practically qualified out of existence by Benedict's admonition that the abbot ought not "disturb the flock committed to him, nor should he arrange anything unjustly as if he had unlimited power" (RB 63:2). For an abbot to tell a community that a particular monastic is judged to be holier than the others and is worthy of a higher place is sure to disturb the community. To raise a monastic's rank for no discernable reason will likely disturb the community to the point of touching off a mimetic conflagration.

One of the effects of ranking a community by time of entry is that it acknowledges the accumulated experience of those monastics who have been living the life the longest and the perspective that these years have given them. This isn't just a matter of age; this ranking acknowledges the number of years lived in the monastic life, not the number of years lived overall. A thirty-year-old who has lived in the monastery for the past ten years is normally going to be wiser in the monastic life than a forty-year-old who has just joined the community, even if the forty-year-old is wiser overall in life experience. Note that what the senior monastics are given here is not power but respect.

Benedict softens the hierarchy of the monastery further by urging that mutual respect and obedience be practiced within the community: "The juniors should respect their seniors, and the seniors should love their juniors" (RB 63:10). "The blessing of obedience is not only something that everyone ought to show the abbot, but the brothers should also obey one another" (RB 71:1). This exhortation is a clear echo of Paul's admonition in Ephesians 5:21. Even Paul, however, is unable to make this mutual obedience perfectly reciprocal. Although husbands should be obedient to their wives, it seems that wives should be a little more obedient to their husbands, an attitude often contested today. Children should be obedient to their parents, while parents should try to avoid frustrating their children *too* much. Still, this New Testament notion that a person in authority should be obedient to one in a subordinate position is as revolutionary now as it was then.

Benedict himself shows some difficulty in maneuvering between the radical principle that all should be one in Christ in mutual obedience and the more conservative belief that seniors are normally due a higher respect than those who are younger. The terms used in Benedict's admonition that "juniors should respect their seniors, and the seniors should love their juniors" (RB 63:10) shows a lack of equality. Even if one suspects that, in the end, Benedict would have the juniors love their seniors and the seniors respect their juniors, the implication seems to be, as Kardong suggests, that Benedict "does not consider their relations to be perfectly symmetrical."[6] This asymmetry is strengthened when Benedict goes on to say that a junior should ask a blessing from a senior when they meet one another, and a junior should never sit unless a senior tells him to (RB 63:15–16). In chapter 71, Benedict pushes even harder for respect of senior monastics by saying, "All juniors must obey their seniors with every mark of loving attention" (RB 71:4). Not only that, but if a junior monastic suspects that a senior is the least bit upset at him, he must make it up to the senior without delay (RB 71:6–8). There is no suggestion that a senior might have reason to apologize to a junior monastic, although anybody who has lived in a monastery knows that seniors do have reason to apologize to their juniors at times. For that matter, a monastic who has learned wisdom and humility over many years will be strongly disposed to take the initiative in mending a broken relationship with a junior. In the broader, long-range view, this mutual respect is not quite as asymmetric as it seems. By learning to respect the seniors, a younger monastic should learn to respect the juniors who enter the community afterward.

In spite of the strong language tilted in favor of obedience to seniors, Benedict's championing of younger monks suggests that respect, as well as love, should be shown to them. When he insists that age shall not determine seniority, he reminds us that Samuel and Daniel both judged their elders while they were still children (RB 63:6). Although Kardong thinks the example of Daniel is stronger because of the way he denounced the corrupt elders who tried to judge Susanna unjustly, the example of Samuel is more telling because, as a boy, Samuel was more devout and open to God than the old priest, Eli. Benedict's championing of the young is all the stronger in that boys were raised in the monastery in his day, and so he was reminding the rest of the community that these boys just might prove to be more worthy than some of their elders. When we remember that in chapter 2, Benedict suggested that God might reveal the best course of action to the youngest member of the monastery when the community is discussing a weighty matter, we are constrained to conclude that it is indeed appropriate to see that the goal of community life is to achieve a mutual flow of both love and respect between juniors and seniors. Needless to say, the deeper the mutual love and respect, the less rivalry there will be between persons.

Chapter 69 is the first of two chapters where Benedict discusses briefly, but bluntly, two serious perversions of communal dynamics. That these are the only two chapters that use the word "presume" in their titles attests to the strong feelings on Benedict's part when he wrote them. The title of chapter 69 is "That no one presume to defend another in the monastery." One might think that defending a weaker person is a good thing to do, but that is not the case here. Kardong notes that it is easy for people to form "cliques based on personal loyalties, featuring emotional attachments that override those of the larger group."[7] When such cliques are formed, it often happens that its members defend each other no matter how wrong their behavior. What Benedict is worried about, for good reason, is the divisiveness that occurs when one monastic champions the cause of another. Here it is likely that the champion is taking advantage of a weaker person to create a power base over/against the authority of the abbot and the well-being of the community. As Benedict feared the effect of a conflict between the abbot and the prior on a community, Benedict also feared that one monastic's defense of another could escalate into a community-wide conflict where everybody takes sides. Once again, Benedict uses the word *skandalon* to describe the situation where the two monastics become stumbling blocks to the community. Kardong says that "when the community is tempted to take sides with either the abbot or another power broker there is indeed a cause for great scandal in which many can stumble."[8] In this case, a weaker person, far from being strengthened, is kept weak by a stronger person and is thus prevented from growing through the discipline of the abbot's authority. Indeed, in the end, the would-be champion could be defending a monastic from God! Chittester sees this possibility when she says that "friends who protect us from our need to grow are not friends at all. People who allow a personal agenda, our need to be right or their need to shield, block the achievement of a broader vision in us and betray us."[9] In such a scenario, all mutual love and respect through obedience is thrown to the wind. This chapter makes it clear that the abbot and prior are not the only ones responsible for maintaining the peace of the community. The cooperation of everybody, from the oldest down to the youngest, is necessary.

The title of chapter 70 states that no one should "presume to strike another arbitrarily." As the previous chapter warned against cliquish behavior or favoritism, this chapter warns against unilateral punishment of other members of the community. Only if the abbot has specifically delegated disciplinary powers to another may that person use such powers. It is easy enough to see how chaotic community life would be if any of its members were subject to the whims of everybody who holds a more senior rank. The previous chapter expressed concern that a stronger monastic might take advantage of a weaker one by becoming that monastic's champion, thus using that person as a pawn in a power game. This chapter expresses concern over a more direct abuse of power. Benedict points to the right use of power when he says that everybody is responsible for watching and disciplining the children who, along with the elderly, would be the weakest members of the community. He then cautions his monastics that this discipline must "be done in a moderate and reasonable way" (RB 70:5). Anybody who "flares up wildly at the children" must be disciplined (RB 70:6).

Benedict's teaching that a communal hierarchy should be based primarily on mutual obedience reaches its final flowering in chapter 72. As the last chapter of the Rule except for a concluding bibliography of monastic literature, it is reasonable to believe that this chapter reflects Benedict's most mature thinking about

Christian community and that the sentiments here take priority over the way Benedict approached similar themes earlier in the Rule.

The first two verses of chapter 72 contrast "an evil and bitter zeal that separates one from God and leads to hell" with "a good zeal that separates one from evil and leads to God and eternal life" (RB 72:1–2). Here, Benedict is using the word *zelus*, which is a transliteration of the Greek word used in the New Testament. This word is ambiguous in the sense that it depends on its context for whether it is a good thing or not. *Zelus* describes the intensity with which a direction is followed without specifying the direction itself. St. Paul tells the Corinthians that he feels a "divine *zelus* [jealousy] for them" (2 Cor. 11:2). More usually in the New Testament, a negative connotation is indicated, as when James accuses his readers of "bitter *zelus* [envy] and selfish ambition" (James 3:14). This accords well with Benedict's use of the archetypal presentation of the two ways as presented in Deuteronomy, chapter 30, and other places in scripture. It is zeal which gives us the energy to move our lives, but we must be alert as to which direction that zeal is taking us. Benedict would have us direct our zeal toward God by practicing "this zeal with the warmest love" (RB 72:3). De Waal says that by zeal, Benedict is returning us to the prologue and urging us to "run in the way of God's commands" (Pr. 49). Benedict wants "a dynamic and alive people" who are filled with "this primary spiritual energy, which brings light and fire, passion and fervor, and which prevents what might otherwise be simply plodding." This energy is what Benedict "calls a very ardent love."[10] Again, Benedict shies away from raw emotionalism as he steers us to a deep flame that will not burn out. Benedict rounds out this chapter by affirming the communal dimension of zeal when he prays that Christ may "lead us all together to everlasting life" (RB 72:12). When a group of people is committed to the goal of attaining everlasting life with God *together*, then there is no room for any sort of rivalry among them.

Sandwiched between these verses centered on God as our end, Benedict lists a series of aphorisms on the theme of communal love. The first of these is a direct quote from Romans 12:10: "Let them strive to be the first to honor one another" (RB 74:4). Kardong notes that this same verse was used in RB 63:17. There, it is slanted to enjoin hierarchal respect. Here, the egalitarian intention of Paul's admonition is fully affirmed. Kardong goes on to say that honor "seems to be a rather flat and cold type of love," but by putting it at the top of his list, Benedict shows that he considers human respect "a very high form of love."[11] Honor and respect are not equivalents of love; they are the foundations on which love is built. More important, respect and honor are the very attitudes that dispose us to renounce rivalrous attitudes toward others. On the contrary, honor and respect redirect us in the direction of attending to the well-being of others. In the next verse, Benedict takes us deeper into attentive love of others by paraphrasing Galatians 6:2: We "should bear each other's weaknesses of both body and character with the utmost patience" (RB 72:5). Kardong tells us that although "tolerate" would be a literal translation of *tolerent*, the biblical resonance dictates the alternate meaning of the verb, "to carry."[12] The willingness to carry other people in their weaknesses is a very deep renunciation of mimetic rivalry, provided it is grounded in the full respect due to everybody else enjoined in the previous verse. Not only are we asked to compete in giving the most honor and respect for others, but we are also asked to "compete with one another in obedience" (RB 72:6). Kardong notes the irony here, in that "people do not normally strive to take the last place."[13] But this is precisely the competition enjoined by Jesus many times in the Gospels. Moreover, it is the disposition to outdo all others in obedience that spurs us on to carry the weaknesses of others in charity with full respect for those who are being carried.

Competing in obedience means that "no one should pursue what he judges advantageous to himself, but rather what benefits others" (RB 72:7). Here is the heart of the matter. The zeal of bitterness causes us to regard other people in terms of their usefulness to ourselves. This bitter zeal culminates in championing others or oppressing them. A good zeal leads us to regard ourselves in terms of what is good for other people. What we have here is a paraphrase of Philippians 2:4, the verse that immediately precedes the kenotic hymn that praises the self-emptying Christ who accepted the cross. This reference reminds us that bearing the weaknesses of others could end with our suffering on account of those weaknesses. The fourth step of humility requires that we be willing to suffer to the extent that Christ suffered, but this chapter shows Benedict hoping for something far better. Here, the more individualistic orientation of chapter 7 blossoms into a fully communal vision of humility. We become vulnerable to the weaknesses of others, but we also have to accept the fact that other people are equally vulnerable to *our* weaknesses. Ideally, we will each care for everybody else, and everybody else will care for us. We carry others, and they carry us. We bear their burdens, and they bear ours. This is what it means to "prefer absolutely nothing to Christ" (RB 72:11). We prefer nothing to Christ *only* if we prefer everybody else to ourselves, since Christ preferred everybody to himself. In this way, Christ, whom we prefer above all else, will "lead us all together to everlasting life" (RB 72:12).

CONCLUSION:
THE TOOLS OF
WEAKNESS

Tools are sharpened by friction with other materials. Our spiritual tools are sharpened through friction with our encounters in life. Benedict is quite clear that we learn humility not in a vacuum but in our relationships with God and other people. The insights of Girard's mimetic theory also give us tools for understanding how our relationships work and alert us to those times when we need to make them better.

As we look back to review what tools Benedict offers us for living the Christian life, we see that they are rather few. Prayer and work as humble service to others pretty well sum it up. The seventy-four maxims in Benedict's chapter on the tools of good works can be reduced to these two items. That should not surprise us once we recall the two great commandments of Jesus culled from the Hebrew Bible: "'You shall love the Lord your God with all your heart, and with all your soul, and with all your mind.'" And a second is like it: "'You shall love your neighbor as yourself'" (Mt. 22:37–39). What Benedict has done is take a very few tools that can be used in many ways in different circumstances in life. I think this is how Benedict's Rule gains the flexibility that it is so famous for. Start with the few fundamentals, and run with them all the way to eternal life.

Girard also bases his thought on very few principles, indeed only one: that a human being's desires are derived from the desires of others. Only God is exempt from this law of personal existence. But, although God does not derive any desires from humans or even angels, the Persons of the Holy Trinity share their desires with each other. Unlike Benedict, Girard has not gained a reputation for flexibility; he has instead gained a reputation for rigidity. He has reduced all of human experience to one principle. That much is true, but if Girard has reduced anthropology to the *most fundamental* principle, or even a principle that is among the most fundamental, then he has planted a seed that can grow in many ways with great flexibility. Girard's analysis of mimetic rivalry leading to sacrificial violence not only sounds rigid; it *is* rigid. But it is not Girard's thought that is rigid; it is the human mechanism uncovered by Girard that is rigid. As we examine the ways that Benedict's little box of tools can help us align mimetic desire with God, we see a whole new world opening up with a dazzling array of possibilities that we call the Kingdom of God. I suggest that, like Benedict, Girard has given us a few tools that we can run with all the way to eternal life.

Retaliatory violence and the multiple victims it creates presses upon all of us and forces us to respond in some way. Looking away is one possible response, but that is hardly better than actively participating in collective violence. It is clear that we won't create peace by refraining from throwing bombs at people. We will only create peace by "running in the way of God's commands." There is no question that the forces leading to the victimization of people are very strong. The strength of these forces tempts us to think that we must make the tools of peace more powerful than the weapons of violence. Unfortunately, making these tools more powerful turns them into weapons. In the face of the world's violence, the tools that Benedict and Girard give us seem small and weak. And they are. We really should take comfort in that. These small and weak tools can be used by anyone, anywhere, at any time. They are so simple that they are hard. It takes a lot of humility to rely on them. It also takes much vigilance, as opportunities are never lacking for using them or failing to use them. Every word we speak or refrain from speaking, every act of service we perform or refuse to perform, takes on enormous importance, not only for the state of our own souls but for the state of the whole world. When we devote this much attention to these tools, we will not harden our hearts when we hear God's voice (RB Pr. 10, Ps. 94:8). But if we are vigilant both to our opportunities and to our failures, then each time we fail, we will hear the cock crow (Mt. 26:74–75).

The example of Jesus shows that peace originates in the place of the victim. It is from *this* place where Jesus was crucified that God "highly exalted him and gave him the name that is above every name" (Phil. 2:9). This is a place where nobody wants to be, but it is the only place where we can most effectively use the few and simple tools of peace that Benedict and Girard give us. Indeed, God is at the center of the universe just as much as the victim is at the center of the circle. We certainly can't use these tools to make peace from the edge of the circle where the stones are thrown to the center. Of course, in our day-to-day life, we don't usually see anything quite as drastic as a circle of people throwing stones at a victim. What both mimetic theory and the Rule of Benedict would have us understand, however, is that each thing we do, each word we say, either brings us closer to the place of Christ at the center or farther from it. Normally, we move in and out several times a day. Perhaps we also wait for others to move into the center with us. This is precisely what the Church, the Body of Christ, is called to do.

I will close by looking at Shirley Jackson's famous and troubling story "The Lottery," a story that illustrates religiously sanctioned collective violence before Girard began to write about it. Only at the end do we learn that the annual lottery held by this town is to determine who will be stoned to death that year. One old man states quite clearly that the purpose of the lottery and the stoning is to hold the social fabric together when he pours scorn on those in other towns who are thinking of giving up the lottery: "Next thing you know, they'll be wanting to go back to living in caves, nobody work any more, live *that* way for a while."[1] The custom of the lottery follows the logic of sacrificial violence as defined by Girard by presupposing that anybody can be the victim. Once the victim draws the piece of paper with a black circle in the middle of it out of the box, everybody surrounds the victim and throws stones. During this narration, there are vague references to rituals that used to accompany the lottery, rituals that are completely forgotten except for the single act of stoning the victim. There is no hint that anybody in the town doubts the rightness of the lottery. The closest thing to any doubt comes from a group of girls who are relieved when it turns out that their friend won't be the victim. But they, too, give every indication that there has to be a victim. But then there is one dissenting voice, Tessie Hutchinson, the very person who turns out to be the victim. When she draws the paper with the black circle, everybody else in the town surrounds her to throw stones while she cries out, "It isn't fair, it isn't right."[2]

Let us now imagine a different ending to this story, the ending that the Gospel would have us imagine. Once again, Tessie Hutchinson cries out, "It isn't fair, it isn't right!" But this time, a few people hear the victim's cry, drop their stones, and walk into the center with Tessie. This gesture confuses everybody else, since they are only supposed to stone the one person who drew the paper with the black circle. Most likely, a few stones are thrown. Maybe a couple of them hit Tessie, but most of them hit the wrong people. This adds to the confusion. Then the confusion grows when everybody standing at the center with Tessie repeats the cry: "It isn't fair, it isn't right!" It is harder for those on the edge of the circle to ignore the outcry, and more people drop their stones and walk to the center. By this time, the center bulges, and the people at the edge have to move back. Now the cries of, "It isn't fair, it isn't right!" are deafening, and the people at the edge cannot hear themselves think. The people at the edge become desperate and throw more stones, but with less effect. Any further injuries or deaths from the stoning seem more absurd than ever. More people drop their stones and move into the ever-expanding center. Perhaps the moment comes when everybody is standing at the center of the circle, the place of Christ himself. Then the chanting of, "It isn't fair, it isn't right!" can cease, and all can hear God in "a sound of sheer silence" (1 Kings 18:12) and know that God "is God not of the dead, but of the living" (Mt. 23:32).

GLOSSARY

abbot. From the Aramaic *abba*, meaning father. In the first monastic generations and in Eastern monasticism today, it is used of any monk who acts as a spiritual father to a younger monk. In Western monasticism, including the Rule of Benedict, this term is used for the superior of a monastic community, who is expected to act as a spiritual father to everybody.

acquisitive mimesis. Imitating the desire of another person for the same object to the extent of entering into conflict with that person to acquire that object for oneself.

anchorite. A monastic who lives alone; a hermit.

anthropological. Pertaining to fundamental human characteristics. Does not preclude humanity's relationship with God. Benedict and Girard presuppose this relationship in their understanding of humanity.

atonement. In Christianity, the reconciliation of God and humanity through the death and Resurrection of Jesus Christ. Several theories of the Atonement have been constructed by various theologians. Girard rejects all theories that suggest that sacrifice was *necessary* on God's part. For Girard, the necessity for sacrifice is all on the part of humanity.

Benedictine. A person who follows the Rule of Benedict in a community. The adjective can refer to the principles of Benedict's Rule that inspire both monastics and laypersons.

canonical hours. The seven hours of prayer during the day (known as the day hours) plus a night office as designated by the Catholic Church. **Matins.** The night office. Also known as **Vigils. Lauds.** From the Latin *laude,* praise, in references to Psalms 148–150, the Psalms of praise. Office done at sunrise. **Prime.** Office done at the first hour of the day, reckoning by the Roman system of measuring equal amounts of daylight. **Terce.** Office done at the third hour of the day. **Sext.** Office done at the sixth hour of the day. **None.** Office done at the ninth hour of the day. **Vespers.** From the Latin *vespera,* meaning evening. Office done near sunset. **Compline.** From the Latin *compline,* meaning completion. The prayer done at the completion of the day.

cellarer. The monastic who is put in charge of managing and distributing the material goods of a monastery.

cenobite, cenobitic. A person who lives in a religious community under the authority of a superior and a common rule.

chastity. In monasticism, the abstention of all sexual activity, even activity that would be right and good for non-monastics. More important, chastity is an inner attitude of respect for others that avoids thinking of them as sexual objects (Mt. 5:26–27), or, more broadly, making another person part of one's own agenda in life.

Christological. Theological reflections on Christ, most especially the relationship between Christ's divinity and humanity. When used in the Rule of Benedict, it presupposes Church teachings about Christ but refers primarily to Christ as the basis of virtues such as humility and service.

commodity. Usually has the neutral meaning of any article of commerce. Hyde, Marx, and Bandera all note the potential for commodities to become a source of **mimetic rivalry** when people fight over their relative values. Commodities in this sense are at cross-purposes of a **gift economy.**

compunction. Sorrow for one's own sin but also refers to a longing for God that is not yet fulfilled.

conflictual mimesis. Imitating another person with whom one is in conflict over a mutually desired object.

conversion. Includes the normal religious meaning of turning to and accepting a specific religious orientation for one's life. In monastic literature, it refers to the ongoing process of sustaining and renewing this primary conversion. For a monastic, conversion is sustained by persevering in a committed life in a monastery.

dean. A monastic who is put in charge of ten members of the community as recommended in Benedict's Rule.

Divine Office. A liturgical event featuring the use of hymns, psalms, and canticles.

excommunication. In the Rule of Benedict, the disciplinary exclusion from one or more aspects of communal life. For Benedict, this is always used as a means to restore a monastic to the fullness of communal life. This practice has no ecclesiastic ramifications beyond the monastery and should not be confused with excommunication from the sacraments imposed by a bishop.

gift economy. A social network where goods and service are freely offered to everybody within the society. Theologically, a gift economy is grounded in God's free gifts of creation and grace.

grumbling. See **murmuring.**

gyrovagues. Wandering monastics who never stay long enough in one place to become settled in living the monastic life. Benedict considers them the worst of all monastics.

hesychia. A Greek word that means "resting." In monastic spirituality, it takes on the specialized meaning of resting in God in **peace.**

homeostasis. The ongoing equilibrium of a physical or social system. Both Family Systems Theory and mimetic theory note that homeostasis in a society often has the unstable foundation of gaining its coherence from an **identified patient** or a victim of collective violence.

humility. Popular belief that humility means self-abasement obscures the richness this word has for monastic writers. The first step of humility in Benedict's Rule, that one should be constantly aware of living in the presence of God, makes a much firmer starting point for understanding this virtue.

humor. See **laughter.**

identified patient. Phrase coined by Edwin Friedman. The identified patient is the person in a family system or community who absorbs its communal dysfunction more than anybody else. Physical, mental, and emotional illness on the part of an identified patient may be real, but they are either caused or at least exacerbated by becoming a community's focus so as to avoid deeper underlying issues causing a community's dysfunction.

intelligence of the victim. Phrase coined by James Alison. The privileged viewpoint of the victim who understands the dynamics of persecution that persecutors are unable to see when they kill or expel victims. Andrew McKenna coined a more technical phrase, "the epistemological privilege of the victim," to say the same thing.

Jubilee. The fiftieth year when, according to legislation in Leviticus, chapter 25, all debts were to be forgiven and slaves were set free. Isaiah 61:1–2, read in the synagogue by Jesus in Luke 4:18–19, refers to this Jubilee.

kenotic. From the Greek *kenosis*, meaning "emptying." In theology, it refers to the self-emptying of Christ through entering human nature and dying on the cross as expressed in Philippians 2:6–11.

laughter. Although this can be a good thing, Benedict is very much aware of the destructive possibilities of laughter and humor when they are used to put other people down.

lectio divina. Latin for "holy reading." Reading for the purpose of fostering spiritual growth. Scripture is the primary text for *lectio,* but other reading material of spiritual value may also be used.

literary inspiration. A phrase coined by McNeill. Liturgical texts and religious teachings informing liturgy or any other form of **muscular bonding.**

logismoi. Related to the Greek *logos.* It is usually translated as "thoughts," but this word is not limited to thoughts as mental processes but also refers to one's full emotional involvement with these "thoughts."

messiah. Royalty in the Jewish tradition. At the time of Jesus, there were various prophecies of a coming messiah, many of them envisioning a violent conqueror of Israel's oppressors. Girard argues that kingship is a **sacrificial** institution. The behavior of Jesus in light of messianic prophecies suggests that Jesus radically redefined kingship to the extent of repudiating its traditional meaning.

mimesis. Normally this word means "imitation" or "representation." In the works of Girard, it takes on the more specialized meaning of "imitating the desire of another person."

mimetic crisis. A situation where **mimetic rivalry** has become so rampant in a society that there is a real possibility that the society will destroy itself.

mimetic desire. A desire that is caused and/or intensified by the desire of another person for the same thing.

mimetic doubles. When two people enter into conflict because each is imitating the desires of the other, they become indistinguishable mirror images of each other.

mimetic rivalry. Rivalry where two or more people imitate each other in their desires and attempt to attain the desired objects for themselves.

mimetic theory. The theory of Girard that a human's desires are derived from the desires of others. That is, not only do people copy the external behavior of other people, but more fundamentally, people copy the *desires* of others.

mimetic triangle. A triangle formed by two persons desiring the same object and the desired object. Two men pursuing the same woman in conflict with one another form a mimetic triangle.

monastic. This adjective is now also used as an inclusive noun to refer to both men and women who live the monastic life.

monk. Derived from the Greek word *monachos*, it originally referred to a hermit, one who lived alone, but soon took on the meaning of a member of a male community devoted to the monastic life.

murmuring. Complaining about a situation in such a way that nothing is likely to be done about it. Benedict considers this one of the most destructive vices in a community.

muscular bonding. A phrase coined by McNeill. The unity that humans experience when they engage in synchronized bodily actions.

myth. Usually a story that explains the origins of cultural institutions. Girard believes that these narrations usually disguise spontaneous acts of collective violence that became institutionalized in sacrificial rites.

obedience. Placing one's own will into the custody of other people. In the monastic tradition, one's will is primarily placed in the custody of the abbot or superior of the community. Obedience, however, needs to be lived in relationship to the whole community. In this regard, the abbot must also practice obedience.

opus Dei. Latin for **Work of God**. See **Divine Office.**

participative imitation. A phrase coined by Fodor. **Mimetic desire** is so deep that the subject participates in the subjectivity of another and shares the mutual desire at a deep level in a totally non-rivalrous way. This is most fully experienced when a human participates mimetically in God. The human **self** remains distinct at every level of participative imitation of God.

Paschal Mystery. From the Greek *paschein*, "to suffer," in reference to the suffering of Christ during his passion and death, and *mysterion*, meaning "a divine secret." The suffering, death, and Resurrection of Jesus. In the Gospels, this becomes an open secret, but one whose meaning cannot be totally understood by humans.

peace. In traditional monastic writings, means primarily the peace of the monastic community. Monastic peace is not just absence of conflict but an active cooperation of the members with one another. Broader social issues of peace have usually been a concern of monastics as well. On a more personal level, peace is a harmonious relationship with God at a deep level. See *hesychia.*

poverty. In the Rule of Benedict, poverty is not an absence of material goods; it is the renunciation of personal ownership of these goods. Poverty is acted out primarily through using material goods moderately with good sense for the sake of the common good.

primitive sacred. The religions of early humanity that Girard believes are founded on **sacred violence.** By extension, it can refer to any religious system that continues to perpetuate **sacrificial** structures.

prior. Occasionally means the superior of a monastery in early monastic literature. Normally means a monastic who holds the position of second-in-command. This is the meaning in the Rule of Benedict. Benedict insists that a prior, if there is to be one, be appointed by the abbot.

prophet. In the Hebrew Bible, a prophet is not primarily one who foretells the future, although this happens occasionally. A prophet is a person who expresses a special insight from God as to what God is doing in the present time. Sometimes there are future ramifications to what God is doing in the present. Benedict uses this word loosely for many figures in the Hebrew Bible who can be construed in any way as prefiguring Christ. Without prejudice to the broad biblical meaning of this word, Girard pays particular heed to Jesus' definition of a prophet as one who witnesses to God's truth as a victim of collective violence (Mt. 23:34–36).

purity of heart. A state of being freed of *logismoi* to the extent of having an unclouded sense of God's presence. An advanced state that may be experienced sporadically but is rarely sustained in this life.

sacred violence. Violence that is sanctioned by religious tradition. See **sacrificial.**

sacrificial. In addition to the usual meaning of rituals involving sacrifice, Girard uses this word to refer to an underlying attitude that assumes that harmony between humans and with God requires either the death or the exile of a living being. Is also used in its more positive meaning as referring to a voluntary giving of oneself for the sake of others.

sarabaites. Monastics who live in small households with neither a rule nor a superior. Benedict disapproves of them very much.

Satan. Without prejudice to the existence of a supernaturally evil being associated with this word, Girard uses this word primarily in its biblical meaning of a stumbling block. In this usage, any person can be a "Satan" to another, as Peter was to Jesus (Mt. 16:23).

scandal. Derived from the Greek *skandalon*. Girard uses this word in its biblical meaning of a "stumbling block" or "obstacle." Girard suggests that when two or more people enter into conflict fueled by mimetic desire, they become stumbling blocks or obstacles to each other.

scapegoat. A goat that bears the sins of the Jewish people and is cast out of the temple into the desert according to Leviticus 16:7–26. Girard makes use of this traditional meaning but usually uses this word to refer to the selective blaming of one person or group for the sins and crimes of the whole community.

scapegoat mechanism. An unconscious communal process that happens in times of **mimetic crisis** in which a victim is selected and either killed or expelled.

self. In normal usage, the essential core of an individual's identity distinct from all others. Christian literature accepts this meaning but denies that the self of any created being is autonomous. The human self may be distinct from all other selves, but it is not self-sufficient; it is grounded in the selfhood of God. **Mimetic theory** says that the human self is not autonomous to other human selves either. The self is formed through interactions with the desires of other persons. Each human self functions best when it is aligned foremost with the desires of God and secondarily with the desires of other people.

self-will. Putting one's own will ahead of the will of a superior and the other people in one's community. The contrary to **obedience.**

silence. Absence of sound is only a superficial understanding of this virtue in monastic writings. In its more substantive meaning, it takes on much of the meaning of **peace.** Like **peace,** silence must be actively cultivated. Silence is closely connected to God, as silence, in its positive aspects, makes a person more open to God's communications.

stability. In monastic literature, a monastic's commitment not only to living the monastic life but also to living this life in a specific community.

Suffering Servant. An anonymous "servant" who is the subject of five songs within chapters 39–55 of the Book of Isaiah. Isaiah 52:13–53:12 is particularly devoted to the persecutions that this Servant suffered at the hands of the people. Much Jewish tradition has interpreted the Servant as standing for the whole of Israel in its persecution by other nations. Much Christian tradition has interpreted this Servant as a prophecy or forerunner of Christ. Girard believes that this Servant was a victim of the same sort of collective violence as Jesus.

Work of God. See **Divine Office.**

NOTES

1. Gathering a Community in the Spirit: Introducing St. Benedict and His Rule

1. Gregory the Great, *The Life of Saint Benedict*, trans. Hilary Costello and Eoin de Bhaldraithe (Petersham: St. Bede's Publications, 1993), 174.
2. Francis Clark, *The 'Gregorian' Dialogues and the Origins of Benedictine Monasticism* (Boston: Brill, 2003), 39–143.
3. Ibid., 279–91.
4. Ibid., 203–18.
5. Ibid., 279–80.
6. Simone Weil, "Reflection on the Right Use of School Studies with a View to the Love of God," in *The Simone Weil Reader*, ed. George A. Panichas (New York: McKay, 1977), 44.
7. Ibid., 49.
8. Ibid.
9. Ibid., 51.
10. Ibid.

2. Violence and the Kingdom of God: Introducing the Anthropology of René Girard

1. This chapter is based on an article published in the Fall 1998 issue of the *Anglican Theological Review* under the title "Violence and the Kingdom of God."
2. TH, 8–9.
3. René Girard, *Deceit, Desire & the Novel* (Baltimore: Johns Hopkins University Press, 1965), 1.
4. Ibid., 4. Italics are the author's.
5. Ibid., 6.

6. Shirley Jackson, "Seven Types of Ambiguity," in *The Lottery and Other Stories* (New York: Farrar Straus Giroux, 1991), 209–17.

7. René Girard, *A Theater of Envy: William Shakespeare* (New York: Oxford University Press, 1991), 72–79.

8. René Girard, *Resurrection from the Underground: Feodor Dostoevsky* (New York: Crossroad, 1997), 49.

9. GR, 63.

10. TH, 26.

11. Ibid., 12; cf. ibid., 142.

12. Ibid., 26.

13. Nigel Davies, *Human Sacrifice in History and Today* (New York: Morrow, 1981).

14. Girard, René, "Generative Scapegoating," in *Violent Origins: Walter Burkert, René Girard, and Jonathan Z. Smith on Ritual Killing and Cultural Formation*, ed. Robert G. Hamerton-Kelly (Stanford: Stanford University Press, 1987), 79–80.

15. Gil Bailie, *Violence Unveiled: Humanity at the Crossroads* (New York: Crossroad, 1995), 33.

16. Ibid., 31.

17. TH, 76–77.

18. TH, 145–46.

19. James G. Williams, *The Bible, Violence, and the Sacred: Liberation from the Myth of Sanctioned Violence* (San Francisco: HarperCollins, 1991), 70–98.

20. Raymund Schwager, *Must There Be Scapegoats?: Violence and Redemption in the Bible* (San Francisco: HarperCollins, 1978), 83.

21. Ibid., 84.

22. Ibid., 99.

23. Ibid., 100.

24. Sandor Goodhart, "'al lo-chamas asah (although he had done no violence)': René Girard and the Innocent Victim," in *Violence Renounced: René Girard, Biblical Studies, and Peacemaking*, ed. Willard M. Swartley (Telford: Pandora Press US, 2000), 208.

25. Ibid., 212.

26. Ibid., 213.

27. Raymund Schwager, *Jesus in the Drama of Salvation: Toward a Biblical Doctrine of Redemption* (New York: Crossroad, 1999), 73.

28. Ibid., 75.

29. GR, 195–210.

30. GR 198.

31. Ibid.

32. Schwager 1978, 172.

33. TH, 197.

34. Schwager 1978, 169.

35. René Girard, *The Scapegoat* (Baltimore: Johns Hopkins University Press, 1986), 168.

36. Ibid., 169, 174.

37. TH, 178–79.

38. Goodhart 2000, 204.

39. Ibid.

40. Cf. J. Denny Weaver, *The Nonviolent Atonement* (Grand Rapids: Eerdmans, 2001).

41. Schwager 1999, 197.

42. René Girard, "Are the Gospels Mythical?" in *First Things* 62 (April 1996), 27–31.

43. TH, 216.

44. James Alison, *Raising Abel: The Recovery of the Eschatological Imagination* (New York: Crossroad, 1996), 18–19.

45. TH, 186.

46. Ibid., 187–90.

47. Schwager 1996, 173–75.

48. James Alison, *Knowing Jesus* (Springfield: Templegate, 1993), 37.

49. Ibid., 31–59.

50. Ibid., 39.

51. Alison 1996, 42.

52. René Girard, *I See Satan Fall like Lightning* (Maryknoll: Orbis, 2001), 146.

53. Girard 1986, 1–11.

54. S. Mark Heim, *Saved from Sacrifice: A Theology of the Cross* (Grand Rapids: Eerdmans, 2006), 212.

55. Alison 1993, 92.

3. A Call to Conversion: The Prologue to the Rule of Benedict

1. Esther De Waal, *A Life-Giving Way: A Commentary on the Rule of Benedict* (Collegeville: Liturgical Press, 1995), 6.

2. Ibid., 6.

3. Ibid., 4.

4. Joan Chittester, *Rule of Benedict: Insights for the Ages* (New York: Crossroad, 1992), 20.

5. Kardong, 29.
6. De Waal 1995, 11.
7. Girard 2001, 126.
8. Girard 2002, 126.
9. Schwager 1999, 213.
10. Kardong 1996, 474.
11. RM, 94.

4. A Call to Commitment: The Kinds of Monastics

1. Kardong 1996, 43.
2. Saint Basil of Caesarea, "The Long Rules," in *Ascetical Works*, trans. Sister M. Monica Wagner, CSC (New York: Fathers of the Church, 1950), 250.
3. Ibid., 251.
4. Ibid., 252.
5. Kardong 1996, 43.
6. TH, 359.
7. Julian of Norwich, *Showings*, trans. Edmund Colledge, OSA, and James Walsh, SJ (New York: Paulist Press, 1978), 233.
8. De Waal 1995, 17.
9. Chittester 1993, 34.
10. De Waal 1995, 152.

5. The Authority of Christ: The Abbot

1. TH, 51.
2. Ibid., 52
3. René Girard, *Violence and the Sacred* (Baltimore: Johns Hopkins University Press, 1977), 103–12.
4. TH, 53.
5. James Williams, "King as Servant, Sacrifice as Service: Gospel Transformations," in *Violence Renounced: René Girard, Biblical Studies, and Peacemaking* (Telford: Pandora Press US, 2000), 179.
6. Ibid., 180.
7. Ibid., 183.
8. Ibid., 193.
9. Ibid.
10. Ibid., 36.
11. Kardong 1996, 66.
12. Ibid., 50.

13. TH, 290.
14. Fyodor Dostoevsky, *The Brothers Karamazov*, trans. Richard Pevear and Larissa Volokhnsky (San Francisco: North Point Press, 1990), 289.
15. Ibid., 319.
16. Kardong 1996, 534.
17. De Waal 1995, 170.
18. Chittester 1993, 38.

6. *Mimetic Decision Making: On Calling the Community to Counsel*

1. Kardong 1996, 76.

7. *The Tools of Good Works: The Craft of Christian Living*

2. Kardong 1996, 96–97.
3. Ibid., 97.
4. Ibid., 98.
5. Ibid., 82.
6. Ibid., 102.
7. Ibid.
8. De Waal 1995, 29.
9. Søren Kierkegaard, *Works of Love*, trans. Howard and Edna Hong (New York: Harper & Row, 1962), 39.
10. Kardong, 86.
11. Chittester 1993, 51.
12. Chittester 1991, 51.
13. Schwager 1999, 198.
14. Ibid., 199.
15. Tom Pyszczynski, *In the Wake of 9/11: The Psychology of Terror* (Washington DC: American Psychological Association, 2003).
16. De Waal 1995, 35.
17. Kardong 1996, 96.

8. *Obedience: The Art of Putting Oneself into the Hands of Another*

1. Kardong 1996, 113.
2. Ibid., 106.
3. Schwager 1999, 207.
4. Kardong 1996, 106.
5. Ibid., 107.

6. Schwager 1999, 212.
7. Kardong 1996, 566–67.
8. Chittester 1992, 173.

9. Silence: The Still Small Voice of God

1. De Waal 1995, 41.
2. Max Picard, *The World of Silence*, trans. Stanley Godman (Chicago: Henry Regnery, 1952), 1.
3. Picard 1952, 5.
4. Ibid., 8.
5. Ibid., 8–9.
6. Kardong 1996, 122.
7. De Waal 1995, 42.
8. John Cassian, *Institutes* (New York: Paulist Press, 2000), 220.
9. 1996, 126.
10. Chittester 1993, 60.
11. James Alison, *Faith beyond Resentment: Fragments Catholic and Gay* (London: Darton, Longman & Todd, 2001), 27.
12. Ibid., 29.
13. Picard 1952, 52.

10. Humility: Rising to the Lowest Place

1. Alison 1996, 181.
2. Ibid., 21.
3. Kardong 1996, 136.
4. Saint Augustine, *Confessions*, trans. Vernon J. Bourke (New York: Fathers of the Church, 1953), 2–13.
5. De Waal 1995, 45.
6. Chittester 1993, 62.
7. Kardong 1996, 142.
8. Ibid., 90.
9. Ibid., 148.
10. Ibid., 150.
11. Michael Casey, *Truthful Living: Saint Benedict's Teaching on Humility* (Leominster: Gracewing, 2001), 149.
12. Ibid., 190.
13. Chittester 1993, 69.
14. De Waal 1995, 51.

15. Kardong 1996, 153.

16. Ibid., 459.

17. Ibid.

18. Casey 2001, 188.

19. Kardong 1996, 154.

20. De Waal 1995, 52.

21. Chittester 1993, 70.

22. Rebecca Adams, "Loving Mimesis and Girard's 'Scapegoat of the Text': A Creative Reassessment of Mimetic Desire," in *Violence Renounced*, 287.

23. Ibid., 288. Italics are the author's.

24. Ibid., 294.

25. 296.

26. Alison 1996, 55.

27. Gilbert K. Chesterton, *Heretics* (New York: John Lane, 1905), 130.

28. Gilbert K. Chesterton, *Orthodoxy* (Garden City: Garden City, 1908), 224.

29. Ibid., 224.

30. Casey 2001, 245.

31. De Waal 1995, 55.

11. The Work of God: The Divine Office and Interior Prayer

1. Kardong 1996, 212.

2. De Waal 1995, 56.

3. Kardong 1996, 192.

4. De Waal 1995, 56.

5. Kardong 1996, 170.

6. De Waal 1995, 56.

7. Chittester 1993, 126.

8. Ibid., 126.

9. GR, 11.

10. Cf. Nigel Davies, *Human Sacrifice: In History and Today* (New York: Morrow, 1981).

11. GR, 13.

12. Girard 2001, 79.

13. Ibid., 80.

14. Ibid., 81.

15. Ibid.

16. Jacques Attali, *Noise: The Political Economy of Music*, trans. Brian Massumi (Minneapolis: University of Minnesota Press, 1985), 25.

17. Ibid., 25–26. Italics are the author's.

18. Ibid., 27. Italics are the author's.

19. Ibid., 28.

20. William McNeill, *Keeping Together in Time: Dance and Drill in Human History* (Cambridge, MA: Harvard University Press, 1995), 3.

21. Ibid., 67.

22. Cf. Girard 1977, 126–42.

23. McNeill 1995, 73.

24. Ibid., 75.

25. Ibid.

26. Ibid., 76.

27. Ibid., 77.

28. Ibid., 79.

29. RM, 172.

30. Erik Routley, *Christian Hymns: An Introduction to Their Story* (Princeton: Prestige Publications, 1980), cassette 1, side 1.

31. Heim 2006, 181.

32. Ibid.

33. Schwager 1978, 93.

34. Kardong 1996, 187.

35. Ibid., 188.

36. Ibid., 199.

37. Ibid.

38. Chittester 1993, 89–90.

39. De Waal 1995, 68.

40. Kardong 1996, 175.

41. Ibid., 176.

42. Ibid., 207.

43. Ibid., 208.

44. John Cassian, *The Conferences* (New York: Paulist Press, 1997), 346–47.

45. Ibid., 346.

46 Willard Swartley, "Discipleship and Imitation of Jesus," in *Violence Renounced*, 237.

47. Ibid.

48. Ibid., 238. Italics are the author's.

49. Jim Fodor, "Christian Discipleship as Participative Imitation," in *Violence Renounced*, 257.

50. Ibid.

51. Personal communication from Gil Bailie.

52. Kardong 1996, 190.

12. Healing a Broken Community: Disruption and Reconciliation

1. Girard 2001, 145–46.

2. Bailie 1995, 79.

3. Ibid.

4. Helen Prejean, *Dead Man Walking* (New York: Vintage Books, 1994), 252, n. 20.

5. Helen Prejean, *The Death of Innocents* (New York: Random House, 2005).

6. Bailie 1995, 87.

7. Coventry Patmore, "A London Fête," quoted in Bailie 1995, 83–86.

8. Christopher D. Marshall, *Beyond Retribution: A New Testament Vision for Justice, Crime, and Punishment* (Grand Rapids: Eerdmans; 2001), 66.

9. Ibid., 67.

10. Kardong, 250.

11. Kardong 1996, 250.

12. Chittester 1993, 95.

13. Kardong 1996, 368.

14. De Waal 1995, 118.

15. Girard 1977, 9, 94–95.

16. Edwin H. Friedman, *Generation to Generation: Family Process in Church and Synagogue* (New York: Guildford Press, 1985), 19.

17. Ibid., 20.

18. Ibid.

19. Ibid., 21.

20. Ibid.

21. Ibid., 129–36.

22. Kardong 1996, 237.

23. Ibid.

24. Ibid., 257.

25. De Waal 1995, 88–89.

26. Kardong 1996, 243–44.

27. Kardong 1996, 243.

28. De Waal 1995, 89.

29. Chittester 1993, 100.

30. Kardong 1996, 372.

31. Ibid.

32. Ibid., 374.

13. Mimetic Stewardship of Material Goods

1. TH, 26.
2. Kardong 1996, 273.
3. De Waal 1995, 99.
4. Ibid., 100.
5. Chittester 1993, 108.
6. Kardong 1996, 438.
7. Lewis Hyde, *The Gift: Imagination and the Erotic Life of Property* (New York: Vintage, 1983), 45.
8. Ibid.
9. Ibid., 47.
10. Ibid., 56.
11. Ibid., 47.
12. Ibid., 57.
13. Ibid., 28–32.
14. Ibid., 60.
15. Ibid., 61.
16. Cesáreo Bandera, *The Sacred Game: The Role of the Sacred in the Genesis of Modern Literary Fiction* (University Park: Pennsylvania State University Press, 1994), 267.
17. Ibid., 269.
18. Ibid., 281.
19. Ibid., 293.
20. Kardong 1996, 277.
21. Hyde 1983, 58.
22. Ibid.
23. Ambrose of Milan, *De Tobia*. Quoted in Hyde 1983, 117.
24. Ibid., 135.
25. Kardong 1996, 328.
26. Kardong 1996, 450.
27. Chittester 1993, 119.
28. De Waal 1995, 101–2.
29. Kardong 1996, 268.
30. Ibid., 265.
31. Ibid.

14. Serving One Another Mimetically

1. De Waal 1995, 103.
2. Ibid.
3. Kardong 1996, 398.
4. Ibid., 399.
5. Ibid., 430.
6. Kardong, 299.
7. Kardong 1996, 303.
8. Kardong 1996, 434.
9. De Waal 1995, 137.
10. RM, 243.
11. Ibid., 233.
12. De Waal 1995, 138.
13. Kardong 1996, 435.
14. Ibid., 422–23.
15. Chittester 1993, 141.
16. Cassian 1997, 382.
17. Quoted in Kardong 1996, 319.
18. Kardong 1996, 321.
19. Kardong 1996, 306.

15. Lent: The Gateway to Easter

1. Chittester 1993, 136–37.
2. Kardong 1996, 405.
3. De Waal 1995, 129–30.
4. Ibid., 130.
5. Ibid.
6. Girard 2001, 189.

16. Monastic Mimetic Conflict: The Prior of the Monastery

1. Kardong 1996, 551.
2. De Waal 1995, 173.
3. Kardong 1996, 544.
4. Ibid., 546.
5. De Waal 1995, 174.
6. Chittester 1993, 168.
7. Bailie 1995, 187.

8. De Waal 1995, 174.
9. Ibid.

17. Mimetic Community Order

1. Chittester 1993, 161–62.
2. Kardong 1996, 524.
3. TH, 306.
4. Ibid., 306–7.
5. Kardong 1996, 525.
6. Ibid., 520.
7. Ibid., 573.
8. Ibid., 575.
9. Chittester 1993, 174.
10. De Waal 1995, 185.
11. Kardong 1996, 591.
12. Ibid., 592.
13. Ibid.

Conclusion: The Tools of Weakness

1. "The Lottery," in Jackson 1991, 197.
2. Ibid., 202.

BIBLIOGRAPHY

I. The Rule of Benedict and Benedictine Monasticism
A. Primary Sources on Benedict:

Fry, Timothy, OSB, ed. *RB 1980; the Rule of St. Benedict in Latin and English with Notes.* Collegeville: Liturgical Press, 1981.

Gregory the Great. *The Life of Saint Benedict,* translated by Hilary Costello and Eoin de Bhaldraithe. Petersham: St. Bede's Publications, 1993.

Kardong, Terence. *Benedict's Rule: A Translation and Commentary.* Collegeville, MN: Liturgical Press, 1996.

The Rule of the Master (*Regula Magistri*), translated by Luke Eberle. Kalamazoo: Cistercian Publications, 1977.

B. Primary Sources in Patristic Literature:

Augustine, Saint. *Confessions,* translated by Vernon J. Bourke. New York: Fathers of the Church, 1953.

Basil of Caesarea, Saint. "The Long Rules." In *Ascetical Works,* translated by Sister M. Monica Wagner, CSC. New York: Fathers of the Church, 1950.

Cassian, John. *The Conferences,* translated by Boniface Ramsey. New York: Paulist Press, 1997.

———. *The Institutes,* translated by Boniface Ramsey. New York: Paulist Press, 2000.

C. Secondary Sources on Benedict:

Casey, Michael. *Truthful Living: Saint Benedict's Teaching on Humility.* Leominster: Gracewing, 2001.

Chittester, Joan. *Rule of Benedict: Insights for the Ages.* New York: Crossroad, 1992.

———. *Wisdom Distilled from the Daily.* New York: Harper & Row, 1990.

Clark, Francis. *The 'Gregorian' Dialogues and the Origins of Benedictine Monasticism.* Boston: Brill, 2003.

Dean, Eric. *St. Benedict for the Laity.* Collegeville: Liturgical Press, 1989.

De Waal, Esther. *A Life-Giving Way: A Commentary on the Rule of Benedict.* Collegeville: Liturgical Press, 1995.

————. *Living with Contradiction.* New York: Harper & Row, 1989.

————. *Seeking God.* Collegeville: Liturgical Press, 1984.

Kardong, Terence. *The Benedictines.* Wilmington: Glazier, 1988.

Norris, Kathleen. *Cloister Walk.* New York: Riverhead Press, 1996.

Stewart, Columba. *Prayer and Community: The Benedictine Tradition.* Maryknoll, NY: Orbis Books, 1998.

Taylor, Brian. *Spirituality for Everyday Living.* Collegeville: Liturgical Press, 1989.

Tvedten, Benet. *A Share in the Kingdom.* Collegeville: Liturgical Press, 1989.

Vest, Norvene. *Preferring Christ.* Trabuco Canyon: Source Books, 1990.

II. The Mimetic Theory of René Girard
A. Works by René Girard:

Girard, René. *Deceit, Desire & the Novel.* Baltimore: Johns Hopkins University Press, 1965.

————. *Violence and the Sacred.* Baltimore: Johns Hopkins University Press, 1977.

————. *"To Double Business Bound": Essays on Literature, Mimesis and Anthropology.* Baltimore: Johns Hopkins University Press, 1978.

————. *The Scapegoat.* Baltimore: Johns Hopkins University Press, 1986.

————. *Things Hidden since the Foundation of the World: Research Undertaken in Collaboration with Jean-Michel Oughourlian and Guy Lefort.* Stanford, CA: Stanford University Press, 1987.

————. *Job, the Victim of His People.* Stanford, CA: Stanford University Press, 1987.

————. "Generative Scapegoating." In *Violent Origins: Walter Burkert, René Girard, and Jonathan Z. Smith on Ritual Killing and Cultural Formation*, edited by Robert G. Hamerton-Kelly, 73–145. Stanford, CA: Stanford University Press, 1987.

————. *A Theater of Envy: William Shakespeare.* New York: Oxford University Press, 1991.

————. "Are the Gospels Mythical?" *First Things* 62 (April 1996): 27–31.

————. *The Girard Reader.* New York: Crossroad, 1996.

————. *Resurrection from the Underground: Feodor Dostoevsky*. New York: Crossroad, 1997.

————. *I See Satan Fall like Lightning*. Maryknoll, NY: Orbis Books, 2001.

B. Other Works on Mimetic Theory:

Alison, James. *Faith beyond Resentment: Fragments Catholic and Gay*. London: Darton Longman & Todd, 2001.

————. *Knowing Jesus*. Springfield: Templegate, 1993.

————. *Raising Abel: The Recovery of the Eschatological Imagination*. New York: Crossroad, 1996.

Bailie, Gil. *Violence Unveiled: Humanity at the Crossroads*. New York: Crossroad, 1995.

Bandera, Cesáreo. *The Sacred Game: The Role of the Sacred in the Genesis of Modern Literary Fiction*. University Park: Pennsylvania State University Press, 1994.

Goodhart, Sandor. *Sacrificing Commentary: Reading the End of Literature*. Baltimore: Johns Hopkins University Press, 1996.

Hamerton-Kelly, Robert G. *The Gospel and the Sacred: Poetics of Violence in Mark*. Minneapolis: Fortress Press, 1994.

Heim, S. Mark. *Saved from Sacrifice: a Theology of the Cross*. Grand Rapids: Eerdmans, 2006.

McKenna, Andrew. *Violence and Difference*. Chicago: University of Illinois Press, 1992.

Schwager, Raymund. *Banished from Eden: Original Sin and Evolutionary Theory in the Drama of Salvation*. Leominster: Gracewing, 2006.

————. *Jesus in the Drama of Salvation: Toward a Biblical Doctrine of Redemption*. New York: Crossroad, 1999.

————. *Must There Be Scapegoats?: Violence and Redemption in the Bible*. San Francisco: HarperCollins, 1978.

Swartley, Willard M., ed. *Violence Renounced: René Girard, Biblical Studies, and Peacemaking*. Telford: Pandora Press US, 2000.

Weaver, J. Denny. *The Nonviolent Atonement*. Grand Rapids: Eerdmans, 2001.

Williams, James G. *The Bible, Violence, and the Sacred: Liberation from the Myth of Sanctioned Violence*. San Francisco: HarperCollins, 1991; Valley Forge, PA: Trinity Press International, 1995.

III. Other Works Cited

Attali, Jacques. *Noise: The Political Economy of Music*, translated by Brian Massumi. Minneapolis: University of Minnesota Press, 1985.

Chesterton, Gilbert K. *Heretics*. New York: John Lane, 1905.

———. *Orthodoxy*. Garden City: Garden City, 1908.

Davies, Nigel. *Human Sacrifice: In History and Today*. New York: Morrow, 1981.

Dostoevsky, Fyodor. *The Brothers Karamazov*, translated by Richard Pevear and Larissa Volokhnsky. San Francisco: North Point Press, 1990.

Friedman, Edwin H. *Generation to Generation: Family Process in Church and Synagogue*. New York: Guildford Press, 1985.

Hyde, Lewis. *The Gift: Imagination and the Erotic Life of Property*. New York: Vintage, 1983.

Jackson, Shirley. *The Lottery and Other Stories*. New York: Farrar Straus Giroux, 1991.

Julian of Norwich. *Showings*, translated by Edmund Colledge, OSA, and James Walsh, SJ. New York: Paulist Press, 1978.

Kierkegaard, Søren. *Works of Love*, translated by Howard and Edna Hong. New York: Harper & Row, 1962.

Marshall, Christopher D. *Beyond Retribution: A New Testament Vision for Justice, Crime, and Punishment*. Grand Rapids: Eerdmans, 2001.

McNeill, William. *Keeping Together in Time: Dance and Drill in Human History*. Cambridge, MA: Harvard University Press, 1995.

Picard, Max. *The World of Silence*, translated by Stanley Godman. Chicago: Henry Regnery, 1952.

Prejean, Helen. *Dead Man Walking*. New York: Vintage, 1994.

———. *The Death of Innocents*. New York: Random House, 2005.

Pyszczynski, Tom. *In the Wake of 9/11: The Psychology of Terror*. Washington DC: American Psychological Association, 2003.

Routley, Erik. *Christian Hymns: An Introduction to Their Story*. Princeton: Prestige, 1980. Cassette.

Weaver, J. Denny. *The Nonviolent Atonement*. Grand Rapids: Eerdmans, 2001.

Weil, Simone. "Reflection on the Right Use of School Studies with a View to the Love of God." In *The Simone Weil Reader*, edited by George A. Panichas, 44–52. New York: McKay, 1977.

Index

978-0-595-41245-7
0-595-41245-9

Printed in the United States
73312LV00004B/118-249